Taxis vs. Uber

Taxis vs. Uber

Courts, Markets, and Technology in Buenos Aires

Juan M. del Nido

Stanford University Press

Stanford, California

STANFORD UNIVERSITY PRESS
Stanford, California

© 2022 by the Board of Trustees of the Leland Stanford Junior University.
All rights reserved.

No part of this book may be reproduced or transmitted in any form or by
any means, electronic or mechanical, including photocopying and recording,
or in any information storage or retrieval system without the prior written
permission of Stanford University Press.

Printed in the United States of America on acid-free, archival-quality paper

Library of Congress Cataloging-in-Publication Data
Names: del Nido, Juan M., author.
Title: Taxis vs. Uber : courts, markets, and technology in Buenos Aires /
    Juan M. del Nido.
Description: Stanford, California : Stanford University Press, 2022. |
    Includes bibliographical references and index.
Identifiers: LCCN 2021007120 (print) | LCCN 2021007121 (ebook) |
    ISBN 9781503611528 (cloth) | ISBN 9781503629677 (paperback) |
    ISBN 9781503629684 (ebook)
Subjects: LCSH: Uber (Firm) | Taxicab industry—Argentina—Buenos Aires. |
    Taxicab drivers—Argentina—Buenos Aires.
Classification: LCC HE5651.B8 D35 2021 (print) | LCC HE5651.B8 (ebook) |
    DDC 388.4/13214098212—dc23
LC record available at https://lccn.loc.gov/2021007120
LC ebook record available at https://lccn.loc.gov/2021007121

Cover design: Kevin Barrett Kane

Cover illustration: Fundie Biela

Typeset by Kevin Barrett Kane in 11/13.5 Adobe Garamond Pro

Table of Contents

Acknowledgments

This book could not have existed without Buenos Aires's taxi drivers, their union, and their chambers. My research was originally about all of them; Uber's arrival changed my immediate focus, but probably in the ways that actually matter it all became even more fundamentally about them. They have mostly forgotten me or have never particularly cared about my project, but I owe them my arguments, what career I have so far, and a sensibility to that intelligence, often confused with cynicism, born out of complicity between honorable adversaries. I am also hugely indebted to Mariano, Valentina, Francisco, Ariadna, Pablo, and other Buenos Aires residents living under pseudonyms in this book for their time, patience, and willingness to explain their worlds and reasons, even when—and most importantly when—it seemed there was nothing left to explain. We probably were and remain, in many senses, equals; I addressed them as such, and they always replied in kind. I also thank the court clerks, forensic telecommunication technicians, and Parliament, national, and city administration employees whose time and expertise helped me understand how Uber became something they had to deal with. My last irrevocable debt is to Stef Jansen's immense intellectual rigor, generosity, and supernatural amounts of patience. In ways harder to explain, this book would also not have existed without him.

Manchester's head of anthropology Tony Simpson's monastic calm and infrastructural, professional, and personal support provided a lifeline during the panoply of contracts I held at the University of Manchester since 2016 and the steadiest possible platform for me to lay the foundations of this book. Maia Green, Madeleine Reeves, Chika Watanabe, Angela Torresan, Andrew Irving, Michelle Obeid, Katie Smith, Gillian Evans, Olga Ulturgasheva, Pete Wade, Soumhya Venkatesan, Arran Calvert, and Karen Sykes commented, proofread, recommended readings, lent me offices during the summer, and were of invaluable support. From across Europe and the Americas, Penelope Harvey, Erik Bähre, Keir Martin, Vlad Schüler-Costa, and Diego Valdivieso helped me target, cull, prod, and strategize arguments, read drafts, and organize the workshops and conferences where I presented them. Joana Nascimento, John Foster, Kristian Hoeck, Jasmine Folz, Marisol Verdugo Paiva, Elena Borisova, Ben Eyre, Anna Balázs, Chakad Ojani, Lana Askari, Stan Beneš, Laura Mafizzoli, Eduard Vasile, Skyler Hawkins, Guilherme Fians, Jeremy Gunson, Jérémie Voirol, Noah Walker-Crawford, and Mariela Sánchez-Belmont kept me on my feet. The University of Cambridge's Max Planck Centre took me in at a time of immense uncertainty in the world and in my life, bringing economic, professional, and emotional stability to the last manuscript-editing rounds. I thank James Laidlaw, Joel Robbins, Sian Lazar, and Johannes Lenhard for their role in this process.

Across the years my work benefited from various sources of funding for fieldwork, trips to Buenos Aires, manuscript preparation, and conference attendance. I thank the Royal Economic Society, the Universidad del CEMA's Visiting Professor Grant, the University of Manchester's School of Social Sciences, the UK's Economic and Social Research Council, the Philomathia Foundation, the Royal Anthropological Institute's Sutasoma Award for Research of Potentially Outstanding Merit and its Arthur Maurice Hocart Award, the Society for Latin American Studies Harold Blakemore Award, the American Ethnological Society's Elsie Clews Parsons Award, the University of Manchester's President's PDS, and the Economic and Social Research Council's NWDTC Baltic Social Anthropology Scheme Grant.

This book began to exist as a Stanford project during a conversation with Michelle Lipinski at the American Ethnological Society conference in Philadelphia in March 2018. Her support in the early proposal and draft stages was crucial, as was Margo Irvin's firm stewardship through the enormous challenges of 2020. I thank them and Stanford University Press for believing this project was worth it. Feedback from four anonymous reviewers improved the book by orders of magnitude. Elisabeth Magnus's expert, thoughtful, and patient copyediting worked with my "Argentine-isms" as she tightened the prose, word by word, refining my arguments while keeping my tone. Any and all lapses or awkward clauses are definitely on me, probably "Argentine-isms" I could not let go.

I have not lived in Argentina since 2009, but as South African writer J. M. Coetzee said of his own homeland, I never really left Buenos Aires; I just went somewhere else. Intellectually, the Universidad del CEMA, the Universidad de San Martín, and the Argentine Council for International Relations created spaces for my work to come back home: I thank Ariel Wilkis, Julio Elías, Juan Battaleme, Ambassador Alfredo Morelli, Pablo Figueiro, Nicolás Diana Menéndez, Pablo Miguez, and Gonzalo Bustos for heralding an exciting return to Argentina's spirited, sharp political and economic debate. Lila Caimari and Sabina Frederic made the time for amazing, inspiring conversations and advice as authors and senior researchers.

In Buenos Aires, the United States, and the United Kingdom good friends made the manuscript journey a magnificent one. Gerardo, Bárbara, Natalia, Sofía, Martín, Fernando Martín, Nazareno, Fernando, Pablo, Florencia, and Magui: these decade-long friendships are also, in a way, written into these arguments and into the Argentina that made me and that I never left. Jeffrey, Ed, Dan, and Mark shared summer evenings in Cape Cod, road trips across New England and Appalachia, books, ideas, and linguistic advice. Manchester friend and housemate Richard Glover survived half a house brimming with books, drafts, and half-drunk coffees; friend and fellow anthropologist Mike Prentice, whose work Stanford spotted at that same conference in Philadelphia and who ended up in northern England, proved an inexhaustible source of research ideas and reading recommendations. Finally I wish to thank my parents, Marta and Martín, for an education, opportunities, and more sacrifices than I think I know; and my brothers, Francisco and Joaquín, who in their own way were always beside me for the ride. This book is dedicated to all four of them.

Taxis vs. Uber

INTRODUCTION

A Storm Blowing from Paradise

IN LATE MARCH 2016, Uber's communication manager for the Southern Cone was asked on live radio whether the platform would launch its services in Buenos Aires, Argentina's capital, despite authorities' warnings that it would be breaking the law. She replied, "Yes, definitely."[1] Uber was a contract between private parties, she argued, perfectly allowed in the juridical order of Buenos Aires; it was also an innovative service, therefore outside the remit of existing transportation laws. The company was ready to cooperate with city authorities to develop together regulation fit for twenty-first-century technologies, she closed matter-of-factly. London, Rio, New York, Santiago de Chile, Paris: Buenos Aires's residents geared up for their turn in a world saga by then epic and viral and heady with a whiff of the foretold. Cars ablaze and street fighting in foreign lands flickered on national media, sensational spoilers of a conflict that had not even begun but that announced itself to a city prone to popular protests in the warnings of taxi drivers' union leader, Omar Viviani: "[The company] will have a problem with us, for under no circumstances will we allow their arrival."[2] By then, thirteen-million-strong Buenos Aires was one of the few large metropolises in the world left without any ride-sharing platform.

On March 27· the Twitter account @Uber_ARG went live and tweeted: "Would you like to be your own boss driving with Uber? Register at socio-sar.com and find out more."[3] The evening of the twenty-eighth, Uber officials held an induction session at a hotel downtown; taxi drivers gathered outside, chanting and smashing windows and making primetime news. On March 29· @Uber_ARG tweeted that over ten thousand people had already signed up as drivers.[4] The epigrammatic brevity of Twitter's interface enhanced the effect of its cunning use as the sole source of publicly available information: the result was electrifying. On April 12 around midday, news broke that Uber had tweeted it would be available at 4:00 p.m. that very same day.[5] Right after four, Ignacio Viale, youngest of a long line of TV personalities and millennial enfant terrible, livestreamed in an elaborate PR stunt what was effectively the first Uber ride on Argentine soil. Within hours several taxi driver associations initiated legal action, accusing Uber of unlawful use of public space, danger to public safety, lack of appropriate driving permits and insurances, tax avoidance, and price dumping. Uber is a company, they spelled out categorically, an explicit affront to the company's self-description as an immaterial intermediary made of virtual optima untapped until then.

The following day, April 13, at exactly 11:00 a.m., taxis blockaded twenty-five intersections simultaneously, paralyzing Buenos Aires for an entire hour, and a city judge issued a precautionary ban against Uber effective immediately. By this point Uber had been downloaded ninety thousand times and had processed twenty thousand ride requests, according to the press.[6] On April 14, traffic wardens fined an Uber driver the equivalent of 4,130 USD, withheld his driving permit, and towed his car away. On Friday 15, Uber officials retorted that the company would reimburse its "associates'" fines, doubling down on Twitter: "Find out about us and defend your right to choose. Until next Wednesday, 15 free rides up to 200 pesos. #Righttochoose," adding a link to a blog.[7] The city mayor announced cryptically that Argentines should welcome "modernity" within the framework of the law; and that day, too, newly elected president of Argentina Mauricio Macri declared that "the taxis of Buenos Aires are a symbol of the city and the nation."[8] Uber had been in Argentina for less than seventy-two hours.

Uber's arrival found me there, in Buenos Aires, where I was born and raised and where I had returned seven months earlier to research, of all things, its taxi industry. I had left Argentina as an economist trained by the Universidad del CEMA, one of the unshakable neoliberal bastions of the Southern Cone, to retrain as a social anthropologist in the UK. As part of my doctoral project at the University of Manchester, on August 2015 I arrived in Buenos Aires for a year of fieldwork on the taxi industry's political economy, its union life, and its drivers' "urban charisma": that wily jaded iconicity animating urban taxi drivers everywhere, from Johannesburg to Sao Paulo, from Jakarta to London.[9]

From the second someone described Uber's arrival as "imminent," an avalanche of economic intuitions, blasts of moral outrage, partisan accusations, and cultural anxieties barraged the industry I had come to know very well by then: notions of monopoly, choice, efficiency, empowerment, innovation, opportunism, competition, and freedom combined in a brutal rhetorical siege. Ferocious, principled, spiteful, and occasionally compassionate, most of these arguments were, strictly speaking, unfair, inconsistent, unverifiable, or misdirected. Some were hyperbolic to the point of caricature. Yet together they framed a field of contention where, regardless of their truth value, it became increasingly difficult to meaningfully counter their claims—to respond to them. The taxi industry's arguments, even enhanced by governmental support, were increasingly not exactly opposed but rather explained away, subsumed into the very workings of that attack from all directions, and effectively neutralized. As Uber hit half a million downloads in May 2016, I decided that the company and the taxi industry in and of themselves were not as important to me, to public debate, and to current anthropological, economic, and political thinking as the conflict that entwined them.[10] The reasoning, arguments, and anxieties that wrote the taxi industry off became the focus of my project, and that project became this book.

The lines of this conflict were set by the intuitions, aspirations, and exasperations of a certain Buenos Aires middle class. In strict socioeconomic terms, these were residents able to take taxis regularly or casually and used to circulating with a given ease in a relatively middle-class city, thus a prime target for Uber's service. But this was never a strictly socioeconomic conflict or one solely about alternative ways of moving around, so its rhetoric and intensity exceeded the bounds of that middle class's transportation practices and economic possibilities.

A city founded for capitalist trade and for much of its history wealthier than its European counterparts, Buenos Aires today stamps its residents' imagination with the watermark of a thwarted prospect of wealth and cosmopolitan modernity, its outlines all the more vivid against the knowledge that from all evidence something fell apart somewhere down the line. The exact forensics and chronology of the country's downfall are contentious battlegrounds, but Argentines on the whole agree that the story of this lower-middle-income nation, whose cultural, political, and economic epicenter always was and remains Buenos Aires, should really have played out very differently. Argentina's famous 2001 economic crash summarized this frustration in the quotable war cry *Que se vayan todos*: let them all go. Targeting primarily the then-president, who indeed fled the headquarters of the executive power by helicopter that day, the phrase extends to established parties and structures of political action and representation. It also symbolizes a decades-old disillusionment that transcends politics and seeps into the experience of a certain Argentine middle-class life, yearning for some sort of answer or purge. I was fifteen in 2001, and part of the generation of Argentines that shortly after spiked enrollment in economics and kindred degrees in higher education to at least give that yearning a frame.

Between the crisis and Uber's arrival, Argentines were ruled by the left-of-center administrations of Néstor Kirchner (2003–7) and Cristina Fernández de Kirchner (2007–11 and 2011–15). The fiscal expansionism, historical revisionism, economic isolationism, and increasingly choleric populism of these years bitterly divided the city's middle class, shaping how residents linked their political experience as individuals, as a social group, and as Argentines to those frustrations and disillusionments. On the whole, the city of Buenos Aires opposed both administrations. Economically liberal in a broad, nonfanatical way; culturally liberal in a globalist, self-conscious sense; and politically pluralist in an unreflexively self-defined manner: the portion of the middle class holding these positions experienced these years as an era of "hyperpoliticization," contrived and cynical culture wars, mismanaged natural potential, irrational nationalism, unstrategic regionalism, and the factionalist and grossly inefficient bloating of the public sector. Huge political actors in Argentina, trade unions fed these frustrations, less as sectorial representatives and more through their reactive, allegedly opportunistic political and partisan enmeshment with the running of the country since the 1930s.

By 2016, taxi drivers' union leader Omar Viviani was a political ally of both Kirchners, which, together with his uninterrupted three-decade rule over the taxi trade, epitomized the vices that exasperated this part of the middle class. They also blamed him directly, derivatively, and just in case for the excesses, real and exaggerated, of a trade involving millions of transactions per day in an unpredictably volatile city at the level of the street. Meanwhile, in December 2015, right-of-center Mauricio Macri had become president of Argentina, voted in on a technocratic manifesto that passed for an electoral platform. He promised the nation, "a team of millions," the resumption of international trade, respect for the institutions and rule of law, and Herculean infrastructural investments. In a poetic, logistical, and cultural sense, Macri's triumph paved the way for Uber's arrival barely three months later; together, the company, Macri's administration, Viviani's ominous shadow, and the anxieties of an electorally relieved middle class would frame the experience of Uber's conflict in 2016 Buenos Aires: these people, as "a People," wanted Uber.

This frame would very quickly evidence immense contradictions, inconsistencies, spurious correlations, and a myriad other fault lines. The same middle class expressly decrying informal economies, tax evasion, and disregard for the law, who found in Macri's administration a viable answer to these concerns, was now enthralled by a service ostentatiously flouting a raft of fiscal, commercial, and civil laws and overtly defined as illegal by several courts and by Macri's own government. As the conflict gathered pace, however, it became increasingly evident that to focus on these fault lines as such amounted to indulging in a pedantic, self-serious literalism that would have spectacularly missed what was actually at stake. Propelling the arguments, just out of view, choice as a moral good, the axiomatic virtue of competition, technological determinism, popular legitimacy, and other by now instinctive grammars of late capitalism reinforced each other, preempting, dissolving, subsuming, and pathologizing the very possibility of disagreeing with the stakes they claimed.

I took that frenzied tangle seriously, or seriously enough not to take it literally, and followed its arguments, passions, and actions through to their logical and material conclusions. I did not seek to figure out who was "right" or whose arguments were sounder or more resonant with the academic urge to pontificate in the key of resistance. Rather, I set out to explain why and how it became so difficult for the taxi industry to make their case before the tribunal of popular opinion—to be afforded the bare dignity of being heard, even with a judicial injunction and government action on their side. Beyond Uber and beyond Buenos Aires, my goal here is to understand how people reflect on their reasons, and the reasons of others, when they come to disagree through the rhetorical resources of late capitalism. This conflict shows exceptionally well how certain ways of reasoning reorganize who can take meaningful part in the common experience of public life, or not, and how one can meaningfully disagree. In the material, emotional, and rhetorical reshuffling that the Uber conflict triggered, the taxi industry, that is, those who disagreed, were assigned the part that was there but was silenced, the part that existed but could only ever utter white noise, the part that was around but whose reasons were disavowed, or in other words: the part that had no part.

The Part That Had No Part

What does it mean to say that the taxi industry became "the part that had no part" in the common experience of Buenos Aires in 2016? To understand this argument, let us begin with the premise, developed by philosopher Jacques Rancière, that people and institutions participate in a "distribution of the sensible": a sort of allocation of roles, parts, times, and scopes delineating how each can rightfully and meaningfully participate in the common experience of the social life they share.[11] This distribution is not just a code, or a list of roles written down somewhere: it comes to life as people engage with each other in spontaneous yet patterned ways through buildings, laws, databases, ethical duties, arguments, expectations, and of course, taxi rides. This is a social experience, including but going well beyond political theory or a constitutional article.

That the experience is common means that everyone knows how they, and others, belong in that experience, and that they know their parts are relative to the whole and to each other's. It does not mean it includes them all as equals, and certainly not in the same way: someone writes laws, someone obeys them; someone is called upon to address a public health crisis; someone can drive someone else for money, and someone's arguments inform what counts as a fair taxi fare; someone can take someone to court, demand reimbursement from an insurer, or complain about a taxi driver who has "taken them for a ride," and for each of these parts there will be different kinds of language, tones, moments, and spaces that can and will count, and others that will not. This last point is crucial: when defining the distribution of the sensible as "a delimitation of spaces and times, of the visible *and the invisible*, of speech *and noise*, that simultaneously determines the place and the stakes of the form of experience," Rancière reminded us that there is always a part that is there but that has no part.[12] Be it Roman plebeians or the homeless of a wealthy Western capital, this part is physically and even institutionally and formally there, but in a way it comes not to count as others do. It may speak the same language as the others, but its words are not intelligible on a par; it may utter refined arguments, but others can afford to not engage it in debate at no moral loss; it may scream back the utterances of other parts, even verbatim, but when coming from its lips those same claims sound as noise.

What exactly does being a part but having no part entail, in general, and in Uber's conflict in Buenos Aires in particular? After all, by early

2021, nearly five years after the company's first ride in Buenos Aires, taxis continue to exist pretty much as they did before, the union is still there, the government still manages the trade with the same laws, and offshoots of the original legal case against Uber continue to make their way through the same courts and are still subjected to the same judicial authority. In important formal, political, and institutional ways, which were the ones that mattered to Rancière's thought, most activities, roles, expectations, and reciprocal relations between the industry, its authorities, its customers, the union, remain unchanged.

Yet this was a conflict that engulfed political parties, influencers, news commentators, and public opinion at large, playing out in streets, social media, and PR blitzes as much as, if not more than, it did in courts. What I argue here is that, from the perspective of the part that defined public debate around Uber's arrival, that is, the segment of the middle class outlined above, grew the arguments, intuitions, and exasperations that progressively reshaped the common experience around this conflict. It was this reshuffling that wrote off the taxi industry and its arguments. Half-baked associations between the taxi license and ideas of competition, anxious technological determinism, and an unbridled, feverish, and increasingly pervasive obsession with "what the people want" that precious few public institutions dare counter effectively overrode the industry's attempts at talking back in a conflict where its livelihoods were at stake, even as taxis drove that very middle class around every day. The logical, rhetorical, and affective experience of that middle class and its economic, cultural, ethical, and political arguments subsumed the taxi industry in a process whose meaning and consequences it could barely influence, let alone control. It was in that experience, too, that this exclusion was no longer up for debate; the experience became common in the other sense of the term, common as in naturalized, taken for granted, beyond disagreement, or in other words: depoliticized.

In Rancière's thought, always at society's level, this depoliticization takes place through statewide institutions and logics of government that disavow genuine disagreement.[13] Put simply, these are the politics of our times, of spreadsheets and consultants, where actual change seems impossible—a postpolitical order of "technocratic mechanisms and consensual procedures . . . [where] political contradictions are reduced to policy problems to be managed by experts and legitimated through participatory processes," pathologizing real disagreement.[14] Certainly, Macri's project for Argentina fits quite well this definition of a postpolitical government. Yet this alone cannot explain how the taxi industry came to be written off, even if that segment of the middle class that so desired Uber did vote for Macri, not least since his cabinet and administration, as well as judges under his wing, publicly endorsed the taxi industry's argument.

This is where ethnography as a method and anthropology as a way of understanding how things matter gain the upper hand. To grasp how the taxi industry was disavowed not institutionally but in public debate, casual conversation, and trivial transactions, we must focus on how, in the throes of the Uber conflict and independently of any governmental projects, that middle class developed what I refer to here as postpolitical reasoning: the logics, rhetoric, and affects that people mobilize to imagine, legitimize, and argue for a common experience where a certain kind of disagreement is foreclosed. Reasoning here does not mean a logico-mathematical sequence, or a positivistic or Cartesian ordering. Rather, it means the process and method of developing knowledge and of organizing and making sense of that knowledge—of excluding, prioritizing, and associating specific aspects of what emerges as known and knowable. With the term *postpolitical reasoning* I seek to capture how, through particular ways of knowing, certain possibilities of disagreeing come to be disavowed.

Postpolitical Reasoning: Nonexperts, Affect, Neoliberalism

Whereas postpolitical orders, the ones Rancière was properly concerned about, are led by canonically defined experts, postpolitical reasoning is a nonexpert way of knowing that does not necessarily seek to make an expert adjudication or to address the adjudication of experts, however defined, when disavowing certain stakes or when pronouncing itself in terms of truths. This is not to say it is random or illogical, but simply a reminder that, through whatever means at hand, "nonexperts" are working through the same questions "experts" ask.[15] The answers nonexperts produce put pressure on popular imaginations (and governmental projects) not necessarily because of their "truthfulness" or accuracy, but because of how they organize what others can know. For example, among this middle class, the courts' technical struggle to interrupt Uber operations passed for evidence of the company's self-description as an immaterial mediator beyond politics. That this argument may "actually" be spurious is beside the point: it mattered because in *this* form it framed the middle class's reasoning of their experience, and in *this* form it made it harder for the taxi industry to talk back. In this sense, this book argues for an attention to the sense nonexperts make of economic and political processes.

Similarly, because of their proximity to what people see as relevant, affects, broadly speaking emotions, motivate, propel, and galvanize postpolitical reasoning. Postpolitical technocrats of the kind Rancière imagined may certainly act on emotions, or even codify them in governmental projects or stir them in others, but their statist framework requires that they work through forms of knowing deliberately and ostentatiously separated from emotion. Meanwhile, anthropologists have long known that things like suspicion, exasperation, and excitement are not just cultural accidents added onto the bare bones of experience: they define experiences and shape their effects. When residents insisted, with caustic irritation, that Uber was "everywhere in the world except *here*," the factoid that Uber was not *really* everywhere in the world was completely incidental to the work such statements were doing to place the company's presence in a rhetorical zone of beyond-contention. Tracing how affects contribute to generating the categories of postpolitical reasoning, this book contributes to a growing academic literature concerned with affect as a form of knowing.[16]

Last, postpolitical reasoning constantly invokes principles such as the inherent virtue of competition, the axiomatic goodness of individual choice, and the "natural" "forces" of economic processes. These tropes are all buried in the intuitions of late capitalism. Developed by a clique of philosophers in the late nineteenth century who gave them the language and iron-clad certainties of physics, they were always moralizing claims about aspects of life that should be understood as beyond disagreement.[17] In the mid-twentieth century they also served as the philosophical spine to the governmental project we now call neoliberalism. Through the latter's institutions and market interventions these tropes expanded around the world and took on the aura of an eternal righteousness.[18] In this sense, postpolitical reasoning shares an ideological repertoire with postpolitical government. Yet, whereas the latter promotes neoliberal administration, postpolitical reasoning remains within the diffuse argumentative space where these tropes tend to tangle themselves up, explaining and doubling for each other, enhancing the experience of their instinctive, ordered righteousness with a "spare and logical clarity."[19]

My first aim in tracing these tropes individually is to understand how each contributed to postpolitical reasoning. The slightly stylized narrative resulting from this decision was a small price to pay to serve my second aim here: to develop through these tropes a viable alternative to the ever-popular genre "critiques of 'neoliberalism.'" I seek disciplinary precision, an argumentative strategy and a grammar to understand the moral, natural, and instrumental invocations usually lumped together in the term *neoliberalism*.

In recent years, the bandying about of the term *neoliberalism* in social science scholarship has rendered the term increasingly confusing and vague, multiplying flagrant contradictions within arguments and often in the same text.[20] This imprecision is particularly salient in the most activist scholarship, whose constant denunciation of "neoliberalism" is quickly losing explanatory power and jading everyone outside of its most fervent practitioners. To say that Uber, its practices, its CEOs, or even Argentina's government are "neoliberal" is probably true, a truism by now, and places us on the right side of what is an increasingly moralized, moralizing opposition. Yet even if we were using the term with canonical precision, it would tell us little about why masses of Buenos Aires's broadly law-abiding middle class *instinctively* understood that their "right to choose to use Uber" should trump the judicial system's admonitions against it. This is probably what many of us, including the activists, are actually concerned about. Historically anterior, logically much more specific, and rhetorically far more complex than "neoliberalism," the tropes I retrace will teach us what was actually at stake in postpolitical reasoning. As a result, the word *neoliberalism* barely features in the book beyond this introduction.

All these features were often indistinguishable from each other; I have tried to capture their entanglement by speaking of the "logics, rhetoric, and affects" of postpolitical reasoning. My analysis does not seek to make a moral claim or to be intelligible to contemporary anthropological mandates to "speak truth to power." Truth and power are immensely complex categories, and I have not let the middle class's emergence as the powerful actor here reorient my analysis to defend "the weak," even if I did march alongside taxi drivers against the company and even if, at heart, I agreed with them. I saw my ethical duty not in determining whether, for example, Uber's algorithms were "actually" fairer or more efficient than the taxi industry's arrangements but in tracing the logical, rhetorical, and affective associations that allowed a self-styled beleaguered middle class to reflect on fairness and efficiency as a problem to be foreclosed through algorithms. This is, in a sense, nothing other than a return to the canon of the British anthropology tradition I am trained in. It always mattered little whether, as Evans-Pritchard infamously said, "Witches, as Azande conceive them, cannot exist."[21] But the point, in this tradition, is that it also matters little whether the "truth" is that they "can" exist; the anthropological duty is to figure out how, why, and in what circumstances a particular group of people think of their relations in terms of something such as witchcraft, or fairness, or efficiency. No other discipline is better equipped to shine this kind of light on "truth" and "power" however defined.

Last, certain readers will notice that in developing the case for postpolitical reasoning I draw on what some social scientists call antipolitical events or processes.[22] We are talking about similar issues; *postpolitical reasoning* captures better the temporal horizon and teleological aspirations of this thinking and emphasizes foreclosure and disavowal rather than antagonism, although at times the difference is cosmetic. My choice also allowed me to capture the echoes between this reasoning and Argentina's incoming administration in 2015: technocratic, postpolitical, and, in the specific sense of an institutional and ideological project, neoliberal. I turn now to examine the economic, political, and cultural features of that part of Buenos Aires's middle class that by 2016 longed to disavow the kind of disagreement a conflict over a ride-sharing app epitomized.

Argentina: The Rise of a Middle Class

With a third of its forty-four million inhabitants concentrated in the Greater Buenos Aires area, Argentina's relatively unpopulated landmass, the size of India or of Alaska, California, and Texas combined, occupies the eastern side of the Andes at the south end of the Americas. Inhabited since 11,000 BC by several Native American nations, what is now Argentina came under Spanish control in the early 1500s. Lacking in gold and gemstones, the region remained a colonial borderland, existing to safeguard and provide the logistics for the transit of silver from Potosí, now Bolivia, to the port of Buenos Aires, founded in 1536 at the confluence of the River Plate with the Atlantic Ocean, on the edges of the world Europeans knew.[23] In the early 1800s, after the expulsion of Spain from most of South America, the loose entente of the United Provinces of the River Plate emerged in the area. This proto-Argentina lost and gained people and land for years, but in 1853 the remaining and new provinces sealed the project of a shared nation in the form of a constitution. Its capital would be Buenos Aires, the city whose port was the union's only gateway to Europe and that belonged to the homonymous province, at the time expanding southwards and apace with the extermination of Patagonian peoples, and already encompassing some of the most fertile land in the world.

Argentina lived the second half of the nineteenth century as one grand modernizing, positivistic project. Oligarchic administrations reproducing themselves by dubious, exclusive, and outright violent electoral practices launched a colossal political, economic, territorial, and sociocultural overhaul of the nation, its parts, and its relation to the world.[24] These years saw the military incorporation of the Patagonia, a land three times the size of the United Kingdom, and territories in the Gran Chaco region into Argentina's capitalist production structure; the genocide, displacement, confinement, and cultural absorption of native peoples; a state-sponsored explosion in immigration from Europe, in particular Italy, Spain, Germany, and central Europe, such that foreigners outnumbered locals in several cities; and the cultural and political consolidation of the modern nation-state through the secularization of free, universal education in the Spanish language, compulsory military service, and the expansion of state bureaucracy techniques and infrastructures, from censuses to postal services.[25] Like the US, Canada, and parts of Brazil at that time, Argentina offered the masterminds of nineteenth-century statecraft a brutally emptied, virginal canvas onto which the universalizing views of physics and engineering, the science and craft of objective progress, could play out their expansive, tentacular fantasies. The themes were *grands travaux*, "civilization," and the taming of a nature that, after all, existed to be tamed and brought in line.[26]

This era produced enough material traces to foster belief in the no-nonsense fable of purely technical progress. Statistical and economic knowledge, one way to tell a story, say that by the turn of the century Argentina was among the wealthiest nations in the world, its GDP per capita surpassing that of several European countries.[27] Argentina "boasted the highest per capita income on the continent, the most extensive urbanization, the largest middle class, as well as the best newspapers, universities and publishing houses," and being Argentine would until 1955 be conflated with upward mobility.[28] Meanwhile, Buenos Aires's political, economic, and cultural predominance over the entire nation, effectively its depot and backwater, was already by 1910 discussed as irreversible.[29] The rail network, telegraphs, phone lines, banking, electricity, and basic and advanced infrastructures were set up from, toward, and in favor of the Autonomous City of Buenos Aires, its own federal district since 1880 and "Goliath's head."[30]

It is in this time and space, where opera houses, an education, industry, and palatial coffeehouses socialized the children of illiterate Lombard or Basque farmers into an expanding middle class, that many Argentines today anchor the birthright to a cultural cosmopolitanism that is peripheral but not exotic, secondary but intelligible to the core. Borges, football, tango, beef, polo, and five Nobel prizes merged in the modern landscape of progress, where Argentina joined the countries that mattered through ballroom dancing, high literature, and scientific innovations—that is, the terms on which "proper" peoples counted.[31] This is a stylized, depoliticized reading: entire regions were desperately poor, and political violence had already taken forms that would prove lasting. But this was the case in many developed societies at the time as well, and the question is less about whether the nation excelled in absolute modern virtue, though in some ways it allegedly did, than about Argentines finding the means of understanding themselves in relation to those who counted.

Peronism: A Political Democracy

Intellectuals across Argentina's ideological spectrum agree that around the early 1930s a deterioration that would prove to be systemic and durable began creeping into economic production, fiscal and monetary stability, the quality of national politics, and the experience of democratic life.[32] This was not at all a linear development: certain regions, classes, and industries enjoyed at that time a bonanza they had never known, gained a political influence continuing to this day, or retained privileges they had always had. But from the Great Depression onwards, the historical memory shaping the experience of the middle class that concerns me here becomes significantly more complicated, haunted by more intricate ghosts and splintered along several lines at once.

A military coup in 1930, which we now know was only the first of six, exposed the fragility of the bourgeoning democracy. The autocratic government counted within its ranks an astute, charismatic bureaucrat by the name of Juan Domingo Perón, who would rise to national visibility during the next coup in 1943. The politically disaffected working classes found in him a shrewd interlocutor and ally that turned them into the democratic mass of twentieth-century Argentina.[33] Three presidencies by popular vote, the first right after that second dictatorship transitioned back to democracy, and his marriage and political alliance with the equally charismatic Eva Duarte consolidated Perón as the nation's greatest political myth, defining Argentine politics to this day.[34]

It is as impossible to exhaustively examine Peronism in this book as it is to explain this conflict without understanding how Peronism shapes

Argentine political imaginations.[35] I hope readers interested in Peronism itself will find in this fragmented approach a complement to the reams already written on it, and that readers interested in the other contributions this book makes will be able to place Peronism's relevance within the arguments I put forward. Peronism's long-term impact for my purposes here begins with a reinvented trade unionism and a cradle-to-grave welfare state, both copied from continental European models; the populist, charismatic, and mediatized political culture of mass democracy; and an explicit, purposeful, and celebrated intervention of the state in economic matters vaunted as a unique balance between communism and capitalism. Together they reinvented how middle classes understood their relation to the state, partisan politics, and democracy. Immigrants arriving during the Second World War joined first- and second-generation Argentines in trade unions shaped to funnel their demands to the state and to provide them social and clinical assistance. The Peróns' immensely personalistic style catalyzed the intensification and extension of the state's reach and role across Argentina. This was an era of state-mandated economic and fiscal redistribution, including forceful expropriation; of expansion of civil, political, and economic rights, often through proselytizing school reading material and infrastructure and entire provinces named after one or the other of the couple; and of sophisticated technical and industrial know-how put to the service of the state and its multiplying agencies, as happened in twentieth-century European mass democracies, except that in the Argentine version Peronism and the state became a little more entwined.

Argentine middle classes then and now split in fierce opposition or loyalty to the couple and then to Peronism. Politically intense and ideologically immensely labile, the movement is broadly taken as the natural party of government in Argentina. Since the 1950s, for its detractors, Peronism is the experience of a democracy they need to live through in explicitly political and partisan terms in spite of themselves. Peronists' record with public finances, debt, and inflation is not particularly better or worse than those of other parties, and they are not the only ones to engage in economically interventionist or fiscally expansionist policies. Partly because Peronism is an exceptionally effective cultural machine that operates through multiple venues, from propaganda to public festivities, Peronism's detractors tend to see these policies less as such and more as a high-intensity realpolitik of self-perpetuation. This imagination extends to trade unions, the exact same ones that integrated parents and grandparents of the non- or anti-Peronist middle class today into the fabric of Argentine political, social, and cultural life. That the middle class associates them with opportunism and a recalcitrant and self-serving reactivity makes it even harder for Argentine political imaginations to supersede Peronism.[36]

Markets, Democracy, and the Missing Link

After another military dictatorship ousted Perón in 1955 and banned the party, Argentina entered a half a century where hyperinflations, devaluations, sovereign debt defaults, and more dictatorships, factionalism, and political instability, very often simultaneously, confirmed that this was an increasingly unequal, polarized, and internationally marginal country. These were the years when cultural and historical memories fused with the personal experiences and political subjectivities of the current middle class. Some among them argue that a fine Argentina among the worthy of the world never existed as such; some others see in this process the historically inevitable, even desirable, "Latin Americanization" of Argentina. A large segment of Buenos Aires's middle class, however, has not renounced that birthright to belong to those who count: these people are living now the harrowing experience of a teleological aberration, constantly confirming not that they are poor or underdeveloped but that they are *becoming* poorer and underdeveloped. As Argentine scholar Marta Savigliano argues, they find this experience "incomprehensible. . . . We can't believe it ourselves. . . . The experience of becoming less and less developed, more dependent, increasingly poor, more harshly exploited, economically and politically more polarized, of losing dignity, . . . is hard to admit."[37]

This is the cultural and identity bedrock for the middle class whose experience this book will trace, a people similar in some ways to the middle classes of other middle- and high-income countries but watermarked by these anxieties. This is the Argentine segment more likely to imagine and define itself as apolitical and either to lack a class consciousness or to have a consciousness of itself as a noble moral-ethical collective of citizens who want "the best" for their country. Politically jaded, they understand in theory the tensions of capital and labor but receive explanations of the country's industrial, economic, monetary, or political instability in those terms with impatient skepticism. Ideologically, they do not stray from a center akin to that of European social democratic parties: these are people who, in twenty-first-century Buenos Aires, support proudly and as a matter of principle universal and free public education and health care, maternity leave, and most social benefits, but who, knowing these to be grossly underfunded or insufficient, with a pained nostalgia and a yearning for some stability have for decades been turning to private education and health care.

This segment of the middle class is in fact able to satisfy most of its immediate and secondary needs in several markets. It is also the one that, in a country where entire regions are below the poverty line, thinks of itself as self-empowering. This self-empowerment, however, is not the axiom of an intolerant libertarianism, but rather a weary end point for those who would love to rely on the public sphere but who have had to pay a bribe to access a basic service, who have seen someone they know access safe employment in public administration through nepotism, or whose life savings have been destroyed by a national currency mismanaged into hyperinflation. These people imagine their self-reliance in opposition, not to the possibility or principle of a shared public space, far from it, but to a broad category of "the political," referring to politicians and parties but also to structural processes, practices, and institutions that they see as tainting and corrupting the public sphere, conflating the political condition with factionalism, vice, and excess.[38]

Allergic to partisan dogmatism, this segment is also the most likely to think of economic and political conflicts, theirs and the nation's, in terms of a readily stylized, principled republican common sense that channels exasperation more than it serves as pragmatic guidance. This was their situation in mid-2015, toward the end of Fernández de Kirchner's second term, when I arrived back in Buenos Aires. Monthly inflation was reaching double digits, again; the country had technically defaulted on its debt, again; restrictions on access to foreign currencies and imports had been set up overnight, again. Experts on inflation-outsmarting strategies, currency exchange, and country-risk rates well before these years, middle-class people found themselves having to register as importers to buy one book from abroad and unable to use their ovens for lack of foreign spare parts.[39] National index–reinventing propaganda, the crumbling of basic infrastructure, an ill-designed economic isolationism, and the ostentatious privileging of political and partisan allegiances in the running of the country turned these years into an experience of an unremitting, exhausting political intensity for this segment of the middle class.

Well into the twenty-first century, this middle class's historic worldly aspirations merge with the moral economy of a cosmopolitanism heralded by a superficially ecumenical, globalist Left whose normative legitimacy gained traction during, and in some senses through, the Kirchner administrations.[40] By 2016, this cosmopolitanism, iconically mediated by Apple, Amazon, Facebook, Netflix, and, of course, Uber, was readily available not only in the developed world to which this middle class claimed a birthright but also across the river, in Uruguay, a country these people thought of as a stable, quaint, long-lost Argentine province, as well as in Brazil, Chile, and other countries these Argentines would rank themselves above. This conjuncture passed for maddening proof of a link between that teleological aberration and a meddling political intensity that needed to be urgently disallowed.

The Kirchner governments also spanned the consolidation of social media platforms as accelerators of the formation of a certain public sphere and a certain way of inhabiting that public sphere as political subjects.[41] By the time of Macri's and Uber's arrival, the Argentine middle class had the cultural and infrastructural means to expertly circulate in the shrill, endogamous cacophony of a Twitter timeline and to trade in hashtags, epigrammatic currency of the moral economy of social media. That #Uber-Love was a trending topic in Argentina while a judge banned Uber from the Autonomous City of Buenos Aires was not just expert PR but evidence for these people that this was a battle whose neatly moral turf they had to defend from a fuzzy political they had to shut out. In this sense, we can characterize this segment of the middle class as a missing link: between the moral economy of the market, in a nonfundamentalist, self-styled commonsensical way, and a democracy that, instead of being kept alive through politics, needed to be protected from it.[42] These are the people whose reasoning I trace in this book, and who I suspect would find this description fair. It is the reasoning and not the people I follow; for ease of narrative I will refer to them as "residents" or simply "the middle class," knowing that the reader knows whom I am referring to.

Ethnography as Method, as Writing, as Home

This book is ethnography driven and privileges storytelling as narrative strategy, but it is not written in the conventional, ethnographic vignette sense of contemporary anthropology. This is a deliberate approach. My purpose is not to capture the vagaries of a life followed at infinitesimal distance or to claim that such closeness constitutes epistemological precision or a commitment to "truth." Reasoning is a weird object of knowledge, broken, intermittent, and scattered across people, documents, business strategies, and internet cables: I took the authorial decision to distill and dissect subplots, people's lives, techniques, histories, and affects, to form mostly self-contained chapters, following each other as in a movie reel. This separation, if artificial, was the only way to disentangle this reasoning and trace each strand's progression beyond its breaking point precisely to capture how it remained persuasive beyond that breaking point. In giving these strands a narrative clarity I do not seek to legitimize them, give them an intellectual or moral authority I do not think they have, or imply that these were the only arguments at play. There are always other ways to think about, define, or challenge a given claim, problem, or circumstance; I traced *these* because they determined to a great extent the social life of the conflict. As a result, the narrative is more visibly stylized than in other ethnographies: this is because it is an argument and not a portrait. An argument about arguments, at that.

This ethnography involved my fieldwork in Buenos Aires between July 2015 and August 2016, and well into early 2017 in terms of archival data collection. As per current anthropological practice, all names are pseudonyms and all events and statements have been anonymized except for declarations by governmental, political, or institutional authorities, Uber employees, and taxi industry representatives uttered expressly for, and available now in, the public sphere in the form of mass media interviews, press releases, freely available tweets, blog entries, and journalistic op-eds, adequately referenced throughout the book.

To understand the taxi industry I conducted regular participant observation at two "taxi drivers'" bars, as they are known in the city, one of them conveniently located at a gas station taxi drivers used regularly. I also interviewed all senior and midcareer officials at the taxi drivers' union, shadowed the work of doctors and road technicians during checkups and training sessions, and underwent the three-week course sponsored by the union and the state to become a taxi driver. I also interviewed the leaders of two of the chambers of commerce that taxi car owners belong to, and one of them generously offered me access to their printed archives from the early twentieth century. Taxi riding in Buenos Aires is a private affair involving one passenger, or one party of passengers, and the driver; to analyze how users understood the transaction, I worked with about twenty regular taxi passengers and took about seven hundred taxi rides on my own.

From the moment Uber's "imminent" arrival was announced in March 2016, I began tracing the company's activity on social and traditional media, particularly press releases, a work involving fragments, snippets, rumors, and op-eds from all sides of the partisan and political spectrum. Media narratives always occupy certain cultural and political spaces, especially in those polarizing years. The culturally conservative and economically liberal national daily *La Nación* was the predominant source of online and printed information for the middle class that dominated postpolitical reasoning. Also, its editorial line and most prominent journalists favored Uber to the point of practically campaigning for it; I paid particular attention to this material, but whenever relevant I included voices and arguments from outlets read by other segments of the middle class, often more critical and nuanced—*Perfil, Clarín, Página/12, Infobae*—in the development of this, my own, narrative.

I registered on Uber's website to receive its newsletter and other documents produced by the company but never even downloaded the app. Uber remained illegal, or at least in several courts at once, during all this time, and hundreds of Uber drivers were stopped by authorities, were fined, or had their cars seized. I attended the company's training sessions for new drivers, collected and analyzed fliers and promotional material, and interviewed Uber drivers and passengers and the same city authorities I had worked with regarding the taxi industry weeks earlier. As the conflict emerged, I participated in several protests against Uber alongside taxi drivers and witnessed several others from the perspective of a resident trying to move around. Nonconfidential legal cases in Argentina are freely accessible to the public; aside from interviews with relevant court clerks, my analysis of the legal case is based on the court files uploaded to the government's portal, www.ijudicial.gob.ar.

Buenos Aires remains the city I have lived in most of my life. "Home" is never just a neatly defined geographical place but also a way of carrying oneself, a more or less self-conscious elaboration on difference and sameness and a way of knowing and of understanding knowledge about something.[43] As a middle-class, adult male with the canonical physical appearance of all those markers in Buenos Aires, I was also at home with the practices and tacit laws of taking taxis and interacting with mostly male drivers, with the taken-for-granted way that bodies like mine can circulate in Argentine urban spaces, and with the tones, inflexions, and complicities of River Plate Spanish, even those I did not use.

Strictly speaking, this is not a book about the middle class, however circumscribed, but about a kind of reasoning I encountered most intensely among bodies who first and foremost fitted a certain socioeconomic definition of middle class. On the whole, this is the segment of Buenos Aires's society that through the inflation, devaluation, currency restrictions, and economic volatility of the country between July 2015 and August 2016 never ceased to be comfortably and regularly able to take a taxi. These residents were mostly professionally trained or university educated; were gainfully employed, sometimes to a managerial or directorial level; were diverse along the sex/gender and LGBTQ+ continua; and had sufficient disposable income to holiday in Uruguay, Brazil, or even Europe and the US and some savings in euros or US dollars. Socioeconomically, this is the segment that was home to me. A subset of this universe partakes in the cultural-political anxieties, intuitions, and exasperations I detailed above: here belonged my informants outside the taxi industry, and, if with reservations, I also inhabited these markers comfortably and was readily associated with them by my interlocutors.

From these homes emerged this project in the form of this book. Only seven hundred of the thirty-six thousand-plus taxis in Buenos Aires are driven by women, and the trade and its spaces of socialization, the union and *propietario* (taxi license owner) chambers are strongly gendered and geared toward men. Women were often quite literally crowded out: women's toilets at gas stations were used by men all the time, the tone and content of WhatsApp and Facebook groups confirmed among the members that these were "the boys," and the relentless, puckishly homoerotic undertones to the overtly and overly (hetero-)sexual banter sought to reproduce comradery among men who spend their days alone in a car. Possibly the most sexist manifestation of these ritualized interactions was that participants dissolved into complicit, mockingly prudish silence the moment a woman was within earshot. I do not mean to celebrate these gender dynamics, or to explore or deconstruct them in ways that hundreds of studies are doing much more exhaustively than I could. My point is that fitting the orthodox appearance of a man naturalized my penetration of spaces, discourses, and practices of a trade operating through bodies that were in a sense like mine.

But maleness, like home, is never absolute, and at another level my body was fundamentally unlike theirs. The River Plate Spanish I speak is not particularly inflected with the markers of middle-class speech, but taxi drivers are uncannily able to suss people out. In their terms, my hard-core inability to socialize over football, the appearance of someone who can afford to engage in regular physical activity for leisure, an odd grammatical turn, and something about my gait betrayed me as a slight but definite outsider. "You probably play rugby," a taxi driver characterized me the day we met: in Argentina, and especially around Buenos Aires, rugby is a quintessentially middle- and upper-class sport, an arena of cultural and social capital reproduction that was indeed my home, for I had played for years and retained links to the game.

Such patterns often map onto verified or suspected partisan and political loyalties and cultural spaces of belonging; in this context this description amounted to drawing a line. "You will probably know more about the industry than us, but you'll never be a *taxi driver*": I was thus sentenced beyond appeal during the first week by a taxi driver the reader will encounter in coming pages and will rightly intuit became my favorite informant. They were far from poor but thought me a pretty posh boy; I self-consciously performed the mannerisms of the place I had been assigned as I retorted, in a register deliberately far too sassy for that place, that this had never been my intention *anyway*. Redrawn onto this turf of chicanery, lowbrow trickery, and repartee, the line that separated us generated more than it foreclosed. I learned about a life I studied and they lived, and my project grew out of my commitment to playing along in a game whose rules I could fiddle with at leisure, so long as I played right and did not try to win.

This line thickened and hardened at the taxi drivers' union, an actively militant Peronist space. I was received with a generosity and openness I did not expect, and with a defensive, frank curiosity about the ideological adversary they intuited in me. At heart forever taxi drivers, union officials knew the middle class's airs and rejection of unions: they drove its people around for a living. My situation as a doctoral student at a British university complicated the nature of this relationship, legitimizing my presence there as an intellectual, and thus less explicitly political, endeavor, but also awkwardly associating me, not a Peronist but an Argentine after all, with the wrong side of the historically tense relationship between the United Kingdom and Argentina.[44] In the hierarchical environment of this union, official authorization from one of the directors had smoothed away explicit resistance to my work from the outset.

As time went by, however, from our different ideological and political positions (which were far less incompatible than they seemed, but were definite on both sides) grew a "cognitive complicity": we shared through our differences a frank commitment to understanding their work and, soon after the problem of Uber, in the terms that mattered to them.[45] They knew that I knew their industry from the other side of that line but that I did so in ways "my kind" probably never would. I marched against Uber alongside them with genuine conviction and a sliver of loyalty that, ironically, would be quite at home in the Peronist ways I was always fascinated yet slightly exasperated by. I agreed seldom with their methods but quite often with their reasons, and I remain convinced that the taxi drivers as a union and as a whole understood better than anyone else what was actually at stake.

But I will never be a taxi driver, as we know, so I reflected on these stakes from a vantage point that probably does not exist outside this book: an intimacy with those anxieties, imaginations, and intuitions, shot through with an industrial knowledge that the middle class does not have. The logics, equations, and axioms of neoclassical economy whose instinctive, cruel utopianism bewitched those residents had been my theoretical hearth for years: they work in this book as perspectival lines imposed by the experience I sought to capture. I knew them in ways beyond the reach of social scientists in general, ways involving years of advanced mathematical training that confirms to neoclassical economists the eternal righteousness of their approach and sets the tone of their near-divine convictions. Defamiliarized from these certainties by real life, which has a way of catching up, and by a disciplinary reinvention, I journeyed back to them as an anthropologist, developing on the way that distance proper to the discipline: a manner of knowing how others organize knowledge about themselves, a genre that, in and of itself, becomes home.[46]

Glossary and Chapter Breakdown

Taxi, one of the most universal terms in the world, designates wildly different industries and relations in different places. In Buenos Aires as of 2021, all taxis are four-wheeled vehicles, and no other kind of transportation is referred to by that name. *Taxi driver* refers to anybody who drives or is institutionally able to drive a taxi. Taxi drivers are divided into two mutually exclusive collectives: *propietarios*, owners, who own the vehicle they are driving or the vehicle someone else is driving for them; and *choferes*, who do not own the vehicle and instead drive for someone else. At the street level, the difference is often invisible and irrelevant: a resident who hails a taxi is unlikely to ever know, or care, whether the driver is a chofer or a propietario. At the industrial level, however, the difference determines the kinds of economic, bureaucratic, and social relations someone enters or is barred from. I use *taxi driver*, or *taxista*, Spanish for *taxi driver*, to refer to the collective, and the more specific *chofer* or *propietario* when the situation requires it.

The urban agglomeration "Buenos Aires" spans two adjacent jurisdictions: the Autonomous City of Buenos Aires, federal capital of Argentina and jurisdictional authority of the taxi trade, and the Province of Buenos Aires. The border between them is a highway, and the whole is culturally, infrastructurally, and economically integrated, much as Washington, D.C., is to Virginia and Maryland. When the jurisdictional distinction matters to particular aspects of the argument, I will speak of the province of Buenos Aires or the city of Buenos Aires. By "Buenos Aires" or "the city," I mean the agglomeration as a whole. *Porteño/a*, person from the port, is the demonym for the Autonomous City of Buenos Aires, but in common parlance and in this book I refer to residents of the whole area as such.

This book is divided into eight chapters. The first three examine what the taxi industry and transaction are like in Buenos Aires, what kinds of bodies and knowledge they are made of, and how they belonged in the common experience before Uber arrived. The first chapter, "The Terms of Engagement," analyzes how the trade became a public service through the taxi license, a unique number carrying with it the prerogative of driving someone for money in the Autonomous City of Buenos Aires. The constitution of the license as an effective fiscal, economic, and bureaucratic instrument is tied to a murder, in late 2001, and to the astuteness of Omar Viviani, leader of the union of taxi drivers and by 2016 known across Argentina as one of Fernández de Kirchner's most visible allies. His capacity for "audacity and calculation" both confirmed his condition as a Peronist Big Man and assured the frustrated middle class that Uber would never arrive.

In 2013, a pedestrian's death in an accident involving a taxi driver in an alleged hypoglycemic shock presented the industry with the question of how to minimize the likelihood of such a thing happening again. Chapter 2, "An Intractable Question," examines how union delegates and employees, ophthalmologists, clinicians, road safety instructors, and university professors leveraged a hierarchy of techniques, knowledge, and reasons to approximate an answer to a question whose answer cannot ever be univocal. The fact that the question was tackled, however, and the attempt to answer it turned the management of these bodies, cars, and people into a political problem, including and excluding certain voices and actors and reproducing the relations between the union, the propietario chambers, the taxi license system, and the political economy of the industry.

Chapter 3, "A Most Perfect Kind of Hustling," examines how taxi transactions happened in Buenos Aires in late 2015 and early 2016. Over thirty-six thousand outwardly identical taxis roamed the city as a completely interchangeable whole, providing 1.5 million rides per day. Wholly disembedded by these circumstances, the taxi transaction played out for passengers and for drivers alike as one with no past or future and one where it was impossible for the two parties to pin each other down. Together with the processes explained in the previous chapters, these dynamics reproduced the passengers' experience of their part in the common experience as victims to opportunism and other abuses they could not control.

The rest of the book traces the logical, rhetorical, and affective triangulations Uber's arrival enabled among that segment of the middle class that progressively cast the taxi industry as the part with no part in the emerging common experience of Buenos Aires's public life. Hours after arriving, Uber was taken to court by the taxi industry. "On Gladiatorial Truths," the fourth chapter, examines how, when faced with a legal case and the institutional legitimacy proper to representative democracies, the middle class argued that Uber's popularity was in itself evidence of its rightful place in Buenos Aires's order of things. The moral legitimacy of "what the People want" shifted the nature of the problem: a *political* question concerning who belonged or not, and how and why, to be sorted institutionally, was now set in the distinct *moral* bedrock of the issue of free economic choice, intrinsically good and perversely hard to trump. These citizens' claim constituted what I call a gladiatorial truth: a truth claim based on the moralizing bottom line of minimally mediated popular legitimacy, measured in actual vocal support or its late capitalism proxy, consumption.

Although for legally strategic reasons the company presented itself as an innovative complement to the taxi industry, the middle class saw the two of them as direct competitors encased in a structural opposition. Uber's condition as a triumphant outsider, thriving "around the world" and managing to break in the Buenos Aires market, affronted the political logics the taxi industry existed in and reproduced. The fifth chapter, "The Stranger That Stays as Such," shows how Uber worked as an economic "stranger king," where an association between economics, "outsideness," competition, and objectivity, logically flawed but affectively very powerful, opposed in popular reasoning the politics, "insideness," monopoly, and partiality that the taxi industry had come to epitomize. This opposition inserted the Uber conflict into anxieties about Argentina's place in the world, further stylizing unverifiable claims into a rhetoric hard to politicize.

"A Copernican Phantasmagoria," chapter 6, analyses how the middle class understood Uber relations as an "ordered, orderly order" made of propositions in a grammar of efficiency, supply, and demand that revolutionized how movement could be inhabited and known from within in Buenos Aires. Produced by the company's interface for each and every one of its users, these propositions were unverifiable and could not be debated: one accepted or declined them. In this sense, I argue that Uber operated as a phantasmagoria, an order that fabricates relations and the means to understand those relations. Uber transactions added up to an empty nowhere that resisted external ordering and that reproduced itself through users' interactions within its own logics. What resulted was a paradox: an infinitely inclusive order that was, in fact, impossible not only to give an order to but also to meaningfully engage.

Shortly after the taxi industry initiated legal action, the company was ordered to cease its operations in the Autonomous City of Buenos Aires. Uber flouted these orders, launching discounts and claiming to stand for freedom of choice. Chapter 7, "The Political on Trial," follows how, as an industrial conflict became a case of contempt of court, the justice system made several attempts to shut down Uber's operations. Their successive failures to do so passed for hardening evidence among the forementioned segment of the middle classes that Uber existed in, and reproduced along with itself, an order of relations that could not be reduced to or contained by existing juridico-political orders and that the only possible, but also morally and naturally rightful, way to engage it was to work with its forces rather than against them.

Elected on a technocratic, prototypically postpolitical platform, Mauricio Macri's administration reinforced the preexisting narrative among the middle class of the reconstruction and normalization of a previously "hyperpoliticized" life. "The Scarlet P," the eighth and last chapter, examines how these tropes helped develop the reasons to write off a present of power outages, currency devaluations, and other vaguely interrelated experiences as steps punctuating the road toward betterment and normality. Uber's arrival, the taxi industry's opposition, the union leader's salience, and other factors played neatly into this rhetoric; the taxi industry's resistance in courts, on the streets, and in the media was now also explained away as an inevitable and obvious friction that porteños were to wait out. The industry engaged in what I call indexical reflexivity: an active, strategic performative work, visible and intelligible to, and aimed at, those whose categories organize the distribution of the sensible that explains one's disagreement away. This work involved performing a particular kind of civility during protests, insisting on the legal routes of the case and on the fact that the judicial power largely agreed with them, and pursuing other strategies to retain a place in the experience of debates worth having and to remove the mark of the Political, Peronism, and the Past foisted upon them by those who disavowed their claims.

As I write this in January 2021, the conflict continues and has spread to other provinces; by the time this book reaches its audience Uber may already be gone, or fully entrenched in Buenos Aires's economy. These scenarios make little difference to the contribution I expect this book to make. Uber was not the first technology to enthrall these anxious Argentines in this way, but several factors converged in this time and place to make this conflict over a ride-sharing app an exceptionally illustrative example of the rhetorical resources late capitalism offers to foreclose disagreement. The terms of the common experience at stake begin for us in July 2015, at a bar near a petrol station where a few taxi drivers who knew the difference between being serious and being literal used to meet every day.

1

The Terms of Engagement

JUST UNDER THIRTY-SEVEN THOUSAND taxis circulate in the streets of Buenos Aires, a place where up to thirteen million people go about their lives on any given working day. Taxis are cars and are most often hailed in the streets as they roam. Taxistas, taxi drivers, signal their availability by a brightly lit red LED sign spelling LIBRE, free, at the top right corner of the windscreen. Would-be passengers raise an arm from the edge of the sidewalk; if they notice each other, the now passenger steps in, the LED sign is turned off, and a transaction is concerted in seconds, an estimated one million times a day, between two strangers who in principle know nothing about each other and who will most likely never meet again.

This chapter examines what a Buenos Aires taxi was as of early 2016. The industrial, economic, political, and historical patterns that informed the industry were tied to the taxi license, a government-issued permit granting certain people the right to drive others for money and rendering this transaction intelligible in a certain way. Taxi drivers are either propietarios, who own the license, or choferes, who drive for them and belong in the taxi drivers' union. This used to be an immensely informal trade, but by linking informality to criminality through a sensational murder in November 2001, Omar Viviani, the union leader, reshaped the political, economic, industrial, and labor relations of the trade into a "trickle-up" economy that consolidated the union's power. Epitomizing the charisma, audacity, and political skill of Peronist leaders in the Argentine imagination, Viviani had by 2015 propelled himself from a tiny, relatively irrelevant union into national politics. Knowing little of what actually went on in the political economy of the trade but certain from their perspective of how Peronism and unions shaped politics in Argentina, the middle class was convinced that so long as Viviani was there Uber would never arrive.

The Number That Rules Them All
Big Sky

To most topographies of Buenos Aires the neighborhood of Villa Ortúzar does not exist, at least not concretely. It is, however, one of the official and smallest forty-six neighborhoods of the Autonomous City of Buenos Aires, where the lowlands of wealthy Belgrano fuse with Villa Urquiza, before the maze of Parque Chas and La Paternal's full industrial decay. Colegiales and Chacarita hem it in from the south and southeast. The name Villa Ortúzar sounds remote to Buenos Aires ears, and its own residents and real estate agents refer to it for indexical, vanity, or marketing reasons as Belgrano, Colegiales, or Villa Urquiza, which are on the whole comfortably well off, beautiful in their own ways, and known cultural references.

Dubbing it in the 1920s the neighborhood with the "Big Sky," Borges already saw in Villa Ortúzar the encryption of that Buenos Aires he mythologized as he brought it to life: three or four regular square grids, all slightly skewed to the west, mapped onto the pampa that the horizon fused with in the mid-nineteenth century. It is not obvious where Villa Ortúzar ends, but three avenues transect it diagonally, two of which intersect, and jacarandas border its two-lane interior streets, trimmed yearly by the city council. Late nineteenth-century through mid-twentieth-century one- and two-story homes are interspersed with small warehouses and depots, the family-run businesses of butchers, locksmiths, tailors, and other small-scale trades, one private and one public school, a kindergarten, and some new developments. The neighborhood has one community-improvised square, at a corner, where an old café was demolished years ago and neighbors installed a children's playground and painted a mural. The Buenos Aires subway, operational since 1913, did not open its Tronador-Villa Ortúzar stop until 2003; the empty, incongruous vastness of the station only enhances the feeling of a place tucked away.

Property here remains affordable and units of land are comparatively big, so along the wide, easy-flow avenues, family houses have been reconverted more or less thoughtfully into car mechanic repair shops, garages, ironmongeries, furniture shops, and a funeral parlor, or outright demolished and replaced with an enormous supermarket with its own underground parking lot, car dealers, gas stations, and car washes. At the corner of an inside street and one of these avenues, someone named Dionisio has owned what porteños call a *café de barrio*, a neighborhood café, for twenty years.[1] It was already a café when Dionisio bought it, and had already been one when the previous owner acquired it in the sixties and for as far back as anyone remembered, even before the beautiful houses had been reconverted. I had been told a group of taxistas gathered there every day.

The café was spacious and almost empty when I found it, except for two men at a table by a window talking loudly, one drinking beer and one drinking wine, and the waiter, pottering around, in and out of the conversation. I ordered a coffee from the table next to them, nodded and greeted everyone in a way that casually wedged me into the conversation. I asked them if they were taxi drivers; they said they were, and I replied I was told they would be there: I was there to research them. "Another one?" The youngest of the pair raised his eyebrows. "There was some journalist here a few months ago," he said; "she wrote an article about us." "I know," I replied, and explained who and what I was. They invited me to join their table and expand on what I was there for, and, amusingly, how long it would take.

As the night went on, more taxistas trickled in, and by about 9:00 p.m. there were seven of us plus the waiter, who was also Dionisio's son and an honorary taxista as far as socializing went. They all anticipated and answered my questions with impeccably performed candor, but the tempo was set by the youngest of the first two, a histrionic, brilliant storyteller with a raspy voice and expansive manners. "What do you need to know? I'll tell you anything," he guaranteed several times, baiting me with "What else?" after he considered a question had been sufficiently addressed. "You could get me a beer, after all these pointers I'm giving you!" he intimated, less to demand a quid pro quo than to envelop me in a playful moral frame, all the more persuasive for the complicity it allowed.

We were all interrupted only once when a mousy man came in, gave this same taxista an envelope, and socialized clumsily before driving away in a taxi. I said my goodbyes to the four or five left at the bar after four hours; "See you tomorrow," the younger of the first two yelled as I left, winking conspiratorially. That he did and several times more, for that very table at that bar became a prime site of my fieldwork, as did the lives of the very first two drivers I met.

A Trade Divided in Two

At some point between September 2015 and March 2016 there were exactly 36,941 taxi cars working in the Autonomous City of Buenos Aires. Although within certain mechanical parameters different car models can be turned into taxis, in the whole of the city there is conceptually only one kind of taxi, painted a certain shade of yellow from the lower rim of the windows up and a certain shade of black from there down. The taxi fare in Buenos Aires is universal and set by the government, and from most perspectives, especially the passenger's, all taxis and all taxistas look the same.

To each car is assigned a unique natural number, called the taxi license, between 1 and some number beyond 38,000; this license grants the prerogative to pick up a fare anywhere within the legal boundaries of the Autonomous City of Buenos Aires. As I write this book there are virtually no taxis without a taxi license in Buenos Aires: I speak of owning one or the other interchangeably. I recognize this statement works against the grain and intuition of much intellectual work on South America emphasizing illegality, informality, and a general effrontery with regard to law, but I present evidence to support it later in this chapter. Governmental and industrial figures estimate that there are three hundred "fake" taxis in the city, by which they mean cars that look exactly like taxis, and are put to work as taxis, but are not properly declared as such, or are running on an invented license number. Three hundred is still less than 1 percent of nearly thirty-seven thousand, and passengers would in principle not be able to tell them apart from official taxis. Their existence therefore does not detract from my argument in this book or from the taxi license's role as the main organizer of economic, political, and cultural relations in this trade.

The taxi license partitions the universe of taxistas into two mutually exclusive camps: propietarios, literally "owners," who "own" a license and, as I will explain later, also the car that is assigned to it, and who are effectively self-employed; and choferes, "chauffeurs," who do not own a license and are driving for someone who does. Owning the taxi license was the only thing the drivers I met at Dionisio's had in common: in principle they responded to no one for their use of time, and on the whole they were able to sit still—a luxury in an industry that trades in motion. Slightly over 60 percent of taxis in Buenos Aires are driven by their propietarios, virtually all second- or third-generation Argentine, from Buenos Aires or the provinces.

Andrés, the histrionic taxista mentioned above, was fifty-two years old, porteño, and a lifelong resident of Villa Ortúzar. He had been driving the taxi he owned for thirty-four years. His father was a taxista too; at age sixteen Andrés slunk out with his dad's taxi at night, "to see what was happening, make some money on my own. Just for a couple of hours." He eventually inherited the taxi license. He often announced with gravitas that he was a *real* taxista: there was nothing he liked more, ever, anywhere, period. By 2016 Andrés owned three taxis: a Chevrolet Spin only he drove, and two Renault Clios assigned to choferes who drove for him, one of whom was the mousy man who had handed Andrés an envelope at the café: inside was the daily rent for the car.

Like Andrés, many propietarios enter the trade through fathers, uncles, brothers, or husbands already in it. Andrés's son, a firefighter by training and employment, acquired a taxi license in his early twenties and drove his taxi on weekends and whenever his chofer was off. Often families go in the business together. Valeria was fifty-two and had grown up in an upper-working-class family in Godoy Cruz in the province of Mendoza. Trained as a nurse and having worked all kinds of trades, she had come to Buenos Aires in her late twenties, gotten married, and had two kids. She and her husband had a comfortable economic situation: their children went to private school and they lived in a big house in La Boca. With sudden restrictions on all imports into Argentina in late 2011, their business became immediately unviable and had to close down. Valeria had driven all her adult life; she and her brother acquired a taxi license in mid-2012, and she had been driving their taxi since. Incidentally, most of the other seven hundred women taxistas in Buenos Aires are also propietarias.

Most propietarios who are not Argentine are Uruguayan and thus linguistically, phenotypically, and culturally indistinguishable from River Plate Argentines even to River Plate Argentines themselves. This was the case with the other of the first two drivers I met, Mauro, sixty-seven years old. He had crossed the River Plate from Montevideo, Uruguay's capital, at age eighteen and had trained and worked as an accountant, where he met his wife. They married, had three daughters, and started two businesses of their own in Villa Ortúzar, one selling and repairing shoes and one selling and repairing bikes. When trade was liberalized in the 1990s both of their businesses collapsed, along with much of Argentina's industry. Mauro bought a taxi just before Argentina's 2001 meltdown and had been driving it since; in 2015 he had a three-year-old Chevrolet Corsa.

Value, Investment, and Freedom

Buenos Aires's residents imagine taxistas on the whole as marginal individuals, unruly but not necessarily uneducated, who fell from the productive layers of the national economy and who, out of a poor work ethic or desperation, have, or can do, nothing other than taxiing. Recent, more fanciful versions of this notion also evoke convicts and petty criminals driving rogue taxis. A moral commentary comes with the general characterization as tricksters, in the conversational and anthropological sense of the term—recalcitrant, opportunistic, and casually devious, as a collective and as individuals. This impression would shape the reception Uber had in Buenos Aires later on.

If grossly exaggerated, these assumptions do evoke some features of taxi life. The taxi license works effectively as a fully tradable commodity, and as implied above, movements in its market are closely correlated with Argentina's economic woes. Still, whereas the turnover for choferes is high, propietarios often remain in the trade for a long time, even those who, like Mauro, entered the trade in circumstances of hardship they have long ago overcome. This is because owning the license in this industry is an investment that actually pays. Andrés made about 18,000 USD a year with the car he drove, plus about 10,000 USD for each of the cars with choferes assigned. Mauro made less, as he had only his own taxi, but with the addition of his wife's income as an accountant, now that their children were adults, they led a comfortable life: during my fieldwork they spent two weeks in Villa la Angostura, in Patagonia, where one of their daughters, a biologist, conducted research for the Argentine National Research Council, and two weeks in Iguazú, Misiones, visiting their other daughter, who was a chef at a five-star hotel. They drove to both towns, among the most expensive tourist destinations in Argentina in international terms, in Mauro's car. They were saving money for a trip (which later happened) to Freiburg, where their third daughter worked at a laboratory. Andrés's daughter was studying to be a lawyer at the University of Buenos Aires, where tuition is free; Andrés helped with study-related costs. Mauro, Andrés, and Valeria all had private health insurance with extensive coverage, which they paid for monthly; they all owned their own homes, Andrés and Mauro right in Villa Ortúzar, where each member of their respective immediate families had or had once had his or her own room. They all had smartphones, most had GPS technology in their car, and none of their taxis was older than three years.

A second reason for staying in the business is that taxistas, especially propietarios, tend to attune themselves to what they explain as the freedom of being a taxi driver. Part of this freedom, as I will show in chapter 3, pertains to the form the taxi transaction takes in Buenos Aires; but for these people it evokes the flexibility of self-employment. Andrés had never had a boss, other than himself, and said he "didn't need one." He started working around six every morning and stopped for coffee during rush hour. He drove some more and, after a meal his wife cooked for their lunch (his triglycerides had tested alarmingly high, and except for the beer he'd have at the end of the day with us, he watched his food intake closely), he drove a few more hours before meeting us at the café. Mauro preferred to begin his day around the tail end of the night and the small hours of the morning: he had always been an early riser and, slightly insomniac with age, sometimes would go out at three or four in the morning, explaining, "I might as well make some money if I'm not going to sleep." Eager to avoid the evening rush hour, he was usually off the streets by 4:00 p.m.

Finally, the taxi license is also a reservoir of value. In late 2015 it changed hands for a market rate of about 18,000 USD, and it was at one point in the late 2000s worth 33,400 USD. Although its value fluctuates in inverse correlation to the country's economic circumstances, it has remained an attractive, broadly speaking safe investment. Propietarios tend not to let go of it, and sometimes licenses barely make it to the market before being transferred to a friend or some kin. Sometimes, also, propietarios hire someone to run the business aspect of having an employee, repairs, insurance, and expenses in exchange for a fixed monthly sum, taking a step back but holding on to the license.

By the time of its popular trial as the perfect icon of an alleged monopoly over a kind of movement in Uber's shadow, the taxi license was in fact the result of a dense knot of governmental, political, economic, and cultural relations. To pull its strings in some logical sequence let us begin with the problem, 160 years ago, of how to monitor strangers joined fleetingly in the space of a car on the western shores of the River Plate.

History of a Public Service

Mobility and transience are inherently difficult to rule: authorities need to hold relations and their parts still long enough to frame and classify them, making them intelligible in certain ways.[2] After retracing colonial attempts to do exactly this since the 1600s, Argentine historian Alberto Parapugna tells us that the Vehicle Plates law, passed on August 27, 1859, by the government of Buenos Aires and requiring all stagecoaches to pay a yearly sum to the city council in exchange for a uniquely numbered car plate, was the first "modern," universal attempt to link up databases, bodies, numbers, and vehicles in motion in unequivocal ways.

Since any mobility in urban environments often involves strangers, and since taxi mobilities involve transacting strangers, asymmetric information, moral hazard, and legal responsibility compound the sheer danger of being encased in a moving vehicle guided by someone one knows nothing about. On February 28, 1860, a new law required all coach drivers offering transportation services to "always display a small numbered plate wherever it is deemed most visible"; compliance would be monitored at all times, still or in motion, except when the vehicle was occupied.[3] In 1861, it was added that "all coaches providing transportation must be numbered on both sides [of the exterior], and the numbers must be three inches long," and that "inside the carriage and in a visible spot will be placed a sheet of paper containing said coach number, the company's name, details of the inscription in the municipality's registry, and approved fare." The last article of the decree states that "coachmen must have a sufficient number of business cards imprinted with the serial number . . . and the officially approved fare" to hand out to passengers.

Fare setting, already in place by 1861, rendered movement knowable by qualifying the economic nature of the transaction and even its material conditions: in 1866, fares were standardized for point-to-point journeys within a given area of the city and doubled for nonpaved roads.[4] The mandatory adoption of taximeters by all coach drivers, from then on known as taxi drivers, was instructed in 1905 by a municipal decree to "guarantee the strict application of fares and avoid abuses to the detriment of the public."[5] Later on, anyone driving a taxi was required to have his or her photograph printed and displayed inside the car; also, choferes would be hired after a suitability examination and production of police records.[6] Already by the 1930s the municipality-issued serial number, linking up this information held in governmental offices, was known as the taxi license. The number of licenses issued increased apace with population: in 1901, there were 2,822; in 1935, around 3,800; and in 1942, about 4,200.[7]

In 1942 the efforts to streamline the trade were streamlined themselves, and taxis were declared a public service under the authority of the

Autonomous City of Buenos Aires, reaffirming that "no vehicle might provide this service without the corresponding license."[8] Within Argentine legal doctrine, public services are loosely defined as standing in a peculiar, case-by-case determined relation to the state.[9] For the taxi industry this means, first, that although in common parlance taxistas "own" and "sell" the taxi license, they can only ever hold and transfer it: it belongs to the city as a legal entity. Taxi licenses are effectively permits, and with no monetary compensation whatsoever the government can recall any of them for reasons such as criminality, unpaid taxes, failure to renew the professional driving permit, evasion of union charges, and fraudulent transfers.

Second, the city government alone has the prerogative of setting the price, or value, of the transaction: the taxi fare. The algorithm combining time and distance to compose the taxi fare is universal, uniform, and programmed into taximeters by five officially designated companies serving the whole city. Third, it means that in principle, and to a much larger extent in practice that even most locals realize, the government of the city of Buenos Aires determines most material and organizational aspects of how the service is conducted, from the types of cars that are permitted to the frequency and costs of vehicular checkups. The city government is the ultimate guarantor of the service.

Finally, the city government alone controls license supply. This authority would be framed as a monopoly in the arguments that the conflict over Uber generated, as chapter 4 shows. More interesting for now is the recent history of this authority. In a fraudulent maneuver inside the city government in 1992–93, about four thousand licenses were outright invented and then granted to people. To make matters worse, Buenos Aires's taxi fleet grew by four thousand as a result but the highest numeral remained the same because all four thousand were duplicates of already existing licenses. To keep the scam relatively under the radar, existing numbers were cloned: these licenses were identical to existing ones in everything that made them official while singular in everything that pertained to the new cars they were being sold to. Honest people accessing the industry now held taxi license numbers identical to already existing taxi licenses held by other honest people already in the trade. Either of them would find out, at the point of vehicular checkups or taximeter adjustment, that these licenses already existed under someone else's name. Renumbering cloned licenses seemed the least unfair solution, which led to a total of now genuinely uniquely numbered licenses surpassing thirty-eight thousand. The taxi industry deemed this supply far too high and lobbied to translate this total into a formal cap, set in 1998: no new taxi licenses have been issued since.

As a governmental device and prerogative, the taxi license is also a disciplinary mechanism. There is a hotline people can call to denounce anything from excessive speed to "having been taken for a ride." Also, often propietarios forget to renew their paperwork, or are found not to be transferring licenses properly (a transaction that includes a payment of a fraction of the value into the city's coffers). In such cases, the propietario is summoned to the government's taxi administration, eleven miles southwest of Buenos Aires's downtown and on the edges of the city proper: "This is the worst punishment there could be: you're forcing them into stillness, for at least half a day, to come and explain themselves," as a government official told me. The third time this happens, the taxi license is revoked and destroyed. With an upper cap and such downward pressure, the total number of taxis declines one at a time, explaining the gap between the 36,941 operational taxi licenses at a given instance during my stay and numbers over 38,000 circulating on the streets.

The Taxis' Law

Law 3622 of the City of Buenos Aires, sanctioned in 2010 and known as the "taxis' law," was drafted by parliamentarian Claudio Palmeyro, a former taxi chofer. All laws are by nature standardizations; this one had the task of standardizing ten laws, eleven ordinances, seven decrees, and seven legal resolutions, at times contradictory and often obsolete, referring to the trade until then. As it enshrines common practices as law; indexes and tables mechanical, material, and professional requirements; and sets benchmarks for the provision and control of the service, this law constitutes the taxi license as a unique form of investment in Argentine society. Taxi licenses can be legally handed over from one citizen to another via a transaction that is not technically a sale, for one cannot sell that which one does not own, but a transfer of the right to operate a taxi associated with that number, met with a monetary transfer of the market value at that time. In what is a relic from past times and also a logical conclusion, taxi licenses can be inherited by immediate family (spouses, children, siblings, or parents) upon death without incurring inheritance tax, because they do not count as property. For this same reason, although they have a market value they are nontaxable and nondeclarable in tax returns.

The law uses the taxi license to shape the distribution and concentration of resources in the industry. No physical or juridical person can hold more than two hundred licenses, less than 1 percent of the total fleet of the city, keeping the industry atomized (it is rare for a single person to hold more than fifteen or twenty) and limiting the institutional and economic influence any single actor could deploy by hoarding means of production. Also, every single license must at all times be attached to an actual vehicle (as mentioned above, there is no taxi without a license and no license without a taxi) and to someone's name as driver of that vehicle, whether chofer or propietario. No physical person can be signed up for more than one car, for the sensible reason that no organic being can drive two cars at the same time. Any accumulation of licenses forces the owner into a labor relationship, or many labor relationships, creating jobs and, as I will show below, social charges and taxes for the union and the state respectively. Tying the license down to a vehicle and a human, both of which come with monthly expenses that can be covered only by actually using the license and the car to make money by taxiing, which is what the taxi license is for, also limits the incentive to use licenses purely as reserves of value. Thus constructed, the law not only removes incentives to scale up and monopolize but forces the circulation of the vehicles, people, and transactions it was designed to qualify.

This law also creates a database shared by all institutions in the trade called the RUTAX, which works simultaneously as census and genealogy centered on the taxi license. For every taxi license in existence the RUTAX tracks ID and other details of owners, choferes, and vehicles but also taximeters' unique codes, vehicular and professional checkups' expiration dates, social charges payment records, and full employment and driving history. Taximeters break, cars get renewed, choferes are hired and go, but they are all recorded in the license, which binds them together along with the history they constitute.

Administratively, this law completes the political, governmental, and cultural process that in the mid-nineteenth century began constructing and qualifying the economic transaction of selling someone a ride. It constitutes a monopoly in the sense that it excludes and distributes bodies and objects from particular interactions; but as I will discuss in later chapters, the moralization of the term *monopoly* obscures the history and governmental logic of making certain relations visible in particular ways for particular reasons. The taxi license forced those in the trade into a certain architecture of labor, political, economic, and institutional relations vis-à-vis each other and urban

residents at large. It defined the political economy of the industry, constituting the infrastructural means of providing a certain kind of movement,
and shaped the possible and likely interactions in the common experience
of Buenos Aires for residents and drivers alike.

If I speak of an administrative blueprint and governmental logics as if
they translated into literal empirical objects, it is because the taxi license,
brought to life through all these facets, was taken extremely seriously. Nobody outside the trade ever imagined that the taxi industry, the trade of
alleged tricksters living on the margins, could embody institutional virtue, or
probably virtue of any kind. Yet by a fabulous twist of fate enabled partly by
their practices, what could have aged as wishful legal thinking materialized
into an impeccable governmental exercise: the taxi license would consolidate
the political, partisan, and industrial order of the taxi industry that residents
knew, even if residents themselves never knew how.

Audacity and Calculation
A Gentlemen's Agreement

Georgina Barbarossa is a famous Argentine comedian and TV presenter,
and because she was already famous by November 2, 2001, when her husband Miguel Lecuna was stabbed fifteen times inside a taxi at the corner of
Mario Bravo and Gorriti streets in the neighborhood of Palermo, the case
made national headlines.[10] Lecuna, a wealthy entrepreneur, was heading to
the house he shared with Barbarossa when two men burst out of a white
van, jumped into the back seat of the taxi, stabbed him, threw his body
out onto the sidewalk, and drove off in the taxi. Forensics later determined
that Lecuna had attempted to resist the robbery, that he had been targeted
at random, and that whoever was driving the taxi was in cahoots with the
attackers. Earlier that year two women had been robbed by taxi drivers, one
also raped. Perpetrators in both those cases already had criminal records and
committed the crimes with actual taxis, properly and lawfully registered as
such, that the impostors had "rented" from the propietarios.

These crimes are intelligible as part of a very specific kind of informal
economy. In common parlance, the notion of informal economy has ac-
creted notions of illegitimacy, illegality, and marginality to become "a catch-
all term to describe many economic pursuits and logics that are part and
parcel of capitalist relations."[11] Informality, in general, evokes the negation of
regularity and predictability. Yet many economic activities defined as informal involve highly streamlined labor, financial networks, and transactional

patterns and often constitute predictable, reliable, and stable relations.[12] Also, as Goldstein's analysis of the sophisticated, visible, and durable networks of wealth, labor, and political loyalties in a Bolivian market show, all attempts at separating them underestimate the extent to which formality and informality depend on each other, even at the heart of the state.[13]

Those impostors could work as such because of a particular pattern of informality quite common in Argentina at the level of relations of production.[14] Evolving historically from a gentlemen's agreement between propietario and chofer, the taxi industry's employment relationship since at least the 1980s was one of singularly low levels of formality *at the point of employee registration*. Choferes were issued with a little notebook that propietarios would sign, often in pencil, as sole record of the chofer's employment: no tax declaration, social security, or pension payments. This labor was invisible to the state, to the choferes' union, and to anyone passing by as the chofer drove about in broad daylight carrying out his otherwise perfectly legal and legitimate job. Argentines refer to labor that is both legal and legitimate, even official, but unregistered, as working *en negro*—"in the black."[15] In case of discord the employment relation was literally, with an eraser, erased from the records: as a member of the choferes' union said, during those years choferes were the cheapest spare part.

Together with the restaurant and construction industries, taxi driving was one of the most *en negro* industries in Buenos Aires. With them it shared also that the builders, restauranteurs, and propietarios themselves were often "real," declared, and made visible to the state and the taxman while their employees were not. Often, propietarios simply did not pay attention to the drivers who rented their car or did not check IDs. If the chofer was caught committing a crime or any violation that would normally include the owner of the taxi in a responsibility chain, propietarios would claim that the chofer was in a trial period, therefore legitimizing the nondeclaration of his or her labor to the taxman and disengaging themselves from the chofer's wrongdoing.[16] Often, too, propietarios were in on the crime but would argue they could not know what was being done with the car while out there. Connivance is hard to prove, so the taxi would be seized by the police and returned to the propietario for a fine. Barbarossa's husband's case took a surreal turn when the taxi's propietario declared in court that "I just lent the car to [the murderer who was driving]. . . . I knew they were out to steal, but not that they would kill—how would I lend my car for that?"[17]

Lecuna's murder gruesomely crowned what became through it a saga. It also happened exactly six weeks before Argentina's economic crash in December 2001. To the rapidly shrinking economy, spiraling unemployment and employment *en negro* were added the four thousand fake licenses thrown on the market by city government insiders, increasing competition among taxistas for a decreasing pool of clients. Taxi licenses were so cheap they were virtually being given away, as Mauro recalled his own purchase. Work fell by 50 percent and taxis sat idly at corners as the few residents left with jobs and sufficient income to afford taxis were too afraid to hail a taxi on the streets. The "Radio Taxi" modality appeared, whereby these same taxis would form a company, with offices and a phone landline, additional controls and internal rosters and checkups, "gridding" themselves so as to create the intelligibility between strangers that the taxi license was not providing.[18] Potential passengers would then phone for a car, be given a car plate and unit number, and wait to be picked up. Between crimes, cloned licenses, and mass unemployment, nobody clamored more fiercely for controls than taxistas themselves—propietarios and choferes alike.

Fifteen years after these crimes, the government, union, and taxistas themselves estimate that informality in the industry, whether involving "fake" taxis or choferes' unregistered employment, concerns two hundred to three hundred taxis—as said before, less than 1 percent of the city's fleet—while work *en negro* surpasses 40 percent in other urban trades. "The guy 'whitened' the entire industry overnight," Andrés decreed as he vaped theatrically at Dionisio's. To whiten is to bring out of *en negro* economies and into the relevant official labor relations. The guy was Omar Viviani, leader of the Union of Taxi Choferes of the City of Buenos Aires, from now on the taxis' union, since 1983.

A Sleight of Hand

Comparatively speaking, Argentina is a highly unionized country. Trade unions as they exist today were born under Juan Domingo Perón's leadership as part of a military government in the 1940s and consolidated during his first democratic presidency (1946–52). As Argentina recovered from the Great Depression, Perón widened and intensified the geographical, technical, and institutional reach of the state, inserting hundreds of thousands of working-class immigrants and first-generation Argentines, until then politically unaffiliated, into the mass democracy of the rapidly industrializing nation.[19] In this project, trade unions were to funnel and organize workers' demands through state-legitimized channels in the manner of their continental European counterparts. As a material reality and a political and cultural concept, the Argentine welfare state emerged through Juan Domingo Perón's leadership, the indefatigable social and iconic work of his wife Eva Duarte de Perón, known as Evita, and the administrative capillarity of trade unions. Among the latter was the taxis' union, founded in January 1950 by Evita herself. Trade unions and Peronism remain entwined in the Argentine political imagination, although several unions today oppose Peronism at political and partisan levels.

Omar Viviani began working as a chofer in 1971, when he also joined the Unionized Peronist Youth and started his militancy in the taxis' union and in the Peronist party. Argentine unions derive clout from numbers and spatial penetration, jockeying for affiliates and their contributions over a scarcely populated landmass of over a million square miles. Unions representing activities that cut across industries and regions, like the union of metalworkers or construction workers, are historically very powerful, and their power is readily intelligible in terms of sheer numbers. The taxis' union's potential for expansion has always been doubly limited by definition: the workers of a very specific industry contained within the boundaries of the Autonomous City of Buenos Aires, the wealthiest Argentine district by far, but in the jurisdictional limits that matter to representation home to only 7.5 percent of the national population. The enormous levels of work *en negro*, thus skirting union charges, further ate away at any possibility of economic and political expansion. By the time of the crimes the union was headquartered in two rooms in a derelict late nineteenth-century two-story house, with a small balcony and wooden floors, in a neighborhood not unlike Villa Ortúzar.

Argentine unions have different motivations to "whiten" workers; success in doing so depends on each union's abilities to shift people from "one side of the line to the other."[20] This ability is a form of power: that of reconstructing the possible fields of action of others.[21] Five days after Lecuna's murder, as the press demonized taxi drivers and called for an end of the "taxi mafia," which surely the union and Viviani were responsible for institutionally but also in never-specified yet unspeakable ways, Viviani spoke to the press: "There has to be [legal responsibility and liability] for the chofer *and* for the propietario. . . . It is unacceptable that we all [choferes] are brought under suspicion because propietarios do not register choferes."[22] Towing away the taxi was not enough: propietarios failing to register their choferes should have their taxi license revoked. Incidentally, his union had presented a law project requesting exactly this in April of that year to fight workers' exploitation, a project now revived to fight "both informality and criminality."[23] Lecuna's murder, the robberies and rapes, and choferes' informality were now logically aligned as results of the same propietario exploitative practices. In grouping the choferes his union represented with Lecuna and those women on the victim's side, he reoriented public fury toward the government and particularly toward the propietarios, his opponents in the political economy of the trade. Yet he also handed them a solution, pegging criminality to informality and both to the element that had created the trade and had been devised to do what it was obviously failing to do: the taxi license.

And so it was. After a man was stabbed fifteen times in late spring but before the austral summer of 2001 was over, by a single sleight of hand in plain sight Viviani reshuffled virtue and blame, cleared himself, and reinvented labor practices in one of the most informal industries in the city. Propietarios registered their choferes en masse. The union, the government, and the propietarios' chambers consolidated and sifted all trade databases entry by entry on the premise that, if there cannot be a taxi license without a car, there also cannot be a car without someone legally registered as driving it and thus generating taxes and, in the case of choferes, also union charges. In turning the taxi license into what it was actually always meant to be, namely, a device rendering relations visible to public institutions, Viviani encrypted in those five digits the political economy of the taxi trade.

For example, as I mentioned earlier, Andrés has three taxis. He is registered as driving one of them as a propietario. The other two are driven by choferes, cleared by the municipality and registered for that specific taxi as choferes. To be a chofer is to be subjected to the union's collective negotiations (there is very little incentive for choferes not to join the union anyway). By Argentine labor law dating back to the Perón days, unions are in charge of pension schemes and life and health insurance and are entitled to union dues aimed solely and explicitly at the reproduction of the union. These are calculated as a percentage of the pretax salary: a part of that percentage is deducted from the salary of the employee (chofer), and the employer (propietario) pays the remainder. This money is paid into the union coffers.[24]

Viviani's legerdemain engineered a "trickle-up" economy, where the industry crystallized in patterns that drew resources from workers up into the organizations that represented them.[25] The emerging newly legal world of labor relations not only secured a flow of monthly income but also multiplied overnight a political base of affiliates, crucial to the existence and reproduction of the union. Moreover, these charges were calculated as a fragment of the minimum wage for the industry, set by the taxi law I mentioned earlier, irrespective of how much the registered chofer drove, if at all. This minimum wage was set as 5,350 times the *ficha*, the single monetary unit that the taximeter advances for every two hundred meters on a taxi ride: charges are thus universalized, predictable, and indexed by inflation automatically every time the city government reviews taxi fares.

This trickle-up economy even brings propietarios with no choferes under its aegis. Mauro has been driving his own car for over a decade, yet during his yearly vehicle checkup among other paperwork he had to redeclare that he himself was driving the car: signaling oneself to be exempted from the union's charges is an ongoing process. Also, by law, every time a taxi license is transferred from propietario to propietario, a tax set at sixteen thousand times the ficha (around three minimum wages) is transferred to the union for the training and medical checkups I analyze in chapter 2.

A Mediation Machine: Peronism and the Political

> Peronism is as indispensable as Borges . . . in the sense that it is impossible to understand Argentine literature subtracting the crucial piece that Borges is. It is impossible to understand Argentina since 1940 without [Perón's] fundamental part.[26]

"I am not a Peronist, far from it as you know, but Uber will never arrive in Buenos Aires. Do you really think Viviani would let it through?" Andrés's prophecy would not age well, but most residents, even those yearning for Uber's arrival, would have agreed with the logics and intuitions behind this claim.

Strictly speaking, Peronism is the name of a political movement whose partisan form is called Partido Justicialista, started under Perón's leadership. Most Argentines would agree with intellectual Beatriz Sarlo's description of Peronism as the most powerful myth organizing the political in Argentina since the 1940s.[27] Just about anything else ever said about Peronism or Perón is more or less bitterly contested. Its inflamed rhetoric, iconography, relentless modernism, cultural intensity, and political traction and divisiveness compare in potency if not content to those of Atatürk in Turkey or Tito in former Yugoslavia. The movement's foundational myth resists any kind of ordering, featuring Perón's exile in seven countries plus a rocky island on the River Plate; Argentina's neutrality during World War II and Perón's known sympathies for the Axis; the nationalization of strategic industries; the birth of Argentina's nuclear energy technologies; women's vote; land and property expropriation; and the incorporation of the masses, Eva Perón's "shirtless ones" (*los descamisados*) into Argentine political and cultural life. Death only aggrandized Peronism's mythical grip: Perón's corpse was ominously mutilated, and Evita's was copied four times in wax, smuggled out of Argentina, and made to spend a long season interred under a pseudonym in Milan to avoid its desecration by raging anti-Peronists. She now rests in the Cemetery of Recoleta, Buenos Aires's finest, among the grandest oligarchs of Argentina's nineteenth century, whose descendants she so antagonized.

Peronism has been described as a party, a movement, an ideological collective, and even an aberration unintelligible "rationally."[28] The question of its nature bedevils academics because for eighty years something named Peronism has outlived coups, proscriptions, hyperinflations, and plain electoral defeats while programmatically and culturally embracing nationalists, conservatives, liberals, neoliberals, populists, social democrats, and those who would elsewhere pass for socialists, most often simultaneously.[29] No book can define Peronism, or its cultural and political impact, in any exhaustive or definitive way; I will not even attempt this, not least since this is not a book about Peronism. Certain aspects of Peronism, however, were crucial to the life of this conflict, to how residents understood the distribution of the sensible and the taxi industry's part in that distribution and in the conflict Uber would later trigger. Besides, Argentines themselves understand Peronism intuitively; we must explore how this intuition made sense of this conflict, or, in other words, what kinds of implications, commonsense truths, and seasoned affects were built into Andrés's prophecy.[30]

First of all, Andrés, Mauro, Valeria, and all propietarios belong to one of six propietario chambers, associations of various sizes of those who own the means of production, that is, the taxi license and the taxi assigned to it. These chambers work as cooperatives, offering legal, financial and administrative advice to their members. In the political economy of the trade, they by definition oppose the union, which represents labor and whose numbers dwarfs those of the six chambers combined. In partisan and political terms, most of these chambers are not Peronist: Andrés's prophecy was signaling his personal convictions but also this partisan distribution within the trade. This does not mean chambers are diametrically opposed to Peronism, but this is only because the latter's ideological content is so labile. The chamber Andrés belonged to boasted a proud history of "actual" socialist militancy and an institutional continuity, integrity in government operations, and solidarity ethics; from these noble heights they scorned what they saw as the union's phallocracy, opportunism, and mass-based bravado.

Andrés also evoked a cultural link between this particular union, unions in general, and Peronism. As mentioned earlier, Argentine unions were shaped to funnel workers' demands and integrate them into the welfare state Perón imagined, and to a great extent achieved, for Argentina. Acclaimed welfare institutions of a mass democracy, with *mass* both in the sense of universality and in the mid-twentieth-century sense of political masses, workers' unions and the millions they mobilized became the political and electoral backbone of Peronism as a national force, and of the Partido Justicialista as its most emblematic partisan materialization. The relation between Argentine unions and Peronism in the last eighty years is extremely complex, but two aspects matter in terms of the cultural imagination at play here. First, most Argentines take as common sense that Peronism and the unions reproduce themselves through each other, that most unions are allies of Peronism, and that Peronism needs their numbers to survive. This alleged symbiosis is electoral, partisan, institutional, and affective: union leaders are as likely to take executive or legislative roles under the banner of Peronism as they are to march down Buenos Aires's avenues, paralyzing the activity of thirteen million people to perform support of one Peronist politician over another, or over a non-Peronist. Second, both the taxi drivers' union and Omar Viviani were resoundingly, possibly even iconically, Peronist.

Peronist leaders after Perón perform a particularly cunning variant of the "Big Man." They are mostly but not exclusively men who, like Perón himself, rely on nontransferrable qualities such as charisma, eloquence, and an impeccable sense of timing to reproduce their power, but especially, as we shall see, the order within which this power makes sense.[31] Argentines intuitively understand these qualities, a realpolitik of "audacity and calculation," as quintessentially Peronist.[32] This notion may be tautological, but its pull on the Argentine political imagination is as old as Peronism itself: when an earthquake devastated the city of San Juan in 1944, then-minister of labor Perón bypassed the myopic political establishment in Buenos Aires and San Juan, including his autocratic superiors, to orchestrate a reconstruction that was imperfect and institutionally problematic but that "got things done."[33] Peronism stands out in Argentine popular political intuition as the political form that cuts to the chase, less worried about due process or ideological integrity than about outcomes and realpolitik: people may loathe it or passionately defend it, but few, if anyone, question its working as an exceptional "mediation machine, able to process conflicts, incorporate its preferences, and translate them into the res publica."[34]

Viviani's use of a murder to reinvent the labor, fiscal, and political landscape of the trade epitomized this mediation machine exceptionally well within the taxi industry. Older drivers remembered Viviani as a chofer sardonically: an enduring irony of Argentine trade union life is that often union leaders become rentiers of the trades they represent, and Viviani has not driven a taxi in thirty-five years. I never met him; I knew from union directors that he knew about my research and had approved of my presence there. The union's lawyer told me that nothing escaped him, the accountant assured me that he was good with numbers, and the union's director of legal affairs added that he had a shrewd sense for legal matters. Strict, caring, and fatherly, he was said to know everyone in the union by first name and to arrange impromptu breakfasts with union officials. Archive interviews spanning his entire career show a charming and quick-witted man, unfailingly poised with his red moustache and a paternal smile. Some say he owns two companies in Italy, others say he owns three, and many claim he secretly owns all taxis in Buenos Aires. His brother was murdered to intimidate him, or committed suicide; since 1983 he has been reelected leader five times, always in fair and democratic elections, except that since the time one adversary in the early 2000s allegedly came home to a front of shattered windows he has run unopposed.

But by mid-2015 Viviani was also quite well known outside of the taxi trade, where the political intuition of Peronism as a realpolitik mediation machine also thrived. Argentina was approaching national elections, and Viviani was on the forefront of national political life. For reasons logically different from but intimately attuned to those of Andrés, vast swaths of Buenos Aires's middle class also thought Viviani would never let Uber in.

Peronism and What Could Happen Here

Viviani was certainly known to Francisco, a shop clerk in his late thirties. He also knew Uber was available in the UK, where I live, a natural prop for conversations that inevitably returned to "The union will never allow it." He had been born in an agricultural town 160 miles west of Buenos Aires and his parents and grandparents were Peronists. Like many other non-Peronists he spoke ironically of Perón's popular nickname "the General," evoking the loyalty, honor, and leadership of martial life but conveniently distilled from Perón's origins in a military dictatorship. As a boy Francisco had played soccer in the local youth association "Evita," and his townspeople, like many Argentines across the land, celebrated every seventeenth of October as the day of Peronist Loyalty.

His mother had had an administrative role at a local factory, his father worked as a welder, both were unionized, and to this day Evita's portrait hung in their dining room. Both had gone to school when state-issued reading books featured sequences such as "My mother loves me," "Evita loves me," and Evita loves my mother," all quite pedagogical in many ways, not least since their Spanish version requires only three commonly used consonants, M, V, T, and three vowels, A, E, I: *mi mamá me ama, Evita me ama, Evita ama a mi mamá.* This was before the military coup of 1955 that under the name of the Liberating Revolution overthrew Perón's second presidency. The coup leaders accused him of treason, proscribed his party, outlawed political and cultural references to him or his wife, and removed their names from the public sphere, including two provinces they had named after themselves, Presidente Perón and Eva Perón, now the provinces of Chaco and La Pampa respectively.

Francisco had been living and working in Buenos Aires since his late teens. He did not lead an actively political or partisan life but had never voted for Peronism at any electoral level. He defined his origins as working class but himself more as a *laburante*, River Plate Spanish for "someone who works," a cross-class, morally economic category less concerned with toil than with work as an ethical imperative and a civic duty, perhaps akin to "striver" in the UK or "taxpayer" in the US. *Laburantes* tend to resent unions for reasons similar to Andrés's; Francisco referred to them as "leeches."[35] He did not belong to any union, but once members of the union his coworkers at the shop belonged to came round to "request" that the owner close down during a strike day, even though employees who wished to strike could simply do so. Although Francisco did not want to strike, the owner had to send everyone home out of fear union members would damage the shop, merchandise, or worse.

This vignette captures the extent to which trade unions, which people like Francisco intuitively conflate with Peronism, are seen as capable of configuring, disrupting, and controlling the experience of the distribution of the sensible in Argentina, incorporating their own preferences for that

experience into the res publica—or else. In principle, the problem is less
the fact that unions defend their perspectives, stake claims, or present their
arguments, ultimately the reason any political organization exists, and more
the means they deploy in order to do so. This rationalization is enhanced
by the general perception among much of the middle classes across political
lines that union bureaucracies are in it for themselves and would, for gain,
deliberately pursue a course to the detriment of their members. Many union
leaders are known for their fabulous wealth in real estate, land, cars, businesses, and even soccer teams, whose often gaudy ostentation scandalizes
the simmering resentment of self-described *laburantes*. On this particular
front, Viviani was conspicuously discreet.

Like most residents, Francisco had no idea that the taxi license was taken
seriously; he was in fact convinced the opposite was true. He believed my
explanation that Viviani had leveraged it to reconstruct the entire trade
only because he would have believed anything about Viviani if it pertained
to self-perpetuation. Also like most residents, he was convinced that Viviani controlled the entire taxi industry—not only effectively, as perhaps in
some ways he did, but also institutionally and programmatically: very few
residents knew the political economy of the taxi industry in any detail,
and most assumed Viviani spoke for the whole industry and represented it
politically. This conflation would lubricate the intuitive links residents made
between their frustrations with taxi drivers at street level and the excesses of
the union-Peronist mediation machine. It would also catalyze the transfer of
resentment from symbols, rhetoric, and partisan allegiances to the concrete
materiality of the taxi industry and its relations when Uber arrived.

This transfer would gain spectacular impact, too, since by late 2015,
barely three months before Uber's arrival, the broadly known partisan and
political borrowings between unions, Peronism, and governmental institutions had for other reasons materialized in Viviani, of all people. Under the
elastic political label of Peronism, Néstor Kirchner's presidency (2003–7),
and then his wife Cristina Fernández de Kirchner's (2007–11 and 2011–15),
faced the political and economic reconstruction of Argentina after the largest
sovereign debt default in recorded history on December 2001. These were
hugely divisive years: the historical schism "Peronism versus anti-Peronism"
was reorganized along the lines of "K" and "anti-K," that is, "Kirchnerist"
and "anti-Kirchnerist." In two opposing, hyperbolic characterizations, the
K project was either a sovereign, popular project for a truly independent
and inclusive nation or yet another instance of Peronist populism, fiscal

profligacy, economic short-sightedness, and ideologically motivated persecution. Francisco belonged in the latter camp.

During these times, Viviani sided with the Ks and was appointed general secretary of the General Confederation of Labor (CGT by its Argentine acronym), a sort of mecca of Argentine unions. This is a politically very strategic and sensitive position, requiring its holder to be diplomatic, understand national policy, and cope with intense media scrutiny; and during Fernández de Kirchner's second mandate it was under even more pressure as the confederation broke into two, one side supporting Fernández de Kirchner and the other opposing her. Viviani remained loyal, adroitly holding onto his position through the mounting inflation (or in the terms endorsed by the national government, "price dispersion"), falling employment, collapsing infrastructure, and growing factionalism. He was rewarded with a position on the ballot for the Parliament of the Autonomous City of Buenos Aires, under Fernández de Kirchner's aegis, for the December 2015 elections. By then all Argentines knew that the leader of a tiny, territorially circumscribed, and comparatively powerless union had managed to project himself into the capital's Parliament: this was the man whose audacity and calculation Uber would have to face if it tried to enter Buenos Aires.

Peronism: Not for Just Anyone

On October 19, 2015, Viviani, already on the ballot, claimed that Kirchner's iteration of Peronism "understands what Argentina needs to continue growing, developing, creating jobs and redistributing wealth," adding they would win the elections in the first round.[36] Three days later, Fernández de Kirchner's candidate won by too slim a margin to avoid a second round, and Viviani lost, or never won, the parliamentary seat he was running for. The second round for the presidency would be held November 22, between Fernández de Kirchner's candidate, Daniel Scioli, and Mauricio Macri's broad coalition, Cambiemos, Let's Change, encompassing technocrats, centrists, historically right-of-center politicians, and, although it appealed to both non- and anti-Peronists, some converted Peronists in its ranks.

In the throes of the election campaign, Macri, who was chief of government of the Autonomous City of Buenos Aires at the time, erected a monument to Perón. What had that been about? I asked Francisco. He did not know. This was perhaps Macri's attempt at audacity and calculation: a tactical nod at Perón's mythical potency and material impact on the nation in the minds of millions of supporters about to cast their vote?

That the symbol rang hollow mattered only to media and academic political analysts. As chapter 8 will show, Macri's technocrats were less invested in engaging, or understanding, the symbolic density of Peronism than in managing it through polls, surveys, and spreadsheets, where probably a stubborn correlation between the national electorate's affinities and the variable Peronism recommended erecting a statue to him. The statue was perceived as a blunder, which only reinforced the notion that in Argentines' experience of the distribution of the sensible, only certain actors can pull certain calculations off.

Statue or not, Macri's coalition won. He took office as president of Argentina on December 10, 2015; in early February 2016, fifteen Peronist parliamentarians from seven provinces broke ranks with Fernández de Kirchner, suddenly a toxic asset, and formed their own Peronist sub-bloc. Viviani went under the public radar, resurfacing nine months later to declare that "Cristina [Fernández de Kirchner] is over, that era is done."[37] "He left Cristina stranded in the end, of course!" Francisco grimaced: Peronist loyalties are nationally famous for their versatility, enhancing the opportunistic aspect of Peronism as a mediation machine.

Back in the early 2000s, shortly after the en masse registration of choferes, the union left its derelict headquarters and moved into two six-story, purpose-built buildings, used for the training programs and checkups that chapter 2 examines, legal and administrative member support, and the running of the union. The first floor of the largest of the two is lined with two rows of union delegates, that is, union members with institutional duties. Emblazoned in half-yellow, half-black jackets embroidered with the inscription "Omar Viviani—Sindicato de Peones de Taxi," their sole job is to pore over the RUTAX entry by entry, taxi license by taxi license, chasing up union charges online, via email, telephone, and the occasional visit, in person or in groups, to incentivize propietarios to register their choferes. The union, the taxi license, and the leader that crafted a whole political economy out of a way of moving around are tightly interlocked.

During my first visit to this building I was shown the meeting room on the fourth floor, empty save for an immense rectangular table with a dark wood veneer and two life-size portraits, one of Perón, one of Evita, hung on either side of the narrow end of the room, visually above the shoulders of whoever presided over the table. Later I heard it was at the taxi drivers' union, at that very table, that those parliamentarians had convened to rebrand their own version of Peronism. Viviani had presided over the meeting.

Windows ran the room's length, and one could see most of Boedo, the neighborhood where the union's headquarters were and Borges's favorite, an older part of Buenos Aires of straight lines and low-rise houses, wide avenues, car mechanics, and a huge supermarket, a near-perfect square grid skewed slightly to the west-northwest. Two floors above that room, at the top, Viviani had his own office, lined with the same windows, towering over the building and over Boedo itself, a neighborhood not really unlike Villa Ortúzar, where my informants met and my project began, except that everyone knows where Boedo is.

2

An Intractable Question

THIS CHAPTER EXAMINES a question that would haunt the Uber conflict: Who gets to drive someone else for money? After an accident in 2013 involving a taxi driver, the industry and the city government reorganized entry and permanence in the trade around the question of how to ensure that such an event, involving a presumed diabetic driver and presumed reckless behavior, would not repeat itself. Taxi drivers' bodies were problematized, that is, turned into the object of a particular kind of attention to render them intelligible in a certain manner and to certain eyes. This chapter traces the techniques, spaces, and rationalities that organized these bodies with respect to that question. Problematizations are always a political exercise: bodies are excluded, certain forms of knowledge are prioritized, specific behaviors are encouraged, and certain exceptions are made in a hierarchical exercise dominated by a certain rationale. A sequence of classes, health examinations, and declarations and interactions with the spaces of the industry and its authorities reproduced the political, economic, and labor relations within the trade: taxi drivers' bodies emerged through the questions asked of them in an ordered relation vis-à-vis the union, the trade, and each other. This problematization does not matter as a "truth" to counter the middle class's imagination of the taxi industry as an unruly, ungoverned trade of tricksters, although it does, effectively, offer a counterpoint. My goal is to examine which bodies entered the common experience of the taxi transaction, how they stayed there, and the perspective from which the industry would attempt to resist its exclusion from debate when Uber arrived: that of an order that was exclusionary and hierarchical because all genuine social orders are.

An Accident

Twenty-two-year-old only child Leonela Noble was born in Tres Algarrobos, a tiny town in the flat pampas on the northwest edge of the province of Buenos Aires, some 320 miles from the spot where she was run over on Tuesday January 29, 2013. She had arrived in the city of Buenos Aires in 2010 to study fine arts and was working as a secretary at a general practitioner's surgery in the neighborhood of Recoleta. On January 29, around midday, she phoned her mother, Sandra Fewkes; Mrs. Fewkes later told the press her daughter was on her way to cash a check at a bank on Santa Fe Avenue, yards from her office. The money was to pay for a bus ticket to Tres Algarrobos the following day.[1]

Also in 2010 Santa Fe Avenue's lanes had been repartitioned to allow traffic in both directions, after four decades of flowing exclusively into the city center. According to witness reports collected that Tuesday, a taxi, a Ford Focus, veered out of its lane and past the dividing yellow lines, accelerating as if out of control, zigzagging by some accounts, into the incoming traffic and toward the avenue's intersection with Montevideo Street. Miss Noble would have been around that intersection; in that instant traffic lights were giving right of way to drivers on Montevideo Street, and cars on Santa Fe were standing still. In a matter of seconds and across a third of a block the taxi collided with a motorcycle and two taxis on Santa Fe Avenue, skidded onto the sidewalk, and crashed into a bus and another taxi driving down Montevideo Street.[2]

The policeman that first approached the totaled Ford Focus declared he found thirty-four-year-old chofer Rubén Botta in the driver's seat, staring absentmindedly into the distance; the car doors were shut. When firefighters managed to remove him from the car they found an unwrapped candy clenched tight in his fist. He and four of the six pedestrians injured were transported to the Hospital Fernández, about a mile east, where ER reports stated that Botta had suffered a hypoglycemic shock at the wheel. This report would be crucial during the ensuing trial, as would be the alleged severity of the shock and the veracity of his story overall, for Botta insisted that he had blacked out and had no memory of the accident. A fifth pedestrian was taken to the Hospital Rivadavia, also to the east, and all of these people survived, but Leonela Noble was killed instantly.

Mr. Botta was indeed diabetic, which upon acquiring his taxi driver's license he knew but did not tell. As Leonela Noble's death entered courts and newspapers, popular, medical, and legal debates raged about how exactly diabetes would affect a driver, or whether Botta had had a full hypoglycemic shock, and if so, what the likely organic manifestations would have been, how much time he would have had to react, what his responsibilities as a diabetic patient were, and more. Two days after the accident, Sandra Fewkes, Miss Noble's mother, discovered that Botta had fifty unpaid speeding tickets and other traffic violations.[3] Not only did this call into question his suitability to be a taxi driver, indeed to even drive; it also challenged Botta's account of the hypoglycemic shock as the sole, or main, cause of the accident. Perhaps he was just a reckless driver, irrespective of his diabetic condition; or a diabetic sufferer who was careless about his treatment; or a reckless driver who was careful about his health and had genuinely had an unforeseeable hypoglycemic shock.

Botta's case manifested, in an exceptionally literal way, how illegible bodies in motion can be. Diabetes, its treatment, the ethics of its management in relation to one's job, its effects, and other events of fundamentally different natures were quite difficult to separate and give weight to in the task of determining responsibility and legal liability for Miss Noble's death. Inside the taxi industry and the government, the case raised questions about what those players could and should know about other bodies, what kinds of knowledge should count, and how to organize that knowledge and those bodies with respect to a particular problem. If only in PR terms, these questions were urgent, and they were tackled straightaway.

A Question of Questions

The union's headquarters in the neighborhood of Boedo, which I mentioned in chapter 1, consist of two buildings on opposite sides of the same block, connected internally by a patio. Before my first visit I was instructed to announce myself at the reception of the smaller of the two, swarming with union delegates in black and yellow jackets emblazoned "Omar Viviani—Sindicato de Peones de Taxi" (Union of Taxi Choferes) on the back. For the purposes of this argument, union delegates are union members with institutionalized political and pastoral duties. "*Compañero!*" a delegate greeted me with wary kindness and no other word. As chapter 4 will show, *compañero* and its plural, *compañeros,* were Perón's vocatives for the working people, his People. The course coordinator was expecting me, I explained, and another delegate was instructed to escort me upstairs to the coordinator's office. He invited me to sit on a row of padded seats while he announced my presence, and I was greeted again with "*Compañero*" by yet another delegate in the same black and yellow jacket pacing up and down the spacious hallway in a casually vigilant way. Sepia portraits of taxi cars from the early twentieth century lined the otherwise clinically blank, creamy-white walls.

Within minutes Malena called my name as she walked down the hallway. She carried herself with that spontaneous authority that makes others unreflexively available; I stood up without realizing. She directed me toward her office, invited me to take a seat, and asked with curiosity about my doctoral project, which we had discussed briefly on the phone. She had already decided she was interested in my work; we shared biographic snippets as we toured both buildings and their rooms, patios, and foyers where everyone greeted her as they sorted files, cleaned the floors, or guarded the entrance. Trained in corporate and administrative law, Malena had worked in the private sector and as a solicitor for much of her life. She had in fact been working for one of the propietarios' chambers, antagonists to the union in the political structure of the industry, when five years earlier Viviani had convinced her to work with him. In the formal distribution of responsibilities, Malena was in charge of the yearly renewal of choferes' credentials, which included every process I list below. In the political and institutional daily life of the union, not much happened without her approval.

A more modest version of the professionalization course and medical checkups I refer to below had been in place since early 2012. The Botta case had changed, or more precisely, accelerated everything, forcing the union to realize, according to Malena, that "we had here an enormous population of which we knew virtually nothing. Taxi driving is an extremely stressful, unhealthy activity: these people spend ten, twelve hours driving virtually nonstop in traffic, snacking on processed food, skipping meals, sitting all day in the car, their sleeping patterns are all over the place. . . . They are time bombs."

This was all known before January 29, 2013, but Rubén Botta's rogue Ford Focus marked the logical beginning of the process whereby taxi driver bodies began to be delineated by the industry's authorities as bodies that needed to be known in particular ways: they were problematized. I speak of *problematization* in the Foucauldian sense of the term: that is, those bodies were set apart and characterized jointly as "taxi driver bodies" to be understood in specific ways.[4] A problematization is never a neutral exercise, or simply a "representation" of the reality at hand; it is always imbued with a particular rationale, and its point is to render certain things visible through certain lenses and to certain eyes. In the aftermath of the Botta case and in Buenos Aires in the twenty-first century, these were the eyes of the union, the propietario chambers, and the city government. The concrete question they asked themselves was "How do we avoid another one?"

The reasons for this triad of deliberating parties were various. In a most obvious sense, the union, the chambers, and the city government were on the front line of public demands for explanations. Also, the taxi industry remained a public service in legal and institutional terms. This is a broad category in Argentina, as chapter 1 mentioned, but in this industry it meant the Autonomous City of Buenos Aires legally owned the taxi licenses and remained overseer of the trade and its relations as a whole. The reasons for the union's involvement are historically and logistically more complex, and a full exploration of them lies well beyond the scope of this book. For my purposes here, readers need to know the Argentine welfare state developed largely through trade unions in the 1940s: as the latter enrolled unaffiliated masses of workers and gave them political voice, they were charged with the provision or management of several typical welfare state duties, like basic health care, life insurance, and funeral costs. Like many others, the taxi drivers' union retains these duties and prerogatives to this day.[5]

The union's sheer numbers and clout in the political constellation of the industry also played a role. A few years before the Botta case, Santiago, an urban planner and lecturer at a university in Buenos Aires, had been hired by the city legislature as an external consultant for many of Mauricio Macri's projects in Buenos Aires during the latter's two consecutive terms as chief of government of the city (2007–11 and 2011–15). These involved the progressive pedestrianization of the financial district, the redirecting of traffic (on streets like the Avenida Santa Fe, where Miss Noble was killed), the demolition of whole city blocks to prolong boulevards, the architectural restoration of palaces and historical properties, an increase in the number of cycling lanes, and the expansion of subway lines. In the early 2010s Santiago's focus shifted to transportation, which he interpreted as being "in need of a new paradigm."

When I interviewed him in late 2015 he was leading an interdisciplinary commission where urban planners, architects, parliamentarians, and engineers examined the "Swedish model of road safety." This model was a bundle of transportation safety policies developed in Sweden that factored in the driver's concentration and health, the chemical composition of asphalt, the vehicle's structure and plasticity, et cetera, in a "holistic" approach aimed at minimizing the number of road accidents and the seriousness of those that happened. The model had been discussed at international forums sponsored by the Inter-American Development Bank, whose technicians encouraged member cities to implement it.

The near-thirty-seven thousand taxi cars in the city of Buenos Aires constituted a prime, single collective allowing planners to "holistically" reflect on traffic. In 2012, the union and propietarios' chambers were invited to collaborate in integrating this model with the existing mechanisms of taxi control and verification mentioned in chapter 1. The goal was to progressively "professionalize" the trade "holistically," incorporating the "needs" of drivers, passengers, and other city dwellers in the city's driving "ecosystem." This integration won the Inter-American Development Bank's Best Practices Award and was copied "around the world," Santiago announced proudly. In that 2012 collaboration he met Malena, who represented the union, as well as the propietario chambers' representatives. They developed the idea of a professionalization course and a series of medical checkups for every single body in the trade, conducted at the union and at the propietarios chambers' for each collective respectively, and launched in 2012. After Leonela Noble's death a psychological test and a sworn declaration of health were added.

From this intersection of professional careers, accidents, awards, and international circulations of "best practices" emerged the union, the government, and the chambers as interpreters of taxi driver bodies with an eye, always, on the question of how to make sure the Botta case did not repeat itself. This was a form of power that did not work through coercion but sought to "operate on the field of possibilities where the behaviors of acting subjects are inscribed: [the exercise of power] incites, induces, diverts, facilitates or hampers, expands or bounds, makes more or less likely, as last recourse blocks or impedes completely; . . . a way of acting on acting subjects."[6] In other words, this power is imbued with a particular rationality Foucault famously designated as governmentality: the "conduct of conduct."[7]

A Taxi Driver Body

Problematizations are always multifarious, diffuse, and scattered, combining different kinds of knowledge.[8] This one in particular involved the deployment of techniques, materials, practical truths, and different sorts of expertise that both depended on and informed these authorities' under-standing of what a taxi driver body was.

Medical knowledge was an obvious touchstone. Certain techniques and discourses were incorporated fairly straightforwardly: visual and hearing examinations that already existed for candidates for any driver's license were transposed into the checkups as a commonsense baseline. Others were adjusted to the particularities of the population being circumscribed. Malena combined and reconciled the union's health insurance records with the registry of choferes. The correlation between those bodies and conditions like diabetes, hypertension, obesity, and other ailments normally problematized in terms of sedentarism was colossal, and taken as evidence that this was not a statistically normal distribution of diseases. The "real" distribution, the one that mattered concretely to the industry, was one where monotony, stress, and other particularities skewed the "normal" in ways that needed prioritizing.

Certain clinical conditions of those bodies were also understood to interact with certain behavioral, psychological, and even socioeconomic and migratory circumstances. With intermittent or deficient access to medical and other forms of care beyond those provided by the union, choferes often had conditions that went unchecked for years. Also, many came from Argentina's northeast, where Chagas disease is endemic, so the condition was included on a list of diseases taxi drivers would have to declare having had or not.[9] Also, always in terms of preventing another Botta case, many latent "risks," that is, biomedical patterns and behaviors deemed more likely to bring about problematic outcomes, were either not traceable in some or most stages, or not traceable in any practical or cost-effective manner. In Malena's words, "Lack of sleep, excess of caffeine, poor diet in themselves all go under the radar unless and until they build up to something measurable. We know they do in the long run, but if a driver has not slept in thirty-six hours and keeps going on coffee or other substances, irrespective of the cumulative damage to his health, he is a danger to himself and others in that very moment." Statistics, epidemiology, geography, medical knowledge, and constructions of normality, together with their attendant techniques, allowed the union, the city government, and the chambers to turn that collective of bodies into a *population* to improve and manage.

But taxi drivers spend most of their time alone, on their own: in order for this problematization to make sense in terms of the Botta case, those *individual* taxi driver bodies, as such, would have to be encouraged to engage in a particular kind of self-care. Malena gave me two examples: "Crisscrossing data, we found that one chofer had never disclosed he had epilepsy, out of fear his taxi driver's license would be withheld. He had been a member of the union for years, a beneficiary and contributor to the union's social security, but we had to withhold his license. Months later he brought us a doctor's note certifying he was being medicated and monitored. He also brought his EEG and ECG as well as other tests, and was then authorized to resume the activity." In a second episode, on the basis of peculiar results in Bender's test, the union's psychologists interviewed a chofer who admitted to smoking marijuana regularly. He was offered counseling by a union psychologist and was informed that he would have to quit his habit, but he refused to undergo counseling, so his taxi driver's license was withheld and he was never let in the trade again.

As these cases show, the conduct of conduct works through circumscription, revelation, and actualization rather than outright sanction. Neither the epilepsy nor the drug consumption was in itself a barrier to the trade; the lie and the refusal to comply were. At stake, thus, was whether these bodies were, or could be made, docile, allowing their practices and biochemical processes to be monitored and ready to show that they were looking after themselves in canonically certified ways.[10] Along the road toward minimizing the chances of another Botta case traveled bodies marked for the rest of their organic lives as sites of asthma, diabetes, neurological diseases, and other incurable conditions. That perpetuity is written into these bodies; the problematization tends to it through the regular checkups these bodies must comply with.

Having delineated both the bodies and the kinds of truths to be read from them, the yearly event of the professionalization course and medical checkup was set up as follows:

- A three-hour lecture;
- An audiometry and a "hearing examination form" where candidates declared having or having ever had cochlear implants, ear discharge, hearing aids, and other potential causes of or remedies for hearing difficulties;
- A visual acuity examination (Ishihara's test and Snellen's test);
- A psychological test (Bender's test); and
- A "health questionnaire" where the candidates, swearing by their signature that their answers were truthful, stated whether they had ever had, or been treated for, one or any of twelve conditions.

Malena allowed me to take these tests as if I were another candidate, with the exception of the audiometry, which took place in a very small room where candidates were allowed in one at a time, and a turn for me would have been cumbersome to organize. The following techniques, spaces, and rationalities organized choferes with respect to the question of the Botta case. Propietarios would undergo a near-identical checkup in their chambers. The events of this day (re)produced choferes as workers, for no one could become a chofer without a checkup, and without being linked with a propietario as license owner; but they also (re)produced every body's respective relation to the union and to the state, and the union's to the state, thereby (re)producing the terms on which this industry worked. These terms included, of course, determining who got to ask a question about order and who was ranked in the construction of an answer and how.

Knowledge and Everyone's Place

I joined the 10:30 a.m. group in the hallway where I had waited for Malena a few weeks prior. Another group had started at 9:30 and still another would start at 11:30. Two delegates gathered us and took attendance at 10:30 sharp, checking against the roster for that slot. One recognized me from previous visits to the union; we shook hands and he patted me on the shoulder, explaining to his colleague that I was to follow the entire sequence of lecture and checkups with that group, authorized by Malena, for university research. The other one nodded, shook hands with me, patted me on the shoulder, and welcomed me to the union.

Thus accounted for, we followed this second delegate up one flight of stairs and into a large classroom, where a young man was setting up a projector. He introduced himself as Juan Marcos, twenty-five years old and one of the first graduates to attain the degree of technician in road safety at the Universidad Tecnológica Nacional, developed by Santiago, the urban planner at the city legislature. We were about twenty attendees, all men, and we introduced ourselves in turn. Some were new to the trade, some less so, and two or three had been choferes for longer than Juan Marcos had existed. Hoisting himself onto a first-row bench, facing us, he announced, "I know I would be very stupid to come here and pretend to teach you how to drive," flicked his projector on, and began the class.

Safety was the first topic, organized around road safety awareness campaign videos from Argentina, Australia, Spain, and other countries, showing via simulations the clinical reconstruction of what happens to a human body in a collision. A driver told how after a grave accident paramedics told him that in the circumstances of that particular collision the seat belt had saved his life. CCTV recordings of accidents, charts, personal anecdotes, all were used as props to discuss prevention, injuries, and blame. Someone told how a woman's water had broken while she was in his car; he had opened the windows and honked his horn rhythmically as he sped to the nearest hospital. A cascade of tales of passengers vomiting, fainting, and having nervous breakdowns filled the room; Juan Marcos curated it into a discussion of legal frameworks and liabilities, the need to save certain telephone numbers and to be able to map hospitals, police, and fire stations.

Next was food, "a big problem for you, on the go all the time. It's hard to eat decent, filling food, and you end up snacking on anything cheap, quick, and easy that comes in a bag that can sit next to you." In his efforts to minimize rhetorical distance Juan Marcos even flirted with some of the rude corners of River Plate Spanish slang. He carried around nuts bought in bulk, fruit, and cereal bars; we commented on the difficulty of getting small portions at the gas stations where drivers usually bought food and how drivers often skipped meals without realizing. Some recommended gas stations or out-of-the-way bars and small eateries that sold individual quiches, salads, or even stews and homemade food for decent prices. The last theme was paperwork and legality. Upon arrival we had been given a booklet whose last few pages outlined in plain conversational language some minor modifications to the taxi law that I have referenced in chapter 1. Juan Marcos discussed them briefly, fielded questions, and ended the course.

We met a few days later and I congratulated him on his success. After teaching the course for a year he knew how to negotiate the encounter: "They see me and think, 'What can this kid tell me about driving a taxi?' And it's tricky because you have only a few hours to elicit an interest in what you have to say." Continuously extricating himself from the "expert" position, he had gone to great lengths to humble himself, to talk down his expertise, and to present his academic knowledge as complementary, rather than superior, to the drivers' embodied and practical knowledge. This was both a strategy and genuine recognition: "These guys *tienen calle*, you can't simply come here and quote a book. They wouldn't respect you or anything you say."

Tener calle has no equivalent in English. Meaning literally "to have streets," *tener calle*, like *tener adoquín*, "to have cobblestones" among tango dancers, and *tener potrero*, "to have field" among Argentine football players, is a form of embodied knowledge that these bodies acquire and cultivate by doing.[11] It is understood as too pragmatic a knowledge, too instinctive and even intimate to be abstracted and transferred, a knowledge that drivers claim for themselves and that they and Juan Marcos know he cannot have. A sort of street smarts, its use involves spontaneity and wits, intuition and dexterity. "They have all these unwritten laws, codes of the streets, and they develop this instinctive sense for danger: they know they are on their own. You are not going to do away with that, and I don't think we should, but we try to work with that to get other points across."

The ostentatious performance of self-awareness and the resort to charm and vulnerability displays allowed Juan Marcos both to remain *in* authority, in terms of leading the class, and to be recognized as *an* authority, in terms of the techniques and rationalities he was presenting to these taxi drivers now enticed to act upon themselves in certain ways.[12] The overall effect was that of a sustained courtship, I told him later to his amusement, but one of a particular kind; these bodies had no choice but to be courted and to wait until the delegate came to pick us up. "All good?" he asked. "All good," Juan Marcos replied.

We left in an orderly line behind the delegate shepherding us up another flight of stairs, where the group was divided into two for the audiometry. Another delegate, forty-five-year-old Facundo, was waiting for me, having obviously been informed I would not undergo it. We had met several times before: Facundo was the one who had told me that during the 1990s choferes were the cheapest spare part. He reported directly to Malena and worked in the general running of the courses. He himself had been a chofer since his late teens, and an interest in the political life of the trade had drawn him to the union in his early twenties.

We walked leisurely around the building and I commented on its organization: classrooms on one floor, medical rooms on another, the audiometry rooms next to the visual examination room, the whole over-seen by the constant presence of union delegates (of a lesser rank, I would find out later), wearing the black and yellow jacket with "Omar Viviani Conducción" emblazoned on it, ensuring that everyone knew where they had to be and what they had to do. "We aimed for this. Normally, in-cluding breaks, they should spend a maximum of five and a half hours here. Everything has to happen in the same day. The only exceptions are choferes whose driver's licenses are withheld and who then have to come back. These people are alone and doing their own thing all day, every day; time spent in classrooms for them is time of foregone income even if propietarios discount the daily rental of the car. Also, even just getting them here, having them come to us to do all these things. . . . Once it's done you have to make the most of it."

The exact word Facundo used to describe choferes, *díscolo*, has no English equivalent. It means unruly and elusive in a nonprogrammatic, idiosyncratic way, evoking refusal and autonomy, often used for horses that refuse to be harnessed, mounted, or reined in. As these groups were moved from floor to floor and from road technician to medical expert, this characterization completed the problematization of choferes' bodies: the sequence had been not only planned but choreographed, as delegates' bodies, walls, stairs, and classrooms organized the circulation of choferes' bodies from beginning to end. Facundo's problematization, stemming from three decades in the trade, had been literally built into the building.[13]

By the time the audiometries were scheduled to end I realized that Facundo's walk had brought us to the room where visual examinations would take place. He invited me to take a seat and mentioned to the delegate roaming that floor that my group should be arriving any minute. This delegate also knew me from previous visits; he offered me a coffee and sat next to me in another row of padded chairs in another pristine hallway. Facundo shook hands with me, patted the delegate on the shoulder, and left us to chat. The previous week two people in different courses had become so uncooperative with Juan Marcos that this other delegate had been instructed to remove them. One had been very aggressive and declared unfit; the other had been told to return on a different day and do it all over again. It obviously was not, always, "all good." A few minutes later my group's delegate was in sight, with the group behind him; he and the hallway delegate greeted each other, and almost imperceptibly, as I merged with the group, the hallway delegate broke free from us, returning to the hallway that had never, really, remained unwatched.

One of Foucault's most famous arguments concerning space is its organization to instill the sense that one is being watched; the whole point is to ensure that one stays in place.[14] At no point in these circulations were taxi bodies unsupervised, uncontained, undirected. But neither were delegates' bodies or, at the end of the day, my own. To the cadence of handshakes and pats on the shoulder at every landing and in every hallway, the delegate bodies within these walls provided a constant reminder, via the yellow and black jackets they had and I did not, that I was a visitor and this was their home.

Exceptions, Rules, and What Actually Matters

My group entered the visual examination room, one of the largest in the building. Drivers distributed themselves in two rows for the same sequence of tests; I sat by Jimena, one of the ophthalmologists conducting the examination. Through Jimena, who was effectively a street-level bureaucrat, two sets of abstract, officially codified policies encountered the concrete reality of the bodies they were aimed at: the techniques of medicine and the stratified rules of the union as a bureaucracy.[15] From both she received a fairly strict, depersonalized "programme of conduct which has prescriptive effects as to what should be done," that is, an expert and hierarchical jurisdiction over choferes' bodies to read and classify them and, on that basis, produce an authoritative truth for each of those bodies.[16]

With over twenty years' experience, she conducted candidates warmly yet with dexterity and in the imperative mode. She explained what she was going to do, instructed them to stand on a mark on the floor while she accessed their file in the system, and reminded them that if they wore glasses or contact lenses they should have them ready for the exam. It was all a single quickly conducted exercise; it was obvious she knew exactly, almost unreflexively, what she was looking for and how to find it. Snellen's test came first, the famous chart of eleven lines of black block letters in decreasing size. Perhaps because it figures in popular culture and seems more straightforward, far fewer drivers struggled with it than with Ishihara's test, which followed.

Ishihara's test consists of thirty-eight square plates, roughly the size of a hand, containing a porous circle made of myriad dots and tiny circles that human eyes should see as forming patterns in the shape of natural numbers between 0 and 100—so long as said eyes can tell reds from greens. If carried out skillfully, to the trained ophthalmologist deficiencies are evident quickly. The test also includes what are called hidden-digit plates where only color-blind people can actually see a number. Jimena kept a stack of the Ishihara plates in a sort of wooden pocket built into her desk: from the perspective of the driver the total effect resembled that of a magician pulling cards from a deck under a table. Sitting by her, I noticed that once or twice, unbeknownst to the drivers, she reshuffled the plates and repeated them, or showed some instead of others. Two drivers were visibly nervous, and one apologized clumsily for it. It was not a problem, she explained, switching to River Plate Spanish informal second person (*vos*), demystifying the setting with jokes, and spending some more time on them. None of these examinations were time consuming in any grand sense.

A few days later I interviewed her at the union's canteen. "Sometimes they give you the right answer and you can tell they can see, but then with the hidden plate they can't see anything—rightly so, because to them, because they distinguish red and green, there *is* nothing to see—but they get nervous and tell you any number. I also had a guy who completely blanked out with Snellen's test. I made him read really small print in a newspaper to calm him down and think himself out of the test examination—his vision was impeccable, and once he was reassured he passed the exam with perfect results. Many have never had an eye examination before, and the setting can be overwhelming." Although practitioners were supposed to spend only a number of seconds per plate, she told me, "My job is to determine whether drivers can see or not. That is what actually matters. Is this guy a danger to himself and others? I cannot deprive someone of their job because of the technicalities of a test. The whole point of this exercise is to see whether a person can tell red from green and letters from afar, and if they cannot, ensure that they have what they need."

The production of truth, as a doctor and as a bureaucrat, requires in principle an aseptic, depersonalized distance, a "strict adherence to procedure, commitment to the purposes of the office, abnegation of personal moral enthusiasms": it is this distance that in one move both makes and legitimizes that truth.[17] Precisely because of Jimena's expert and embodied knowledge of clinical "normality," standards, deviance, and technical proportions between and within tests, and of the political economy of the trade in which these choferes' bodies existed, she could quickly triangulate each body with respect to the truths she sought to reveal and the techniques at her disposal and calibrate accordingly. Paradoxically, it was this authoritative decision to forgo or rearrange techniques that allowed her to reveal the truth required of her, "impartial" and accurate precisely *because* it was deeply personalized and collected idiosyncratically. This syncretic diagnostic realpolitik equalized thousands of choferes' bodies: not at the level of technique, for each encounter was potentially unique, and not at the level of organic capacities, since, for example, 6 percent of candidates were deemed unfit by ophthalmologists in the checkups cycle of 2012–13. But all, fit and unfit, were equalized through Jimena's determination to reveal for each and every one of them "whether they could see or not": techniques, the bodies they addressed, and the ethical duties of care and of professional responsibility produced together a truth aimed at, but not determined by, the question of avoiding another Botta case.

At the far end of the same room, the checkup's last stop was an interview with one of three clinicians in charge of the general health evaluation. I shadowed Natalia as my group went through the interview, then stayed for the next round of drivers. By the time drivers reached her, the results of all previous examinations had been inputted in their virtual files. Via their national ID numbers Natalia located them in the system and asked all drivers whether they had, or had ever had, any of twelve conditions listed on a form titled "psycho-physical aptitude examination": bronchial asthma, bronchospasms, tuberculosis, hepatitis, allergies, diabetes, hypertension, cardiac conditions, Chagas disease, and neurological, digestive, or rheumatic diseases. If they answered yes to any, they had to present evidence that their doctor was aware of the condition, detailing medication, dosages, and/or treatments prescribed. She would sometimes ask general questions about the treatment, uploading this information on the file. Once this was done, or if there was nothing to report, drivers signed the paper form, formally declaring that their answers were truthful, and Natalia signed right underneath declaring that this had been declared in front of her. She kept the paper forms to be archived later, and the driver was free to go.

We discussed over coffee the possibility that people lie or underreport. It was likely, she said, out of the same fears that Jimena had to assuage. Also, the biological trajectories and degrees of visibility of the conditions on the list were very different. By the time a body reached a certain age people tended to know whether they were allergic to penicillin or whether they had or had not had a heart attack; hypertension and milder forms of asthma, however, very often went unnoticed and undiagnosed. "The work is strenuous, and they cannot afford to be sick—they cannot afford to entertain the thought of being sick. Most of them actually do not lack education, but the fear of losing their job terrifies them. Older drivers, because they are old and because they have done it already, care a bit less, but younger and new drivers worry a lot. We constantly encourage them to come forward, emphasizing that we can work with any condition, even a heart attack, but that it's important that we know."

Attention to individual bodies also happened at higher levels and in other forms. Later that day, as I was chatting with Malena, Facundo knocked on her door with some papers and some questions. "You know that older guy . . . ," he proceeded to describe him, and she did know who it was. He did not have his hearing device with him, Facundo explained: "This man is in his early seventies, he's been a chofer for years and everyone here knows him. His hearing is getting worse, and normally he wears a hearing device, but now he's lost it, and came to the checkups without it. We told him we can't let him through." Which ear was it? Malena inquired. I wondered why this mattered until Facundo sighed, "The passenger's ear": the right ear, nearest to the passenger (Argentines drive on the left), so that the man would struggle to hear passengers' instructions. Facundo went through his papers again: "What are we to do? He has a family and absolutely needs the daily money he makes. We can't leave him in the streets either," he expanded more to me than to Malena, who was already on it, typing swiftly. As Facundo and I conversed while he waited for instructions, Malena picked up the phone, dialed quickly, and jotted down something on a Post-it note while she spoke to whoever was on the line. She handed the Post-it note to Facundo, instructing that the man was to be let through, exceptionally, and on the condition that within exactly seven days he showed up to re-sit the audiometry with new hearing aids, which he could get at the union clinic at a given time set aside for emergencies. She had phoned them to check whether there were any slots, and the man was to reference her name upon arrival to the clinic. Facundo nodded and left the room.

The man did as he was told. I heard of people who did not, and had their taxi driver's licenses revoked. Like Jimena's realpolitik approach to diagnosing, these temporary exceptions were as much about the problematization of bodies as about a cultivation of care, solidarity, and comradery for those bodies that integrated them in the political and ethical life of the union— what Argentine militant discourses refer to as *contención*, containment.[18] As in the case of the man with the dodgy ear on the passenger's side, exceptions were always explicitly explained and offered as contingent on the quick resumption of the self's responsibility for care.

Problematization: A Political Endeavor

In a single day in early 2016, these bodies were examined, measured, warned, persuaded, and sorted with respect to a particular question triggered by an accident three years prior. With cosmetic differences, these same checkups took place day after day at the union and in the propietario chambers, revisiting and actualizing measurements and declarations, reaffirming the distribution of roles, bodies, rules, behaviors, and loyalties that made the taxi industry a particular part of the experience of social life in Buenos

Aires. In the most straightforward sense, this was simply because there was no driving a taxi without making oneself legible in these ways. To conduct, enact, or make it through the procedures of this day was to reproduce one's part in the political economy of the industry I began to outline in chapter 1: Malena, Santiago, doctors, choferes, delegates, and everyone involved perpetuated specific relations between capital and labor in the taxi trade; specific understandings of work, health, ethics, and urban movement; and everyone's position, duties, and expectations vis-à-vis the union, the government, and the propietario chambers, as well as vis-à-vis less explicitly partisan and political actors like passengers, traffic, and the built environment. A few weeks after the events recounted here Uber would arrive; we must understand the events of this day and all those relations they reproduced to understand how these different actors understood, and reacted to, the claims and rationalities that were writing them out of the public sphere.

In a less literal sense, the problematization of taxi drivers' bodies also reveals more complex distributions, exclusions, and hierarchies assembling these bodies, institutions, and truths in a configuration whose political condition was subtler. This configuration would come under a brutal Uber-fueled popular siege that the industry never managed to control in the arena of public opinion and debate. Let us return to Miss Noble to make this point. As we know, the goal of binding together these truths, rationalities, and persuasions was to answer, as unambiguously and as definitively as possible, the question "How do we make sure the Botta case does not repeat itself?" But this is just a variation of the question "How will these bodies behave on their own?," itself a logical iteration of the question "How do we know that which we cannot know?"

In any of these forms this question remains unanswerable, especially in any definitive way. But the very point of a problematization, and what makes it a political endeavor in subtler ways, is, first, that a question is asked to begin with, in this form and by these actors; and second, that certain means are deployed to approximate an answer. The governmentality of the taxi industry, that is, the conduct of taxi conduct, joined bodies, vehicles, the possible colors of traffic lights, the geographical distribution of disease, and a diverse group of actors in a dense web of rationalities, logics, and practices always oriented toward that question. Whether motivated by legal liability, moral responsibility, fear of public sanction, duty of care, or self-serving cynicism, the point is that these bodies were ordered differentially, not randomly, and were included or excluded with respect to this attempt to answer the question. Because it ranks, sorts, includes, disperses, and regroups, any problematization is at heart a political endeavor.

A rich array of clinical, technical, embodied, performative, and even dramatic expertise enabled the ordering of these bodies. The hierarchical, exclusive, and authoritative condition of these forms of expertise, even *tener calle*, was enhanced by association with academia, seniority, nontransferrable ability, and, of course, the institutional authority of the union, the propietario chambers, and the government. Many of these techniques and truths were valid, in fact, only because they were legally and institutionally fenced in and signaled outward as legitimate, like an ophthalmological report. To foreground visual acuity, indeed even to call it that, is to include one kind of expert truth in the answer to the question, but also to prioritize certain ways of understanding and sorting other truth claims, necessarily discarding others. When other knowledges were included, as in the case of Juan Marcos referencing drivers' *tener calle*, they fed into the general approach of thinking of taxistas' bodies and their trade with respect to the question raised by the Botta case.

Of course, the original question is just as intractable to these experts; yet as experts, they, and not others, design or work with proxy questions, creating fragmentary truths to collate into a practical, approximate but at least more unambiguous answer: Can this person tell red from green? Is this person's epilepsy properly treated? Does this person understand his vulnerability to hypertension? Can this person see a correlation between her spinal injury and a traffic accident? This is a complex political matter in another sense: in the distance between the proxy question and the intractable question live legal and ethical responsibility, accountability, and even authority and legitimacy. Therefore, knowledge crafted from these bodies has to be intelligible, valid, and legitimate across the public registers of several forums: courts, hospitals, official paperwork, insurance policy contracts, and more. To distribute responsibility and blame, to qualify Leonela Noble's death as homicide or manslaughter, lawyers, first responders, police officers, Rubén Botta himself, and many other actors have to share a regime of truth or at least understand and convert into each other's, partly because a publicly recognized authority, like a judge, is charged with interpreting them. This is one of the reasons why cumulated truths produced during checkups formed a collection growing by the day, alphabetically and chronologically sorted in a little office across the hallway from Malena's office and inaccessible to anyone without her keys.

This problematization included passengers, but it did so within its terms. Considering the auditory capabilities of the driver's ear nearest to them, conceiving of passengers as pregnant, mentally unwell, or otherwise potentially vulnerable bodies requiring taxi drivers to react in certain ways, and encouraging taxi drivers to reflect on speed in terms of the physical integrity of the vehicle's occupants at any given point are all ways of inserting taxi users in the ordering of the taxi transaction with respect to the intractable question. Again, this order was selective and hierarchical: the booklet Santiago authored, by the time of my fieldwork in its third edition, included general courtesy advice, simple phrases in English and Portuguese for foreign passengers, and emergency, police, and first aid telephone numbers and addresses. Its silences also, if by default, were elements of ordering: except for general advice on radio and audio system volume, the booklet, the checkups, and those conducting the latter were silent on the issues of, for example, car deodorant and free mints/water bottles or phone chargers. Juan Marcos told us that city laws required taxi drivers to open the door for vulnerable passengers. It was also illegal for taxistas to refuse to carry devices such as a wheelchair, a cane, or a baby pushchair. But those laws and Juan Marcos himself gave no indication that opening the door to any passenger or having mints and phone chargers to share was relevant to the problematization at stake, or to the public forms of authoritative knowledge that this problematization spoke to. Free water bottles and door courtesy for its own sake could never become a relevant public problem here, or figure in any proxy question: to lie beyond the gaze of the problematization is to not count in its terms, which means here to not count at all.

We could ask whether such amenities *should* count, or whether making them count in some way would allow for a more exhaustive, or "better," answer to the same version or a "better" version of the intractable question. More important than these ponderings was that nobody outside the taxi industry was aware that any of these processes existed at all—the booklet, the checkups, the consultants, the classes. As said in the previous chapter, the experience of the taxi industry in residents' eyes, particularly among the segment of the middle class that used them regularly, was mediated by Omar Viviani, by then nationally famous for his partisan proximity to the Kirchners, his parliamentary candidacy and his salience in other institutions. As chapter 3 will show, when passengers met *díscolo* taxi bodies in the very peculiar transportation market that is Buenos Aires, they engaged in another problematization of sorts: one linking the institutional indolence and opportunism they assigned to unions in general and this one in particular with bodies they interpreted as rogue tricksters nobody was keeping any tabs on. Residents' questions seemed to them just as intractable, to the extent that they never expected the taxi industry to change.

That tabs were "actually" kept on these bodies was frustrating and outright insulting to the taxi industry but also, at the end of the day, irrelevant: all problematizations are by definition partial, fragmented, and set up to interpret the knowledge they produce in a certain way, not to satisfy expectations of truth. When Uber's rating and driver selection mechanisms arrived, mints and a smooth music selection would effectively replace legal duties to vulnerable passengers, but only as the symptom of a larger shift shrouded in the language of empowerment and individual choice and experience. As we will see, this shift hinged on the premise that other kinds of events should count as knowledge, expert in an ultimate sense, and should prevail over, or be allowed to compete with, authoritative knowledge in creating, shaping, and sanctioning the experience of a kind of movement. Residents' own problematization of taxi drivers would find in Uber the technical means to supersede the questions posed by the opacities that the government and taxi industry imagined as inherent to all bodies in motion and sought to render intelligible in the ways explained above. This intelligibility was, ultimately, guaranteed by an ordering repertoire that was kept under lock and key and password-protected files but was also fundamentally public in its grammar and aim.

3

A Most Perfect Kind Of Hustling

THIS CHAPTER WILL EXPLORE how the taxi industry's political economy and city residents meet in the taxi transaction. Taxis are hailed and ridden on the go: the panoply of governmental markers that makes each taxi unique, from license numbers to car plates and standardized colors, and that organizes these bodies and these cars in the political economy of the trade, makes them completely interchangeable in the cultural practice of riding a taxi. Taxistas and their passengers effectively treat each transaction as an event with no past and no future, infinitely elusive in terms of accountability, responsibility, reputation, and other considerations that would tend to pin transacting parties down. From the perspective of taxi drivers, an ethical disposition such that fortune and luck merge with industriousness and discipline in accordance with the maxim "*If* you seek, *then* you shall find" defines this experience. From the perspective of the passengers, in turn, a constant suspicion of being "taken for a ride" or subjected to other forms of opportunism and guile passes for confirmation of the many vices they associate with the industry, setting their role in this shared experience as those who are taken advantage of. This chapter completes the examination of the taxi trade and of the general distribution of the sensible that shaped its interactions before Uber's arrival.

Possibilities in a Ride

One weekday night three months into my fieldwork I hailed a taxi on Quintana Avenue between Parera and Montevideo Streets, in the heart of upper-class Recoleta. I exchanged greetings with the driver and directed him to the corner of Las Heras Avenue and Ruggieri Street, where Recoleta and Palermo merge. The car was silent. We crossed Montevideo and Rodríguez Peña Streets, always on Quintana Avenue, and I suggested turning left on the next road if that direction of traffic was allowed; he said it was, but that in any case, that night, he would make a left turn there even if it was not allowed—a strange resoluteness to voice on a night with little traffic. Finally on Ayacucho Street we hit Las Heras Avenue's traffic light. "My little daughter is in the Santojanni hospital with leukemia, and I need to gather 2,500 pesos [around 180 USD] before eight in the morning," he said, glancing intently at me in his rearview mirror. We rolled down a series of green lights on Las Heras Avenue. "It is a public hospital, they treat patients for free," I said; "Yes," he agreed, "but they are associated with private laboratories that carry out studies faster. We just want the best for her—wouldn't you if it was your daughter?" As he drove on past Laprida, Austria, and Billinghurst streets, he added that this was his only child. His wife was spending the night by her side. He had been driving since the morning to make the cash, otherwise they would lose the appointment. We had by now arrived at my destination and I really just wanted to leave the car, so as he pulled over and stopped the taximeter I tapped him on the shoulder and handed a bit over twice the fare, wishing him luck. Argentines do not normally tip taxi drivers beyond rounding up to the nearest integer. He turned around, leaned toward me, and thanked me. The journey had lasted about sixteen minutes. The friend I was going to meet was already there, and as we headed to a third friend's house I recounted the story. How horrible, she said—you reckon it's true?

Maybe it was kind of true, Agustín told me over coffee days later. He was a chofer in a particular kind of arrangement with the propietario he worked for, which I will explain later. From the moment we met he addressed me with a joking, playful patience. The man may have had a daughter who was sick, he explained, even if not as gravely as he let on; maybe he was a chofer who was behind on his car rent or other bills. It was also possible he had lost a bet and was seeking quick money to repay it. Maybe he just wanted money and tried his luck—*Si pasa, pasa*, If it works, it works, "it" being the story, the pathos, the plea, and the argument, and it did, for I may or not have believed the tale but gave more out of discomfort and an eagerness to end the interaction. We agreed I had probably become one of the stories circulating in places like the bar in Villa Ortúzar where I met the drivers at the end of the day.

Yet none of these considerations really explained how this interaction had actually been possible in the first place. How, through what economic logic, could a taxi driver consider, however abstractly, that he could make a given amount of money in a given amount of time? Crucially, how to tell whether the driver was a desperate man, a consummate performer, or one of the infinite variations in between? As in most cities of a certain size, stories of taxi drivers' cunning abound in Buenos Aires, often having them embody the city's spirit in ways impossible to anyone else.[1] This iconicity was most vividly displayed during the celebrations for the Bicentennial of Independence in May 2010, as taxis rolling down the street with tango dancers atop them represented Buenos Aires to national and international audiences (the Spice Girls would put on a similar performance two years later for the London Olympic Games).

These stories had even been magnified by the entertainment industry. During 1972 and 1973, every Tuesday at ten o'clock Channel 13 aired the series *Rolando Rivas, Taxista*, to this day the most seen Argentine TV production ever. Sixty percent of TV-owning households watched its last episode in December 1973. Rolando Rivas, the main character, was a taxista, male, handsome in a jaded way, and of course porteño, driving the same late 1960s Argentine-manufactured Siam Di Tella that Viviani would have been driving around that time, immortalized since 2012 in the Monument to the Taxi Driver in upscale Puerto Madero. Rivas spoke an impeccably colloquial River Plate Spanish and knew the city inside out, its cafés and love hotels, its cemeteries and shady haunts, cruising the vastness of Buenos Aires with a Baudelairian sense of possibility. Rivas brought together in one character more or less naturalized associations between (auto)mobility, modernity, and urbanity, and between these and freedom construed as autonomy.[2] A vernacular version of unmarked masculinity, Rivas carried only the indelible mark of "being from there," and he convincingly embodied as a taxista that very "there": he even hailed from Boedo, that mythical distillation of Buenos Aires that so occupied Borges and where I went to visit Malena at the union and share the story of that night.

No Past, No Future

Unimpressed and lowering her head so as to stare at me over her glasses, Malena asked if I had taken down the taxi license number, or at least the car plate number. I had not; I had been too distracted and uncomfortable. That was the problem, she admonished me: "People do not know how to take a taxi. The taxi license is at the longest a five-digit number. Even the license plate would do, but people just jump in the car and go." She had been insisting on attaching by electronic or mechanical ways the taxi license number "to the only bit people pay attention to: the taximeter," but as of July 2016 she had had no success. What was the point of even having a car plate, never mind a license, if people did not use it for what it was for?

As said earlier, all taxis in the city of Buenos Aires are aesthetically identical, upper half yellow, lower half black. Painted onto both front doors, the taxi license number is the most visible mechanism of control of all those detailed in the previous chapters, added of course to the car plate number required of any motorized vehicle. Also, in early 2015 the city government incorporated a QR code ID system to its taxi-regulating panoply, imprinted onto a sticker stuck to taxis' windows during their annual checkup. Containing census-like information about the taxi and its driver and owner, the QR code had been implemented with the goal of further individualizing each car to passengers—or to anyone with QR-reading technology, fairly accessible in Buenos Aires by then.

Yet if the taxi license and car plate numbers were unique in the nominal sense, they were universal in that all of the nearly thirty-seven thousand taxi cars had them. The vast majority of taxi rides happened on the go, as taxi drivers cruised and potential passengers hailed them: nobody paid particular attention to the actual license and car plate numbers, just as people rarely notice the car plate number on any vehicle driving down the street in Manchester, England, where I live. The car plate and the taxi license number completed the vehicle in both aesthetic and governmental senses, each for their own reasons, but were not taken into account through the information they contained, merging with the general numeric and chromatic paraphernalia that make a car a Buenos Aires taxi at a glance. As for the QR codes, most taxi users I interviewed actually asked *me*, as a researcher of the industry, what they were even for. Worse, whereas at least taxi licenses are natural numbers between 0 and 38,000 and car plates are an alphanumeric combination of six characters, the QR code's encryption is completely unintelligible to a human eye and impossible to memorize or individualize. It was ill fitted to the fleeting practice of taking a taxi.

In the governmental sense of the term, probably no vehicle in Buenos Aires today is more embedded in structures of identification than taxi cars. But it is through actual exchange behavior that embeddedness happens and particular bodies, in this case cars and people, become enmeshed in relations with others.[3] Transactions are always more embedded in their social context than neoclassical economy would claim: situations where transactors are fully unacquainted and unlikely to transact again and where information about the activities of either is unlikely to reach others with whom they might transact in the future are very unusual.[4] Even in highly capitalist economies, individual agents tend to establish moral relationships and transact with the same people, aiming to create webs of loyalty and mutual responsibility to minimize uncertainty and guarantee durable dealings with transactors one is already acquainted with.[5] Consumers develop trust and producers build on reputation. For those transactions to be effectively embedded and exceed their immediate context there must be, among other things, a shared temporality that allows the bonds of reputation, in themselves a logical link of cause and consequence, to grow on the basis of previous transactions between same agents. In fact, it is often paradoxically through "imperfections" like these that "impersonal" markets actually function.[6]

In the case of Buenos Aires's taxis, ironically, the very mechanisms embedding the taxi, its driver, and its owner within each other and within governmental logics ensured that, from the passengers' perspective, taxi cars were hailed and ridden as completely interchangeable. Through these practices, taxi transactions existed in a sort of alienation even greater than "pure" market behavior: Buenos Aires taxi rides had no past and no future. Taxi drivers could not build on personal reputation for quality of service, however defined, and were also unlikely to be held individually responsible for poor service, except in the extreme case of violence. Moreover, in a city where thirteen million people circulated daily, served by nearly thirty-seven thousand taxi cars and over fifty-five thousand taxi drivers (many cars had two shifts) it was overwhelmingly unlikely that two transacting parties would encounter each other again. Even if they did, it was unlikely they would realize it was a repeat. There was no connection between the passengers in a day or in a year, or between the respective transactions, and they were to each other "a string of episodes without history and without consequence."[7]

With the book's earlier examination of how the taxi license organizes the industry's structure and how bodies enter and stay in the trade as service providers, these particularities of the taxi transaction in Buenos Aires complete the experience of a particular distribution of the sensible: "a delimitation of spaces and times, of the visible and the invisible, of speech and noise that simultaneously determines the places and the stakes of the form of the experience."[8] In other words, different urban dwellers partook in the same general form of the taxi transaction as it happened in 2015 and 2016 in Buenos Aires, but their circumstances with respect to it were differential in persistent, nonrandom ways. The blurring of some differences, the enhancing of others, and the recurrence of certain aspects defined the experience of driving and taking a taxi, but also the experience of urban movement and of Buenos Aires life where the industry encountered the middle class, and where each found and understood how their part fit the whole.

The GNCs

There are 132 compressed natural gas stations dotted around Buenos Aires, commonly called GNCs for the Argentine acronym for this kind of gas, *gas natural comprimido*. In Buenos Aires, more vehicles per capita run on GNC than anywhere in the world, as environmental, energetic, and import substitution policies converge with household and mobility economics. Natural gas abounds in the country's lithosphere, and in late 2015 it offered higher calorific value and lower environmental impact for a sixth of oil's price. Argentina's sizable car industry trades solely in oil tanks: adapting a car to run on gas requires a 1,500 USD initial investment, so only drivers engaged in intensive mileage/day ratios convert their cars, which is why all taxis in Buenos Aires run mainly on GNC.[9] They have little choice, too, as the government sets the taxi fare on the assumption that taxis will run on GNC, and no other fuel would square the equation. One of these stations featured a café-drugstore with snacks, wall TVs, toilets, and ice machines. Pressure gauges and car repair and car-washing facilities lined the edges of the lot, which also featured a sizable parking area. It sat at the corner of a street and a broad avenue and was open round the clock, and for every single one of these reasons it was a favorite among taxi drivers.

Compressed natural gas allegedly has a higher potential for explosion than other combustibles, so dispensers are manned by station attendants and cars must be switched off and empty of people during refueling. When it was his turn in line, Arturo, a chofer in his sixties who was always there at some point before noon, would park neatly by the dispenser, switch off the engine, and dash to the toilet while an attendant filled his tank. Arturo would return as the recharging finished, pay, restart the engine, and head toward the parking lot, allowing the dispenser line to move forward. Turnover was fast, and cars, drivers, attendants, and clients were moving, waiting, filling up, washing, and ready to go. Once he had parked the by then full car, Arturo would mingle with taxistas, attendants, cleaners, and other characters peopling the recurrent social scene of this GNC. He would linger for a while, talking football and placing, paying, or cashing in on little bets. He never stayed more than forty-five minutes, including chatting for about thirty minutes with me.

Arturo was a chofer, which means, as I explained in chapter 1, that he drove for someone else. He paid the equivalent of 68 USD per day for the car at the end of his twelve-hour shift from 6:00 a.m. to 6:00 p.m. A shift normally required two full tanks of gas, plus a refill and a wash at the end of the shift to pass the car on to the next chofer: as taxistas say, Arturo woke up 68 USD in the red six days of the week (Sundays he could drive rent-free, keeping everything he made). I had met Arturo through Héctor, a propietario and longtime frequenter of this GNC. Héctor had employed Arturo as a driver for his other taxi in the past, twice, and had fired him twice for incompetence. To Héctor, competence in this market was straightforward: return the car as and when agreed with the day's rent, keep it clean and free of damage, do not use it for sex or drugs. Repairs, fines, and cleaning were costly in themselves, but since the industrial overhaul explained in chapter 1 this had also been a trade of hefty fixed costs—choferes' union charges, car insurance, and costs associated with either owning a taxi or simply owning a vehicle, like car plate taxes—so immobility meant forgone income that propietarios, as capital owners and employers, had to shoulder.

According to Héctor, "You suss out [incompetent drivers] immediately. First they short-change you for some reason: 'It was a slow day,' 'I had to drive my wife somewhere,' or simply 'I'll pay you tomorrow.' Of course the following day they owe you that day's rent, which is already sizable, plus arrears. It snowballs very quickly." He claimed that choferes could make good money if they stayed clear of nonsense and had excellent personal management: "They start every day 60 to 80 USD in the red, and you have a man driving around, alone, with cash in his hands, for up to twelve hours, who has to manage coffee, lunch, and pee breaks and navigate rush hours, protests, traffic jams, et cetera."[10] Good choferes thus defined could make good savings on Sundays. Arturo invariably spent every Sunday driving just to catch up with car rent, and often it was not even enough. Héctor had reemployed Arturo as "there was nothing [nada] to choose from" and he needed to get the car going and get some money in. Good choferes, the "serious" ones (los tipos serios), were always taken, and as soon as a good chofer was out in the market he or she had three propietarios offering their car. Those eventually moved on to become propietarios, said Héctor: he had started as a chofer himself, over two decades earlier, and had saved for a taxi and a license. He now owned two. The tipping point had been the birth of his first child, and he believed the best choferes were those with a family to feed and bills to pay.

This had been Agustín's case, the one I told the story of the driver with the sick daughter. He was in his mid-forties and had two daughters in their late teens. The eldest was preparing for the exams that would admit her to the Faculty of Chemistry at the University of Buenos Aires. His wife was a nurse, and all four of them lived in La Boca. He had made good money doing PR for a nightclub, later launching an escort agency associated with tourist haunts. He became a chofer shortly after his daughters were born, changing his lifestyle as he aged out of nightlife and its attendant industries. Agustín was one of a very small fraction of choferes who "had the car in charge": they were legally and to all effects choferes, but whereas choferes returned the car to the owner at the end of the shift, or passed it on to the next shift's driver, Agustín was trusted to have the car with him permanently. He washed it, took it to the mechanic, did everything that he would if it were his: "Instead of a daily rental, every X day of the week I pop by the owner's and slide the envelope with the money under the door. I set my own shifts and work when and for as long as I want. As long as the money is there and you don't screw up . . ."

Agustín lived effectively the temporality of the propietarios I described in chapter 1, free to organize his days around his family and friends, medical appointments, holidays, weather and traffic conditions, Boca Juniors' football matches, and so on. He had been working for the same propietario for several years and understood seriousness in the trade, and in the working relation, just as Héctor did: he looked after the car, the money was there every week, and if not, exceptionally, there was a reason and a date for when it would be there.

If You Seek, Then You Shall Find

Agustín's eldest daughter was dating a young man from Rosario, some 250 miles northwest of Buenos Aires, and once ran up a small fortune in phone bills. Agustín noticed only the day before the payment was due; he took off with the taxi and stayed out until he had made enough money to pay the bill. "In no other trade is this even thinkable," he smirked. What if you do not find the money? I prodded him, and he retorted without missing a beat: *Si buscás, encontrás*—River Plate Spanish for the universal "Seek and you shall find," except that its local, taxi driver version is uttered explicitly as a logical sequence: *If* you seek, *then* you shall find. An unverifiable truth supported by the intuitive immensity of Buenos Aires, this imperative worked among taxistas as a personal, irreducible, and open-ended claim to that market with no past and no future, impossible to ever repeat in the exact same way. At stake in the tension between how one sought and what one found was their capacity to, somehow, make it, pay the bills, become or remain a propietario, or at least make it to the GNC for another day.

Passing for common knowledge, this imperative included everyone in the trade, but in different economic, political, and ethical terms. On the one hand, choferes woke up in debt every single day; propietarios were self-employed and/or rentiers. The former's economic horizon was capped by midnight, the latter's less ominously if at all and even then by usually more elaborate considerations. On the other hand, as said above, out in the streets drivers competed for fares as perfect equals, since from the perspective of passengers they were all identical. Also, they shared the turf (the city), the price (the centrally set taxi fare), and the pattern of price increment (the algorithm multiplying the fare to the rhythm of distance programmed into standardized taximeters), and they carved a workday out of the same twenty-four-hour day. "If you seek, then you shall find" framed a horizon of experience where the industrial structure, labor relations, organic bodies, and governmental logics examined earlier in the book came to shape the taxi transaction into the *common* experience of the taxi trade in Buenos Aires. It was common in the sense of shared by all actors in it, drivers or passengers, because and in spite of different drivers' relative position in the trade, and it was common in the sense of naturalized, in the sense of the order there was.[11]

Everyone, propietarios and choferes, found fares by cruising, and how and what one sought and found was subjected to highly idiosyncratic mythologies of production, blending rumor and hunches with variously "reliable" information and seasonal and consumer considerations.[12] Agustín worked rush hours religiously, for why would one not go where the office workers went, to which Mauro, whom I introduced in chapter 1, would reply that it was quite silly to do as the others did, so whenever he could he *avoided* rush hour. Many others also steered clear of the spaces and times of rush hour out of fear of getting stuck in traffic. Héctor hovered around universities with night shifts and nightclubs, which others deliberately avoided.

Students were less likely to have money for taxis but were more likely to be running off to a party afterwards, and drunkards were more likely to vomit in the car, be unpleasant, or haggle for fares, but, like tourists and Argentines from the provinces, drunkards were good targets for "a little tour" or for unexpected tips.

As these bodies floated free from a future reputation or a past to be held to, the edges of how and what to seek were hard to police ethically: in practice, guile, deceit, and charm fused with street smarts and cunning as full technologies of production. Héctor had figured out how to con international tourists into thinking that it was customary to tip taxi drivers in Buenos Aires. Who would not, after all, tip when satisfied with the service? Besides, these people tipped taxi drivers "in their countries" anyway, and if only for these machinations he probably did, in fact, deserve a tip. Also, Andrés was always ready on weekend nights to take more passengers than the seat belts his car had, which he would have been fined for if found; but it was still cheaper for a group of friends on a night out to pay (quite a few) extra pesos to one driver than to divide themselves into two taxis, and he knew exactly where police were located—or so he claimed, but to my knowledge either he had not been found or he had somehow persuaded police officers to forgive and forget.

The city as market and its residents as consumers merged and stood for each other in such strategizing of how to make it each day: figuring out the city was one with figuring out its possible rides. Because cruising for fares meant finding, as the driver of one in almost thirty-seven thousand effectively identical vehicles, one passenger among the thirteen million people going about the city, those mythologies of production engulfed the imaginations of those passengers and of the commodity, the ride itself, in keeping with the romanticized aura around taxis and taxi drivers in a world metropolis.[13] "Rolando Rivas," *Taxista*'s opening track, of course a tango, evoked this romanticism, referring to passengers as strange books that needed to be "decoded."[14] Yet the sussing out of potential passengers was a serious matter. Buenos Aires's residents tended to think of taxi drivers as perpetrators of violence, from catcalling to physical abuse, but much more often they were victims of violence, as any criminal would know they were alone, in their car, and definitely carrying cash. Families with children, pregnant women, and young couples were generally considered good passengers, groups of men of any age less so, and many "looks" considerations entered the equation, from colorism to wardrobe. But drunk people do not necessarily look drunk, much less so in the couple of seconds between being hailed and deciding to stop, and a car covered in vomit was a car immediately out of service for at least a couple of hours that the driver had no alternative but to deal with himself. This had happened to Héctor, who was furious, but as a propietario he called it a day and went home to relax. Choferes had no choice but to clean up the mess, deal with the stench, and carry on there and then. Also, three taxi drivers reported having been robbed by "pregnant" women who turned out not to be, and dozens reported "runners" who dashed out of the car without paying. Such events reminded them all that the common experience of the taxi ride happened between practical strangers, one shrouded in regulatory paraphernalia that went unseen and the other an actual stranger, in the sense of Rivas and of Baudelaire, in a city where thirteen million people went about their day.

Mythologies of Production

Even for the most seasoned taxistas, "If you seek, then you shall find" was haunted by its logical negation: if you did *not* find, it was because you did *not* seek hard or well enough. This haunting had a social and cultural dimension, but its baseline was eminently economic: there were bills to pay. Some times were broadly acknowledged as harder: in January, peak of the austral summer, Buenos Aires emptied out and fares were scarce. Some choferes had propietarios who lowered their car rents during January, but certainly not all. In normal times, as over thirty-six thousand taxis crossed paths with two hundred bus lines, 1.6 million cars within the city proper, and over a million cars entering the city daily from the adjacent province of Buenos Aires, one single accident paralyzed traffic for blocks. Also, there were on average 1,020 street protests in the city during every one of the last years of the second Fernández de Kirchner administration (2011–15) and the early years of Macri's (2015–19): entire sections of the city were gridlocked sometimes for hours, most often with no warning at all, and one bad turn could cost a taxista hours stuck in traffic.[15] When they managed to foresee slow or protest days, propietarios and people like Agustín, whose car rental spanned the week, waited it out over coffee, took breaks, or ran errands. Choferes had no choice but to work.

The tension between how one sought and what one found pointed to another tension: that between how well each self sussed out that ever-changing immensity of Buenos Aires at any given time and what Buenos Aires, as a source of potential rides, could "objectively" offer that self. In a market of millions of unrepeatable daily exchanges with huge unknowns, the success of any strategy or approach could only ever be gauged, or even understood, after the fact. Strategizing was one and the same with working with the hand one had been dealt. To speak of discipline, good management, or strategies was to speak of knowing how to work with contingency and chance in a world of one-offs: here an economy of chance and an economy of control converged. Both the ethics of the industrious, capitalist self-made man and those of the Fortune-worshipping man involve taking risks to decode, interpret, and recast the unknown into a destiny amenable to one's own goals.[16] The ritualized persistence frames the hope that if one invests properly, if one judges the circumstances soundly, if one tries and tries again, a reward will come. At stake in the continuing relationship between a taxi driver and the city, between these enterprising providers and this market, and between these gamblers and their chances, was whether they could work the ethical, affective, and economic horizon of this particularly perfect kind of hustling.

Because as hustlers they were all equals, when they coincided in places like GNCs for coffee, gas, toilet breaks, or socializing, the intensely personal relationship between these hustlers and their lottery was subjected to "an agonistic, romantic, individualistic and gamelike ethos."[17] One day Héctor, usually already larger than life, barged into the half-full GNC café rubbing his hands and sporting an exceptionally satisfied grin. Three foreigners from an exclusive hotel had tipped him generously and requested that he pick them up at their hotel later to show them around the old town for the whole afternoon: a small, guaranteed goldmine. Patting me on the shoulder, he proclaimed to everyone: "See, boy? That's how it's done!" How exactly it had been done we never heard, but we did hear it had happened. Within earshot sat a taxista Héctor had a long-running, low-intensity feud with, the implicit intended audience of the performance. This other taxista was equally boastful, except that of course he, not Héctor, was a liar: "He is always on about these trips he makes and these women he beds, and the truth is I saw him once at a corner shop at a time he later said he had been driving a passenger to Luján," a city some forty-five miles west of Buenos Aires.

This one made so much money in just three hours, that one made enough to pay for his shift with just two trips to the airport, this other one was tipped in USD by a naive tourist: hubristic to the point of caricature, these ritualized retellings of skill nearing wizardry in the negotiations between the self and the impersonal, the indomitable city "out there," animated the heady scent of coffee, oil, and grease and the scene of men chortling, shouting, and sweating with the erotic edge of competitiveness.[18] Someone had "cracked it," found that "quasi-magical formula . . . to exhaust an inexhaustible series of variables"—someone effectively identical to each and every one of them.[19] However stark the differences in economic, cultural, or political capital between a chofer owing three days' worth of rent and a propietario owning three cars, this sensual competitiveness also equalized them.

Mauro believed two-thirds of these stories were lies or embellishment. Years earlier he had decided to not even step into GNC bars, instead filling his tank and speeding off; the café in Villa Ortúzar had a completely different atmosphere, and the drivers worked to keep it that way. Andrés once pointed out the window to a smaller GNC less than a block from Dionisio's café, known for all the characteristics and amenities of the GNC bars as well as its poker rounds; otherwise he and Mauro mostly did not even mention the sensual social life of the GNC. Their silence belonged to a different kind of hustler ethics: one aware of the damage of focusing too much on others who at the end of the day were identical to each one of them, also seeking fortune, if only for that day, and avoiding them like a siren's song.

As I showed above, the political economy of the industry, its governance, and its cultural and social practices helped create the spaces, times, bodies, and relations of the taxi experience that passengers encountered. Although members of the upper layers of the working class, students, and other urban dwellers with fewer resources used taxis occasionally, taking taxis in Buenos Aires regularly was a mostly middle-class, professional affair. These residents were integral to the common experience of the taxi transaction; without them the transaction would not be what it was, but most importantly, it was their share and participation in this experience as passengers, urbanites in motion, citizens, and consumers that made this experience common as broadly shared and naturalized. These were the residents Uber would target in cultural terms, that is, a middle class used to being in the back seat when being driven for money, and socioeconomically, as the population segment that could afford Uber. The affects, expectations, and dispositions that I detail below, made up of the logics I detail above, confirmed to residents their place in this common experience.

Perhaps ironically, considering that not paying attention to the glaringly obvious regulatory paraphernalia of Buenos Aires taxis was a problem of their own making, passengers also conceived of the taxi transaction as one between complete strangers who would never meet again. Valentina, in her late twenties, was a well-to-do financial adviser for a multinational company who used taxis daily to get to and from work and for nights out but also for medical appointments and other errands. It is much more common for the middle and upper classes in Buenos Aires to use buses, subways, and inter- and intraurban trains than in many other metropolises in the world, especially because public transportation enjoys a privileged right of circulation in many of the city's streets and is often faster and cheaper than taking a taxi or using one's own car. Valentina used them all without qualms throughout the day, but if out at night she would use only taxis, requesting to be dropped off right by her building's door and asking taxi drivers to please wait until she was inside the building, common practice among residents of any sex or gender.

Passengers knew their part in the taxi experience was that of lottery numbers; they were subjected to the motives, discipline, and ethical inclinations of not necessarily dubious but fundamentally opaque hustlers. The reader knows from the previous chapter that drivers did not exactly have such opacity; but we must understand that they were certainly experienced as such to trace the triangulations that passengers made, casually yet with full conviction, between taxi licenses, the union, Peronism, and taxistas themselves. Although she did not distrust taxi drivers in any serious way, Valentina worked on the basis that if they could take her out of her way they would, even if only for one or two blocks. "They know you are not going to start a fight, you're already in the car" was the general rationale for not challenging what she took as opportunism. To deter or contain the potential for such abuses she often chatted to drivers about routes from one place to another, as actual inquiry and as performance of her unmistakably local accent, a proxy for her knowledge of the city. Taxi drivers were also impossible to find on rainy days, and she knew from conversations with them that the reason was not only that more pedestrians turned to taxis so as not to get wet, but also that propietarios and those who could help it avoided coming out in the rain, for safety reasons and to keep the car from getting dirty. However regulated they may have been (and indeed, the taxis' law required that as a public service taxis be on the road come what may), they were, in practice, often unreliable.

Francisco, whom I introduced in chapter 1, used taxis mostly during nights out with friends; often, at those late hours, instead of turning on the taximeter taxi drivers requested a flat amount of money, of course much higher than what the taximeter would indicate were it to be activated.

When I pointed out that this was illegal, that I had visited the offices where city officials dealt with taxi complaints and that all he needed to provide them with was the car's license plate or the taxi number, he dismissed me. Did I think they did not know this happened? "They know it's them or a late-night bus." A variation of this happened to me as I exited the National Museum of Fine Arts; as I approached a taxi parked by the entrance, the driver asked where I was going. This is normally part of the conversation once the passenger is already inside; disappointed in my destination, he said he was not "going in that direction." Strictly speaking, he was not going anywhere, as his engine was switched off, but I had to walk a short way up the same avenue and hail another taxi.

As explained earlier in this book, residents assumed that all taxistas belonged to the union, or that Viviani owned all taxi cars, or that his imperium over the industry and the government allowed the industry to go unchecked, all of which logically and affectively linked casual taxi abuses with union or partisan politics. Forced, simplistic, or just inaccurate, these assumptions also contributed to residents' understanding of themselves as having no voice in a common experience defined by tricksters, a politicized monopoly, and the industrial stranglehold of the taxi trade, perceptions creating a latent grammar for arguments that Uber's arrival would catalyze. The idea that the taxi industry constituted a monopoly would gain much traction as a general narrative during the Uber conflict, as chapters 4 and 5 argue. In the terms of this chapter, the idea of monopoly lent a logical framework to an experience of entrapment: passengers felt they had to be on guard by default, that they were unlikely to ever have the upper hand and were unable to complain or resist: that is, that trying to reclaim a voice and a part was too costly, pointless, or both. The conviction that "this was how it was," that one's complaints or challenges could not meaningfully disrupt their place in this shared experience, constituted these impossibilities, frustrations, and dispositions as the common experience from their end.[20]

Understandably, each party's experience folded into the other's: frustrated with passengers thinking they were being deliberately taken out of their way, Mauro and Agustín flipped the problem around, always asking passengers which route they preferred before starting the ride. If the ride cost more than it would have or if they got stuck in traffic, blame fell on the passenger who had chosen the route. Taxi drivers used GPS for the odd street they were unsure about but disparaged it and other traffic-interpreting technologies as ways of dictating their work, their movement, or even the city: these technologies would indicate a shortest route through roadworks and would suggest streets lined up with kindergartens at pickup time, or streets where taxi drivers knew, because other drivers told them or they had seen it themselves, that there had been an accident ten minutes prior. Still, over half the taxi drivers I met used GPS-like technologies, not because they viewed them as exhaustive, or even valid, interpreters of the streets, that is, as interpreters of the lottery they were all trying to decode, but because they wanted passengers to see that the GPS was there. Still, in this cultural, social, and economic setup each party was convinced the other one could not be pinned down, and low-key mutual suspicion prevailed. A passenger accused Agustín of going as slowly as possible so as to be stopped by as many traffic lights as possible, thus raising the final fare: "I just turned around and demanded they pay whatever they wanted and get the hell out of my car."

Playing for Grace

This chapter completes my examination of what a taxi in Buenos Aires was, how the industry was organized and worked, and how the transaction played out. In the common experience of the taxi transaction converged also the partisan, structural, historical, bureaucratic, and phenomenological ways in which porteño middle classes imagined and understood the distribution of the sensible, of parts and possibilities, of speech and silence. Paradoxically, the governmental and aesthetic standardization that rendered taxis much more identifiable than residents imagined contributed in large part to the practice of a transaction with no past and no future, where neither party could pin the other down, which of course, as we have seen, did not mean that parties' experiences were the same, analogous, symmetrical, or even comparable to each other. Passengers made sense of their part in the experience, and of the part of taxi drivers as they saw it, through invocations of helplessness and accusations of monopoly, or entrenched interests, or as we have seen, by invoking a hazily defined but potent association between powerful industry players and a driver who refused to budge for less than a given fare. This common experience would provide several touchstones for the reconfiguration of the distribution of the sensible led by these middle-class residents when Uber arrived.

From taxi drivers' perspective, this was a keenly competitive trade; unable to build on reputation or any other form of capital, they had no choice but to hustle for fares in an environment where what exactly hustling entailed was also for them to figure out. They were on an equal footing with respect to the city and whatever they might find in it, and the only way of gauging a hustler's success was whether they made it to the next day, the next bill, or the next story at the GNC, all of which passed for evidence that, in the trade's ethical imperative, they had sought properly and therefore had found. Drivers like Andrés and Héctor, in their own ways, emphasized the "ethic of fortune" side of hustling, seeing their success in the competition as due to their skill at charming luck their way; others, like Agustín, emphasized the "ethic of mastery" aspect and their discipline at work. To varying degrees, all three of them enjoyed the frisson of being at "the razor's edge of luck" and playing the part of the hustler for fares in a lottery they approached from different angles. The very coexistence of those angles only confirmed that the winning number was never known, or at least not for longer than a day.[21]

Play is quite possibly the right verb: its Spanish version, *jugar*, also means to gamble, bet, or play the lottery, capturing the sensual, urgent commitment to "the ever-present possibility of . . . escaping from the narrow confines of alleged necessity . . . and contact[ing] a realm where hope is alive."[22] Throughout my fieldwork I lived near the famous cemetery of Recoleta, where Evita rests. On my daily route toward the GNC station there was a lottery agency, and every morning a taxi car sat outside. Months before anyone knew Uber would arrive I asked about it in the agency; it belonged to a propietario who ran it himself, a very cordial man who for years stopped there daily and bought a lottery ticket, betting always on the same numbers, before heading off to the park across the cemetery for a bite. "So he likes playing, then?" I asked the attendant that first day, in late 2015. "I'm not sure he likes it," she replied, "but a few taxi drivers come all the time. *Juegan para salvarse*"—they play to save themselves.[23]

4

On Gladiatorial Truths

THIS CHAPTER BEGINS the examination of Uber's arrival that will occupy the rest of this book. On April 12, 2016, Uber made its services available in Argentina's capital. Within hours the union and several propietario chambers initiated collective legal action, accusing Uber of a series of abuses and violations. Their request marked the beginning of a process of translation of grievances, economic harm, and other considerations into the language, techniques, and spaces of law, where decisions are legitimate because the judicial domain is by definition exclusive, hierarchical, and representative.

Meanwhile, the heat of social media campaigns and news of Uber downloads at a hysterical pace enhanced the conviction among part of the middle class that "the people" wanted Uber, and that therefore they should have it. In late capitalism, popular choice is the site of a raw, moral legitimacy that fuels what I call gladiatorial truths: prescriptive truth claims based on the moralizing bottom line of minimally mediated popular legitimacy, measured in actual vocal support or its late capitalism proxy, consumption. Gladiatorial truths obscure rationalities, processes, and techniques of production and subsume political economy considerations to the consumption bottom line. They also harness a universal language that speaks of, and to, a nonpolitical collective, organic and epically equal. Their capacity to depoliticize, proper to the translation of disagreement onto the moral plane of right versus wrong, is deliberately sought after in places like Buenos Aires, where urban middle classes suspect their institutions of indolence, corruption, or other unethical, "overly political" practices. With and around Uber the middle class saw itself, and its place in the emergent order, as a collective that could add up to a people intelligible beyond political lines and organized on the immanence of a moral economy based on consumers' choice.

Something Wicked This Way Comes

On March 27, 2016, a YouTube video inviting people to sign up as drivers for such a thing as Uber Argentina appeared online. The tone of the video was prophetic in the present continuous form of a certain future: *Uber is coming*. Around midday, national daily *La Nación* published a 780-word online article titled "Uber's Imminent Arrival in Argentina: Driver Selection Has Started," where Soledad Lago Rodríguez, Uber's communications manager for the Southern Cone, was quoted as saying, "We don't have an official launch date, but Uber's arrival is imminent. We will make the announcement when that time comes."[1] The Twitter account @Uber_ARG was created that same day. Its first and for a while only content was the picture of a woman in a driver's seat, smiling invitingly over her right shoulder, captioned, "Do you want to make extra money? Do you want to be your own boss driving for Uber? Register at sociosar.com and find out the details. #UberArg."[2]

The complicit, conspiratorial secrecy of the message tantalized the growing popular and media frenzy. The video, the website, and Lago Rodríguez's twenty-five-word statement were shared, retweeted, reposted, and liked online; fragmented and recomposed as news titles; flattened, mutilated, and squeezed into image and video captions; spliced together with fragments of older reports in articles, radio programs, and newscasts as journalists and internet users circulated charts with the history of Uber conflicts elsewhere, as well as infographics comparing both services. Representatives of the taxi industry were suddenly on the national radar, touring news channels and radio stations. Omar Viviani's poised statements were provocatively combined with less institutional declarations by taxi drivers interviewed in the heat of their anger. The general atmosphere was of Macbethish expectation.

Forty-eight hours later, on March 29, news broke that Uber was holding an induction talk with 120 potential drivers in the historic Castelar hotel and that taxi drivers were protesting and smashing windows; Uber officials claimed seven thousand people had signed up as drivers in less than thirty hours.[3] Later that same day, the number had escalated to ten thousand; Lago Rodríguez argued that in spite of "[our] interest in finding a way to work [with the city government] before launching the service, we failed to reach an agreement over how to go about it, as the existing normative framework does not apply to an innovative service like [Uber's]," adding that Uber's team "is always available to continue the conversations while we carry on with the launching of our platform. . . . It is our challenge and goal to work together with authorities in creating a regulatory framework in accordance with the new models of the sharing economy."[4]

City authorities told reporters that Uber would have to adapt to existing laws; taxi associations demanded meetings with both city and national administrations where the latter two should set their position on the issue because "This begins [in Buenos Aires] but is a national problem."[5] Viviani was quoted as declaring that "under no circumstances" would the union allow Uber to come in. On March 30, three days after that first tweet, Buenos Aires's chief of government reiterated that the company had not yet presented any paperwork to the authorities. Lago Rodríguez insisted that existing laws did not apply to an innovative service such as Uber's and that the firm would continue the dialogue with authorities "while they prepared their arrival."[6]

On the tenth day Uber broke its Twitter silence, inviting people to a virtual training session to find out how to make the equivalent of 1,000 USD by driving for Uber during its first week.[7] Nobody knew when exactly that week would be; newly registered drivers were told to "be ready." National dailies reported that "tens of thousands" had downloaded the app as potential passengers and twenty thousand people had signed up as drivers.[8] On April 12, the fifteenth day after the original announcement, I was at the GNC station when newscasts announced Uber had tweeted that it would start running at four in the afternoon that very same day. We were glued to the TV. Four o'clock came, and Ignacio Viale, a young TV producer born into a long-established show business family, livestreamed his experience as passenger of the first Uber trip on Argentine soil.[9]

That evening I met Andrés and Mauro at Dionisio's. For a couple of hours it was just the three of us. "So basically anyone can become a driver? What about taxes? Are they even registered with the taxman?" Mauro asked. "Yes, Mauro, anyone—don't you read the news?"—Andrés barked. To the best of my knowledge "Uber Argentina" did not really exist in any bureaucratic sense, I replied, and the only requirements were a five-door vehicle, a smartphone operating on certain software, and a regular insurance policy. "And all the checkups, the monitoring, the license? Who controls that? Uber?" "Nobody, Mauro, nobody controls it, that's the problem. So all those checkups and licenses, you know what you can do with them?"

Andrés roared, completing the phrase indecorously. Mauro sipped on his wine and we stayed silent for a few seconds. "At the end of the day, I'm not worried. Do you really think Viviani will let this go through? Do you think he will sit it out? Forget it. If they insist with this Uber thing he'll flip the city round," Andrés prophesied. Mauro nodded sagely.

On my way to Dionisio's I had spoken to Francisco on the phone. Had I heard the news? He was ecstatic. Finally! "They couldn't stop it, see? It's just too much. What are they going to do about it?" I did not know, but in the meantime an estimated four thousand taxis blocked several strategic corners, bringing the city to a halt. The City of Buenos Aires's minister of transportation, Juan José Méndez, warned citizens that Uber was operating outside the law.[10] Francisco was following the events by the minute. *Les van a tirar con todo*—no punches would be spared. What would the government do? we wondered.

Less than four months earlier Mauricio Macri had become president of Argentina, after two consecutive four-year terms as chief of government of the Autonomous City of Buenos Aires. Macri's technocratic aura and unrivaled capacity for ideological flatness found in the perennially anti-Peronist city of Buenos Aires a base of support and a stronghold from which to project himself onto the stage of national politics. During these same eight years Cristina Fernández de Kirchner was president of Argentina, and her government and Macri's antagonized each other. Many Argentines resented being forced into this binary categorization, but in the circumstances mentioned in the Introduction and in chapter 8, few had any patience or energy left for the nuanced cogitation that would sustain a middle ground. Besides, when Macri faced Fernández de Kirchner's candidate in the second presidential round of 2015, the choice was only between these two.

Macri's coalition won the presidency and several key executive positions around Argentina. Later in this chapter and in chapter 8 I will examine the interplay between the elections, the new administration, and the Uber conflict and reasoning around it. For now, what matters is that barely four months after this coalition premised on ending years of isolationism won the national and city executive powers, Uber arrived in the center of political and economic power of Argentina. Viviani was now withdrawing his support for Fernández de Kirchner and merging again with mainstream Peronism. Beyond partisan allegiances, not only was the political economy of his trade entirely centered in the Autonomous City of Buenos Aires, which Uber had just penetrated de facto in spite of repeated governmental warnings, but as shown in the previous three chapters the entire governance of the trade was a joint exercise between the union, the propietario chambers, and city cabinets under Macri's political authority since 2007.

This is why we all wondered what the government would do. I found out upon returning home from Dionisio's that as Uber blared on Twitter and on people's smartphones the taxi industry had initiated legal action. Before the twelfth of April was over, while taxi drivers honked furiously in front of the city legislature building, blocked strategic corners at rush hour, and broadly speaking multiplied news material in an already heady week, before even twelve hours had passed since Uber's first Argentine ride, the union and the four largest propietario chambers had taken Uber to court. The juridical device of choice was a writ of *amparo* (protection): an urgent constitutional device designed to directly interpellate the state, in this case the authorities of the Autonomous City of Buenos Aires.

The Making of a Case

In Argentine legislation the writ of amparo is a fast-tracked, rapid, free, and summary legal recourse and constitutional right that any person or lawful association of people has to exercise against anyone who, by act or omission, hurts, limits, or threatens rights and freedoms protected by the national constitution. It works like a kind of right of rights: by definition it protects citizens, as holders of rights, and citizens' rights, that is, the constitutional order these rights articulate and the notion of citizenry they define and endow, as harm to either would render the whole order illusive. The nature of the rights in danger—to live, travel, learn, work, marry, and associate freely, among others—requires writs of amparo to be promptly executed, lest the damage to those rights, and those citizens, become irreparable during the normal temporality of legal action. Often, as in this case, writs of amparo are exercised against the state, appealing to its role as provider, overseer, and ultimate guarantor of these rights.

The writ of amparo's role was to translate Uber's presence in Buenos Aires into a legal problem. This translation was technical, temporal, and spatial, a "complex alchemy" embroidering legal texts, other texts, emotions, claims, and several kinds of disparate objects, flattening and aligning their contours and surfaces into a single whole that thus became the subject of law.[11] Buildings, materials, time frames, languages, and ways of organizing meaning orchestrated the process. This routing was not merely functional, but only it could confer a legitimacy standardized and hedged by ritual: in order for the amparo to even *be* an amparo, for its words and claims to be acknowledged and taken seriously, it had to be constructed in a certain way.

The amparo's seventeen pages spliced together references to the city and Argentine constitutions and several local and national laws and articles within them; national Supreme Court rulings; Uber's social media pages; estimates of how many families in subsidiary trades depended on the taxi industry; the first section of the seventh chapter of the national Civil and Commercial Code; newspaper articles where Soledad Lago Rodríguez, Uber spokesperson in those early days, announced that Uber would carry on with its setup despite governmental warnings of its illegality; and the Universal Declaration of Human Rights. The whole was rendered in a slightly archaic form of River Plate Spanish, inverting the place of certain pronouns with respect to verbs and referencing jurisprudence in roman numerals among other quirks.

The translation of the conflict into a legal claim also created subjects, positioned with respect to each other and to the general case, and from whom the amparo demanded and anticipated certain actions.[12] The claim was that the Ministry of Transportation of the Autonomous City of Buenos Aires, in this frame a legal subject accused of "action or negligence," was failing in its duty to protect citizens' right to engage in free and lawful enterprise and their right to safety. The livelihoods of workers in the taxi industry and its attendant trades, the amparo argued, were at imminent risk from Uber's service, whose unregulated tariffs and unregulated vehicles fit the Argentine legal definition of unfair competition that would quickly destroy the economic lives of those incurring such mechanical and governmental costs. The political economy of the taxi industry, that is, the production of taxi drivers' bodies, the vehicles, the fares and conditions of the transaction, and the laws that regulated urban movement and use of space, provided the bulk of the arguments supporting the translation of Uber into a subject of law. I mean a subject as a theme, as a topic of legal interest, but also a subject in the heuristics of law, an entity that is assigned a responsibility and whose actions are brought under the light of a claim awaiting a resolution.

Partly as a rhetorical strategy to add momentum to the claim, and partly because no political economy is entirely self-contained, the amparo enrolled within its claims larger social and economic processes of Argentine and Buenos Aires's life. The plaintiffs triangulated Uber's unfairness with matters of tax evasion and reflections on informal employment as a national problem.

They also argued that Uber's trade involved no professional standards other than its internal benefit–maximizing processes, thus putting at risk the lives of all residents; and that driving for Uber constituted an unlawful use of public space for unregistered private trade. The amparo also extended into other spheres through moral language, highlighting the incompatibility between the incoming government's goal of fighting poverty and the "complicity of those in government" who allowed or did not impede "the setup of a company that bases its profitability on labor precaritization and tax evasion on a sidereal scale." At the end of the document, signatories requested an immediate block of Uber's app.

Within thirty-six hours the judge replied. In such a scenario "[involving] matters of urban security, consumers' rights, right to work and lawful industry, tributary aspects, conflicts stemming from the use of new technologies, security and coordination of public transportation, foreign companies' business in the city space, policing powers reach and limits, etc.," a writ of amparo on its own could not "absorb or guarantee a rigorous treatment of the conflict." He mandated the rerouting of the issue via ordinary justicial channels. Also, while he refused the request to mandate the immediate cessation of the availability of the Uber's app, a decision chapter 7 will examine in detail, he ordered the government of the Autonomous City of Buenos Aires to take all necessary measures to suspend any activity that the company Uber, or anyone on its behalf, might be performing in the city of Buenos Aires until a definitive decision was reached.

The Argentine name for the document the judge produced was *resolución*. Etymologically related to *resolution*, *resoluteness*, and *resolve*, *resolución* is the noun that corresponds to the verb *resolver*—to solve, to sort out, implying that what is sorted is, in a sense, final. In other words, this document took a preponderant and exclusive last place in the production of a particular kind of truth, legitimate precisely because of the preponderance and exclusiveness of those who enunciated it. Canonically speaking, the institutional order of Argentina defines judges as exclusive and definitive holders of the prerogative to decide over certain matters. Reenacted by process, this legitimacy is, in a sense, socially agreed on as part of society's distribution of labor, of course always at the canonical level: "Entry into the juridical field implies the tacit acceptance of the field's fundamental law, an essential tautology which requires that, within the field, conflicts can only be resolved juridically—that is, according to the rules and conventions of the field itself."[13]

The legitimacy of the judge's answer and of the writ of amparo were thus both intelligible and socially meaningful as part of a process and sequence whose domain was the courts, their paperwork, language, and buildings. The terms of this legitimacy were set by the codes that govern social life in Argentina, from the National Constitution to infinitesimally pertinent edicts on how frequently the floors of these buildings should be cleaned. Yet by the time the judge's *resolución* came out, on Friday 14, April 2016, two days after Uber's arrival, this canonical legitimacy was besieged: first, by suspicions that in the political climate after the elections and amid protests, shattered windows, and the threat of violence, the production of a juridical truth would certainly not be such a hermetic process, and second, because an alternative understanding of the source and nature of legitimacy in general, and in the form of this conflict in particular, was taking hold of Buenos Aires's residents: Uber should stay in Buenos Aires because "the people" wanted it to.

Judges, Politics, and the People:
A Solomonic Judgment

Ariadna was Francisco's partner, and they had recently moved in together in a small flat her family owned in the Barrio Norte area, a quarter of a mile from the Obelisk. She had lived in central Buenos Aires all her life, had studied business management at the University of Buenos Aires, and was now working for the Buenos Aires offices of a multinational bank. If forced onto an ideological grid, Ariadna was economically liberal in a pragmatic, nonfanatical way. She had had to deal with the union of bank employees, famously powerful, from her position at the bank; she was on good speaking terms with their local delegates and did not balk at the premise of unionized labor per se. She had used Uber several times during a holiday in New York with her friends, and much of what Francisco knew of the app itself he had learned through her.

Both Francisco and Ariadna thought "the government" was just going through the motions of a legal case and respecting due process to appease the taxi industry's fury. This is why Macri had come out in support of taxi drivers, argued Ariadna, referencing the cover of national dailies on April 14 quoting the now president declaring that taxis were "a symbol of our city and of the country."[14] Both of them had voted for Macri, Francisco with some conviction and Ariadna out of repulsion for Fernández de Kirchner's candidate.

It seemed unthinkable that Macri's coalition, a merry aggregation of metropolitan technocrats anxious for a loosely defined modernity, would *actually* be serious about opposing Uber.[15] This coalition included Buenos Aires's new chief of government, Horacio Rodríguez Larreta, who declared to the press, "We are in favor of modernity within the framework of the law."[16] Such platitudes featured regularly in his rhetorical repertoire but were broadly taken as implying veiled support for a service that was intuitively, aesthetically, and ideologically much more aligned with his and Macri's stance than with the union's. At the level of grand narratives and elections the tide had certainly turned: Macri's coalition had won the highest executive roles of the land, the presidency and the role of chief of government of the Autonomous City of Buenos Aires and that of governor of the province of Buenos Aires, a separate jurisdiction. Still, as I argued in chapter 1, Viviani remained a powerful and astute political actor who in three decades had outlasted governments of all denominations, including Peronist ones. His mere existence evoked the distribution of the sensible where these residents and much of the middle classes imagined that unions wielded all kinds of power, including public violence resulting in death.[17]

As chapter 1 has argued, in their contradictions, evocations, and shifty certainties, these suspicions and fantasies effectively made the distribution of the sensible as people experienced it, irrespective of how accurately they represented "actual" relations.[18] Regardless of their stance with respect to this conflict, most Argentines already imagined that the juridical gaze, canonically imperturbable, was in fact instrumentally, politically, and poetically aligned with the government of the times.[19] Ariadna conceded that the government was showing skill in managing the potential for complex and explosive forms of public violence, and like many residents also imagined that greater networks were at play in this particular conflict. Yet, in a sense precisely because in all evidence this was a country where residents inevitably thought in terms of such concessions and backstage negotiations, Ariadna thought this particular matter should be left to the people: "Let the people decide, and if Uber is what the people want, then leave it—who would any judge be to ban it?" Francisco was less academically trained in economic principles but more readily embraced the intuitions of late capitalist life: "It's about choice and freedom. Who is the union to stop me from going about my own business? It is not a matter for the government or the judges or whether Macri wants Uber or not." There is a legal case, I argued, and explained why I thought it was actually quite sound: irrespective of residents' mistrust, taxi drivers were highly monitored, their commercial transportation insurances were more than twice as expensive as regular ones, and however devious their methods of operating, they held probably one of the most formalized trades in the city in terms of labor registration and taxes.

This was irrelevant, Francisco insisted, because obviously the people (*la gente*) had chosen Uber. "Look at the numbers!," by which he meant the numbers of app downloads reported by Uber's perennially enthusiastic press releases. If people trusted and cared about professional driver's licenses, types of transportation insurance, and vehicular verifications, they would just not use Uber. It is not about the numbers, I replied, and challenged them: Had they not just voted months earlier for the party that had campaigned precisely on respect for the institutions? Were the Argentine juridical system, the constitution, due process, and the like not institutions worthy of respect? "You know as well as we do the justice system is unreliable," Ariadna scoffed. Speaking as if it were up to the three of us to decide, in that room, the tiniest simulacrum of the greatest Solomonic judgment, Francisco passed sentence: the union, the government, everyone should let the people decide, and if they did not want Uber, fair enough—he raised his hands, palms outward as if signaling fairness, with the full certainty that his side, Uber's, would win.

A Moral Legerdemain

If one can speak of an Uber "side" to the conflict, it is because there is no better distillation of the mood in the grand theater of Buenos Aires toward the end of April 2016 than the infographic published by national daily *La Nación* in late March, titled "Taxis versus Uber."[20] At a certain level, this binary was one of the most barren and uninteresting paths into the conflict. But the capacity of a particular kind of thinking to flatten a tangle of law, materialities, and ideologies into such clear-cut terms, and to accomplish this so remarkably persuasively, is perhaps the most powerful rhetorical device of postpolitical reasoning.

Francisco's argument that the people should decide, and that in fact they were already deciding with their downloads and their ride requests, was in principle a conventional extension of the elementary and intuitive market logics to the complex issue of organizing social life.[21] Let us hold in suspension, for now, what exactly one was to think people were deciding by downloading, consuming, or verbally supporting Uber; or in other words, how all sorts of different "decisions" could be made to pass for each other.

How did consumer choice evoke such a raw, ultimate legitimacy? How could invoking consumer choice redistribute the experience of the sensible?

Market logics are exceptionally sticky and capable of resolving the political, the ethical, and even the real into their own logics.[22] Yet, if we look closely, strictly speaking this was not just about markets. In fact, through a logical and affective legerdemain, "putting it to the people" was barely about economic reasoning. Two centuries before the neoclassical canon consolidated, well before economics as we know it came into being, a certain kind of natural right laid the groundwork for the moral order Francisco was now laying claim to. Seeking to contain the passions that fueled the religious wars decimating Europe, Delft-born Hugo Grotius argued that people have natural rights and obligations to each other. These are prior to any religious or political bond and should be respected as such and beyond disagreement, he added.[23] At a natural and original level we are all equal, and we face each other outside any hierarchical relation of any kind, whether courts, classes, religions, rankings, or bureaucracies: Grotius was trying to create a reason to give a *definitive* end to ongoing conflict.

The first consequence of Grotius's reformulation is the sublimation of the political, now demoted as a secondary feature to an order understood in the moral economy of natural life: first we exist and exchange among ourselves as fundamentally perfect equals, then comes any order and experience thereof.[24] The second consequence is that this order promotes ordinary life as the highest form of life in a society by default inhabited only by interlocking industry, production, and exchange in a "concord and mutual service" that conflict should not disturb.[25] These people are not atomized, self-sufficient individualists: they come to be a people and to understand themselves, their reasons, and those of others through an ethics of freedom *and* mutual benefit.[26] This does not mean they are, or should be, economic equals, earning or having the same; it means they all partake in that industry, production, and exchange as equally detachable from hierarchies sullying the moral economy of mutual benefit.

Grotius slinks into Francisco's living room because these three-hundred-year old notions sustain our academic, popular, and intuitive understanding of a moral economy of popular sovereignty, that is: of an order where it is right that the people (however defined, for now) should decide. Ordinary lives are in this moral economy the site of a slightly mystical, morally irreducible legitimacy: it is immensely difficult to argue beyond it. Grotius, however, never imagined that this order carried with it the expectation of its integral, universal, and constant fulfillment: in fact, it coexisted for centuries with hierarchically complementary forms of order, between master and servant, between the elites and the masses, and between fathers and kin groups.[27] Yet in the last centuries demands grounded on this moral economy have grown in extension and intensity, up to our present-day "obsession" with popular participation in politics.[28] Between Grotius and Francisco's living room, the development of neoclassical economics in the late nineteenth century saw in the Enlightenment peasants' revolt against their overlords not only the revindication of Grotius's natural order preexisting politics under siege but also evidence that those ordinary people going about their business knew better than their overlords what was good for them.[29] Thus neoclassical economics' contribution was to imagine these ordinary everyday lives, not as asocial, amoral, or self-sufficient, but rather as *fully and meaningfully informed*.[30]

In this sense, to the moral aberration of political interference with the nature of those ordinary lives was now added the enshrinement of those lives, already in a sense sovereign, as the site of an irrevocable truth. This argument will return in chapter 6, but two developments are crucial here. First, by constituting individuals as perfectly, soundly informed sites of natural economic life that nobody can understand better than they understand themselves, neoclassical philosophy created the rhetorical infrastructure to bolster direct, unhindered choice as the highest possible moral virtue. Second, by organizing moral virtue on the premise of unhindered choice, that natural economic life that was for Grotius populated by a concord of industry, production, and exchange was now intelligible only through the looking glass of choice's bottom line: the act and moral right of consumption.

Now we can tackle what Francisco meant by "putting it to the people." His reasons were as strategic as Grotius's and as intractable as neoclassical philosophers': in this lineage, it would be a moral aberration for a judge, the taxi industry, the government, or an ethnographer to challenge the legitimacy of people's choice or people's choice itself as the ultimate site of truth, as it would amount to claiming to know better than them what they wanted, what they needed, or what was good for them. Of course, we must consider that Francisco defended the ground of popular choice because he was convinced his preference would prevail; but in this particular case, popular choice afforded a way of bypassing the government, the union, and the political that he imagined in his suspicions and elaborations. The quasi-religious mystique that shrouds popular politics and makes it so hard in late capitalism to argue against what the people want could in this instance deliver a prescriptive, concrete decision: let Uber stay.

Here is the moral legerdemain: this whole argument persuades because it pivots on a logical and affective transposition where one speaks of choice as an *economic* trope in a *political* conflict, but choice persuades us because it is actually and throughout mobilized as a *moral* category. Uber officials shrewdly employed this sleight of hand in a tweet from those early days: "Come meet us and defend your right to choose. Until next Wednesday, 15 free rides up to 200 pesos. #Righttochoose."[31] This "right" to choose was not one that played out in courts, politics, or constitutions; it was the intimate, direct inheritor of that free pursuit of mutual interest, and in late capitalist societies it is a moral good, ontologically anterior and superior to the political and any hierarchies—particularly, as we shall see in coming sections, those interfering with the "free" pursuit of industry and choice, like a taxi license. This is how pressure began piling up on the experience of Buenos Aires's distribution of the sensible: disagreement and its sites, processes, and arguments were replaced by the moral economy of right and wrong.[32] As we shall see, entire arguments, bodies, and institutions are ill fitted to inhabit the terms of this distribution of the sensible increasingly common in postpolitical reasoning. In this moral universe, the fact that the people wanted Uber constituted what I refer to as a gladiatorial truth: a prescriptive truth claim based on the moralizing bottom line of minimally mediated popular legitimacy, measured in actual vocal support or its late capitalism proxy, consumption.

Consumption: The Grammar of Gladiatorial Truth

I will tackle later who counts as "the people" and why. What matters now is that, within the logics detailed above, if one does not want Uber, one can simply not use it: to morally oppose a certain act of consumption is coterminous and identical to not consuming, and the only and supremely legitimate challenge mechanism is to divert consumption. Consistently, all the complexities of Uber's labor relations, fare setting, management, and fiscal practices that the writ of amparo detailed painstakingly and that constituted the political, ethical, economic, and legal terms of the conflict could matter only at the level of the act of consumption. From this perspective, people's choice to continue using and downloading Uber doubled as confirmation that these complexities did not matter to them and thus should not matter at all. Uber's officials' recurrent reference to alleged numbers of downloads—thousands of drivers in the first days, tens of thousands in the first week—also worked to consolidate this sense of choice that we can imagine could be pinned down to those individual citizen-consumers, but was in fact convincing through the vagueness of what "choice" exactly meant and the mystique of a collective with a will. This was crucial: we now transcended the individual citizen-consumer, for this was a problem for the people, but was set in terms that simultaneously destroyed any possibility for it to be a *social* problem, that is, one that concerned Argentines as a sort of whole whose internal relations could not actually be disaggregated to individual parts. Proper use of public space, fairness, risk, violence, and tolerance were denaturalized by the same reduction to the self that claimed to account for all that mattered.

As a rhetorical device, consumption organizes what this choice reveals and veils, and what we can take it to be. Uber was the app that had been downloaded half a million times, "available in four hundred cities around the world," a mode of transportation that one "took" alongside subways and buses, and part and parcel of smart, service-oriented cities of shared accommodation and a general sleek circulation of choices.[33] Even when speaking about driving for Uber, Uber's PR strategy was to insist that people drove when and if they wanted. More than the truth value of this statement, what matters here is that by emphasizing choice, the rhetoric of consumption displaced that of industry and production, even for those who were providing the service.[34] Wildly different processes and politics of production, that is, the circuitry and databases that made Uber exchanges possible and the political economy described in the first three chapters of this book, were equalized in the sense that they were both, simultaneously, evicted from the frame of what could count as relevant and legitimate in a referendum by consumption.

As a grammar for the production and intelligibility of gladiatorial truths, consumers' choice enhances the quasi-religious Manicheanism proper to the issue it partitions in morally irreconcilable halves. When production in the taxi industry did count, it did so through a moral register of excess and vice, consistent with the recasting of hierarchy as intrusive to economic natural life. Sometimes poetically and sometimes consciously, this register merged the political economy of the taxi industry as residents understood it with the Argentine and in particular Peronist political universe residents understood the industry to inhabit, represent, and reproduce. The most furious battleground on this front was the taxi license. Buenos Aires residents had known for decades that the taxi industry worked on the basis of licenses, that is, big numbers painted bright yellow onto black on both front doors of every taxi in the city. They were known as a feature of the trade, even if most people did not really know exactly how they worked or whether they were taken seriously at all, and if so by whom. The moment Uber became "imminent," the term *monopoly* came to define the license in and of itself, as an object-number, and also the hierarchies and processes it allegedly underpinned.

Strictly speaking, the term *monopoly* is an economic descriptor for industrial processes with a single seller or provider. In and of itself it carries no moral connotation; in many cases, in fact, even neoclassical economists argue it is less wasteful or more efficient to frame certain provisions as monopolies, for example certain public utilities. In some cases monopolies are even morally desirable to guarantee even and equal treatment of the many, for example in the provision of governmental services, be they outsourced, like border policing in some countries, or classically reserved for the state, like the provision of justice, "monopolized" by the judicial power. We will return to this latter monopoly soon; but the point here is that through transferences analogous to those outlined above, now that the relevance of even engaging with the processes of production of a ride had been discarded, the "monopoly of taxi licenses" was set in the terms of moral outrage. If the license's legitimacy had been a bit wobbly at the street level before Uber arrived because people doubted its efficacy, it was now completely delegitimized as a matter of principle.

Just how exactly this "monopoly" worked, or what monopoly even meant in a city where these middle classes regularly used over two hundred bus lines, seven subways, interurban trains, and a state-sponsored bicycle system, was hard to pin down in any strict industrial or economic sense. Describing very little, the powerful moral connotation of the term *monopoly* intuitively and affectively qualified the production process of the taxi industry as inherently inimical to the arena of consumer choice, and thus by principle illegitimate. Conversely, as chapter 5 shows, a sense of "competition" that was more intuitive than verifiable gained rhetorical ground with undeserved certainty, salutary and antithetical to forces hindering choice.

Production and the Burden of Proof

Regardless of their descriptive rigor or lack thereof, gladiatorial truths derive their affective potency from the fact that in the logics of "the bleached world of the market" the interests of consumers are rendered as more uniform, universal, and just than those of workers, in this case those of the taxi industry.[35] Universal and non–industry specific, consumption brings to the gladiatorial truths it fuels the aura of a maximum transparency, of a will created openly and modeled on the public festival, where we are all both performers and spectators of the bare truth of choice with nothing to hide.[36] In contrast, the interests of workers are necessarily sectorial, specific, and subjected to production, political economies, and other backstage considerations that are by definition opaque to the blinding monochromatism of consumption's spotlight. They appear as provincial and self-interested: the workforce allegedly has "the primary interest of preserving . . . its jobs, rather than . . . serving the public."[37] Because, as explained in earlier chapters, the taxi industry was built on a taxi license now viewed as a moral aberration, the existence of the industry was now assimilated with hidden plots directly evoking a sort of popular treason.

A near-verbatim example of this point was a radio interview held in late March 2016, when Uber's arrival was still "imminent." Journalist and radio presenter Jorge Lanata had gained enormous celebrity through his investigation into high-profile corruption scandals within the Kirchner presidencies. His interviewee, leader of one of the biggest taxi propietario chambers, argued that the industry was not seeking to stunt competition. All taxistas asked was for Uber to follow the same laws they had to follow, invest in the country, and pay social security charges, just as they did. Lanata retorted that it was inadmissible for taxi drivers to hinder his ability to choose the means of transportation he wanted, just because they were defending their labor: "It seems you are protecting someone's interests rather than the consumers. You cannot defend your work by hindering my freedom." He also pressed the propietario on the matter of "fake taxis," a topic and term suddenly back in fashion. The interviewee replied that there was no such thing and that over 99 percent of taxis in Buenos Aires were "whitened," as I explained in chapter 1, and declared to the taxman and to the state. Lanata replied sardonically that in that case he always ended up taking that 1 percent; the propietario leader asked him to please denounce any unregistered taxis and if he had time to expand on these allegations; Lanata replied, "I don't have time for that."[38]

In its ruthless immanence gladiatorial truth has little time to discriminate between choferes, propietarios, their chambers, the union, Viviani, or even the government, now all conflated as a collective invested in depriving the people of their choice. Those who disagreed with Uber's platform, or with its business strategy in Buenos Aires, or with sorting the matter of the gladiatorial arena of public consumption, were rhetorically flattened, equalized, and cast on the wrong side of a battle set in vague terms but with clear moral, nonpolitical lines. Andrés and Mauro did not even join the protests against Uber; Andrés out of cynicism and Mauro because he was not fundamentally opposed to Uber so long as they played by the rules. Fearing violence from fellow taxi drivers or union delegates if seen circulating when the union and the chambers had decided to go on strike, in the two biggest protests against Uber they simply stayed home and waited it out.

This act of partitioning off the moral outside politics was of course teeming with tensions and contradictions: institutionally, politically, and even personally, all of these actors were positioned in extremely different ways with respect to the Uber conflict, and as this book has shown, with respect to each other. However ideologically and aesthetically aligned with Uber the national or city government may have been, the minister for transportation of the City of Buenos Aires, Juan José Méndez, never wavered in his decision to tow Uber cars away, several per day, fining their drivers the equivalent of 4,130 USD. People who hated the union with unspeakable fervor for the same reasons Francisco did, and possibly with more firsthand knowledge of its dealings, now found themselves morally aggregated with the union's allegedly self-serving bravado, which further delegitimized their claim. These contradictions even involved Francisco, who had voted for Macri's coalition and thus for the government Méndez was fully part of: when the latter announced that Uber cars would be towed away Francisco began referring to him as the idiot in the Ministry of Transportation, wondering whether the government did not have more important things to worry about. Here is the logical, rhetorical, and affective potency of gladiatorial truths as a technique of adjudication and as a grammar to imagine and enact the immanent mystique of an ordinary life deployed to antagonize institutions and hierarchies of any denomination.

Fueled by the solipsistic, heady energy of a public festival celebrating itself, gladiatorial truth's chase for the bottom line cannot, by itself, limit its expansion to a single industry: part of its moral appeal is precisely that of an immanent, unassailable truth, beyond the artifices of argument. Consequently, the taxi industry was not the only logic of production dismissed as a moral affront to what the people wanted. As said earlier, canonically speaking, courts hold a monopoly over the production of the kinds of

truths that juridical truths constitute. Although of course in the actual life
of the juridical field its processes depend on "the spirit of the time, . . . on
the shrewdness of lawyers and on the multi-formed pressure of the press,"
juridical truths are ultimately legitimate because they are exclusive and
hierarchical and involve ordinary lives only in the highly ritualized times,
texts, materialities, and processes of production that I have reviewed above.[39]

In the moral universe of consumer choice, the translations and media-
tions any legal case needs to exist are not only superfluous but also intrusive
and immoral for reasons outlined above, and this delegitimizes courts as sites
of truth as a matter of principle. As said earlier, Argentines in particular are
generally mistrustful of courts, doubting their independence from politics
and parties. Like many residents, Ariadna was convinced that the justice
system or the government (residents work on the basis that this difference
is always blurry) was "playing along" with the legal case to appease taxistas'
anger and minimize the risk of public violence. She gave them credit on this
front, but this skillful management of violence only emphasized the tainted,
illegitimate character of juridical truth in the case of this conflict. Thus to
even insist on the importance of courts was to deliberately, implicitly, or
accidentally reproduce the "monopoly" of a morally reprehensive arc spanning the union, the taxi industry, the court, and even the government that
many of these people had just voted for.

The grammar of gladiatorial truths is modular and protean: its spare,
instinctive, and near-religious clarity is within the reach of those illiterate in
other grammars of the public sphere. In fact, in an era where consumption
often mediates the possibilities for disadvantaged sectors to participate in any
form of citizenship, it is often the only grammar available to lay a claim to
any public stake.[40]. As Uber did with its #Righttochoose campaign, corporations leverage this grammar when it suits them.[41] Like any other grammar,
however, it also shapes what can be debated and in what terms it can be
debated.[42] Culturally and socioeconomically speaking, Francisco, Ariadna,
Valentina, and most of my middle-class informants, university-educated,
urban professional homeowners, moved in a public sphere largely made
by and for them, where grammars other than consumption's bottom line
articulated other claims. Also, as we know, Francisco sought the gladiatorial
arena, convinced its adjudication would benefit him, and it is probable that
in a different conflict (or under a different president) he would have decried
the gladiatorial arena as demagoguery and lowbrow populism. Resorting
to gladiatorial truths was a case-specific tactical move to cast the problem

in a framework that resisted the political in its philosophy, in its rhetorical flatness, and in its affective intuition. Gladiatorial truths open an experience of (non)argumentation where subjects, in the syntactic sense of those who speak and are the core of an utterance in this language, and in the intuitive sense of anyone who has a voice, are much harder to interpellate politically because they are being addressed as moral economic subjects.

Yet gladiatorial arenas as sites of contention and gladiatorial truths as prescriptive claims persuade because even if mobilized for purely functional/ utilitarian reasons they still evoke values at the heart of late capitalist mystique: Are we not, at the end of the day, individuals? Do we not, after all, know what we want? Corporations may occupy this rhetoric more or less cynically (drive when *you* want!), and Francisco and my other informants may certainly not have been constantly engaged in reflecting on themselves as fully informed individuals who should always and forever be "free to choose"—however we define freedom and choice. But as Lanata's interview above shows, the near-religious affective intensity that late capitalism affords to gladiatorial truths shifts the burden of proof, of any proof, onto the shoulders of those who oppose them *irrespective of the actual content of the truth claim itself.* This is how they shape the public sphere and the whole distribution of the sensible. Gladiatorial truths' irreducible, irreducibly moral legitimacy preexists and outlasts the tactical deployment of gladiatorial arenas. The latter do not create that moral legitimacy: they just summon it, which further reinforced the imagination of that core as irreducibly moral, both prepolitical and beyond politics. As I will show in the next section, not all bodies deploy gladiatorial truths in the same manner or can reflect on their terms in the same ways: the ethics of freedom and mutual benefit that has fueled them for centuries speaks to, and reflects, selves that understand themselves and the political in their lives in very specific ways.

A Gladiatorial Truth's People

Popular support for Uber, already a poor proxy for estimating the appeal of a gladiatorial truth in the terms of this conflict, was hard to quantify; different sources claimed that anywhere from 30 percent to 80 percent of Buenos Aires's residents were "in favor of Uber," depending on how the matter was framed, what was left out of it, and how the journalists in question interpreted the answers. With a legal case blaring relentlessly on the news and a minimum of three Uber cars towed away per day, it is hard to even qualify what "in favor" could mean.

Yet Francisco's point in invoking consumers' choice as a ground of contention was never to convince through internal logical precision or to inventory allegiances exhaustively, but to ride an enthusiasm palpable in the public sphere that residents like him inhabited in early 2016. People who thought citizens should decide through their consumption whether Uber should stay or not may not have been able to count or recognize themselves, and thus congregate, in any remotely unequivocal way. Yet Uber tweets, press releases, and promotional emails, social media discussions, footage of protesting taxi drivers, and a general exasperation fertilized the imagination that such a collective existed and that it was of a critical size. Crucially, this collective was not imagined as contained by party lines, and to my knowledge it was not. Both Macri's voters and his detractors would agree that his technocratic agenda, ideological emptiness, and world-oriented developmentalism fit perfectly the discourse of empowerment and micro entrepreneurship, or of labor precaritization and exploitation, that Uber epitomized for each group respectively. Like Ariadna and Francisco, virtually all Macri supporters I spoke to were highly in favor of Uber, and a lot of them were already using it, either openly dismissing the legal conflict or effectively ignoring it.

But many Peronists in general, and supporters of Cristina Fernández de Kirchner in particular, used or supported Uber in spite of what would become a legal ban. The reasons, when voiced, spanned resignation, convenience, a pragmatic "need to adapt to the times" tinged with a sense of irrevocability, and a petty vindictiveness toward taxi drivers. Even some taxi drivers I knew were thinking of becoming Uber drivers, particularly choferes, and at least trying to "be their own boss." Francisco, who now found out that some taxi drivers resented the union, relayed to me with satisfaction that two taxistas had told him they had already signed up as Uber drivers on the sly with their personal cars: "even the taxis" were on board. No single ethnographic vignette better epitomizes the ironies and contradictions of this conflict, the infinitely protean nature of Peronism, or the momentum that gladiatorial truths gather than the revelation, a few weeks later, that a former parliamentarian from the province of Santa Fe, Peronist and supporter of both Kirchner administrations "through and through," had become an Uber driver in Buenos Aires. He agreed to be interviewed by the national daily *Perfil* and declared he would try to explain to his taxista *compañeros* why he had done so, to convince them that Uber's organization was worthy of admiration and that the solution to the conflict, in its throes at the time, was "dialogue" and the regularization of the company.[43] *Compañero* is the vocative Peronists have used to refer to each other ever since Perón used it in the plural to refer to *his* countrymen and women, the working-class masses, implicitly excluding urban elites, intellectuals, the landowning bourgeoisie, and several internal others.

The tension between the horizontal sharedness of *compañeros* and the betrayal signified by a Peronist and Kirchnerist leader turning away from his people, the working masses of the taxi industry, and toward a "neoliberal" platform allegedly welcomed by a millionaire-businessman-turned-technocrat president and partisan adversary is not just ironic anecdote. The creeping inclusion of various others in the growing People who were using, choosing, and downloading Uber despite the ban and official sanctions not only enhanced the rhetorical persuasion of the premise of people's choice but verified in the eyes of people like Francisco the legitimacy of their claim that they should choose (and the legitimacy of that which they were choosing). These others reinforced the redistribution of the sensible to the tune of a People that we could never quantify, and indeed, barely qualify, but that was pulling others into a universality conceived as such not because of numbers or volumes but because of the intensity of their shared condition as a site of moral economic life. They constituted

> a claim that no one could evade. . . . It was precisely this initially unpolitical meaning . . . which facilitated the claim to that greatest possible universality which . . . could no longer be outbid. The numerical aggregate of all [people] . . . switched, without a change of word, into political self-legitimation which did not, however, have to be identified as such. . . . The political usage of (this expression) . . . delivered an ideological surplus which was not contained in other binaries.[44]

This ideological surplus consolidated the moral canon of a People imagined beyond the political. It was a surplus because it did not challenge or deny the terms and language of the taxis-versus-Uber binary confrontation. Rather, it included and subsumed them into the fold of an emergent collective, imagined through the substance of the moral economy I detailed above. This surplus logically accommodated the parliamentarian's transition, symbolic in its irony, without needing to deny or reduce it to treason, or atavism, or even Peronist nature, because it did not deal in political categories. This was one last, grand legerdemain: as evidenced in the quote above, gladiatorial truths do not even need to change words to already resist, in their bareness, the category of the political.

For these same reasons the taxi industry's challenge did not even need to be actually addressed; as this book will show, it was never in fact acknowledged as an equal claim to the stakes, and in some instances, like those examined in this chapter, was actively delegitimized. The gladiatorial run for the bottom line in those early days set the terms of the conflict, and as such it will watermark every chapter from now on: the taxi industry, recalcitrant and self-centered, and a People that did not need to be defined beyond the immanence of the choices it made or interpellated on any grounds other than its sovereign choice, by definition beyond interpellation.

Who belonged in the gladiatorial truths' People? Historically, in Argentina, the People, *el pueblo*, and any of its semiotic variations are Peronist signifiers—crowded ones, too, gathering Eva Perón's literally and figuratively shirtless ones, the Uber-driving parliamentarian's *compañeros*, the working masses whom eight decades ago the oligarchy excluded, who epitomized mass democracy in the mid-twentieth century and who in the late twentieth century suffered in the first person the decimation of Argentine industry. Francisco's people, *la gente*, could in some cases overlap with *el pueblo*: as we have seen, some taxi drivers chose to drive for Uber or did not mind the premise of choice. Yet these collectives were of a different nature. As said earlier, the deliberate, explicit, and strategic invocation of freedom of choice and its mystique as a powerful moral claim reflected more the speakers' sense of their own agency than an inevitable resort to the grounds of moral economy. In other words, certain bodies were more attuned to the logics, rhetoric, and affect of gladiatorial truths than others because they were more conversational in their grammar, and because they could afford to think of themselves and their relations in the terms of that ideological surplus that transcended the political and occupied a pure moral economy of freedom of mutual benefit.

For certain other bodies, the subordination of the political on which gladiatorial truths hinged, intuitive for Francisco and Ariadna, could not quite work the same way. Among the taxi choferes I encountered during the events that chapter 3 details, one lived in a squat and three lived in unpaved, unnamed roads with no numbers. Many depended directly on state support to feed and clothe their children and themselves. The union renewed their IDs, offering its headquarters' address to those living beyond the city proper, as the law required city taxi drivers to have a legal domicile in the city. Union members created a fund from their own money to cover transportation costs for candidates who could not afford the commute. They also organized a ceremony that friends and family were invited to attend where choferes received a diploma, in many cases the first ever since dropping out of primary or secondary school. The separation between union membership and representation and the political and partisan forms of the state, on the one hand, and the premise of these ordinary lives as complete moral economic subjects, one the other, was blurred if not entirely meaningless.

In the rhetorical transferences that gladiatorial truths activated, these bodies, more akin to Peronism's *el pueblo*, inhabited the common experience mostly through "monopolies," "excess," "treason," and "self-interest." That this was "only" a factual, empirical dismissal, because *la gente* was infinitely inclusive at the level of principle, evidenced and reinforced the difficulty to challenge gladiatorial truths without, in so doing, denying these bodies an agency they had in a sense other than the only one intelligible to the moral economy of consumption's bottom line. In other words, those opposing the gladiatorial arena had to respond to the following question: Were these taxistas not individuals *equal* to the others? Were they all not as able and entitled to choose as we were? Equality in principle and equality in fact were separable politically in ways that moral economy no longer had a viable grammar for. To attempt to explain that certain Argentine bodies simply could not be reduced to the terms of gladiatorial truths would amount to saying out loud that those bodies lacked agency, not just socioeconomically but within their nature, in a way writing them off from citizenship of that distribution of the sensible increasingly intelligible in terms of gladiatorial truths, where only certain bodies could swap natures with ease.

The gladiatorial truth that the people wanted Uber, and that therefore they should have it, marked now a shift in this conflict, and consequently marks it in this book's narrative. The chapters that follow examine other arguments, rationalities, and intuitions that, even if they at times contradicted themselves or each other, progressively reinforced the writing off of the taxi industry and its claims from a distribution of the sensible seen in light of Uber's arrival. The gladiatorial arena was only the most strident of these logics, and possibly the most irrevocable one. The unmediated, righteous, and emancipatory connotation of gladiatorial truths is always purging a noxious element: they are called upon as a celebration of popular, purifying power.[45] The irony of the Peronist and Kirchnerist parliamentarian's conversion doubled as a confirmation of the prepolitical universality of *la gente*'s moral economy, further cornering those who did not convert because they did not want to or because they could never inhabit it as the equals they were supposed to be. The only viable alternative gladiatorial truth allowed to the vanquished was to not consume, which in its own terms was also the most sovereign alternative and a sort of equality, too, to the extent that to consume and not to consume were in principle, within these logics, equally moral acts: in this sense, the vanquished were just as included as the winners. Insofar as this was a political problem to begin with, however, not consuming was hardly meaningful and hardly an alternative at all, only the confirmation that the political as such had been foreclosed.

5

The Stranger That Stays as Such

FROM THE OUTSET Uber framed its activities in Buenos Aires as a complement to existing modes of transportation, including the taxi industry, and as an "innovation," therefore allegedly beyond existing transportation laws. Yet the middle class saw Uber and the taxi industry as direct competitors locked in a structural opposition guaranteed, ultimately, by the company's condition as an outsider. Uber seemed impervious to the Argentine logics of the alleged taxi "mafia" that had presumably co-opted police, city administration officials, and others in its self-perpetuation. Following the well-trodden trope of competition as an economic solution to a political problem, the company's business practices, vaunted success around the world, and seemingly unstoppable penetration of Buenos Aires worked as an economic version of a stranger king: an outsider with its own motivations but impartial with respect to conflicts framed as political and local.[1] The claim that "Uber worked everywhere in the world," exaggerated, logically false, and imprecise, further fueled the affective persuasiveness of this structural opposition between economics, objectivity, and competition, on the one hand, and particular political circumstances and monopolies on the other hand, explaining alternative readings away through the stranger king logics.

Retiro
On March 20, 1997, in a public ceremony so unnoticed that it might as well have been a secret, Buenos Aires's Retiro train station was declared a national monument, the highest rank of heritage protection in Argentina.

Inaugurated in 1915 and designed by a team of British architects in a sober yet splendid Edwardian style, as the decree explains, "Retiro represents the culmination of the railway installation project, initiated in the middle of the nineteenth century; its network, linking the provinces to the port of Buenos Aires, allowed the distribution of immigrants and agricultural produce, reflecting the era of Argentina's greatest economic expansion."[2]

That era, broadly speaking the years between 1860 and 1930, opened up the wilderness of an enormous land to privatization, agricultural exploitation, and extermination or displacement of native Americans, a national project led by first- and second-generation Argentines and their European associates.[3] The railway system invented Argentina in all the modern senses of a nation, at the time a prosperous one, thriving as a vast capitalist trade outpost along the exciting frontier of a world trade whose latitude zero was western Europe. Retiro was built right next to Buenos Aires's port, and millions of tons of merchandise, grains, and beasts, as well as enormous amounts of capital and more immigrants than anywhere on the American continent outside New York, passed through Retiro on the way to what porteños still call "the interior": the entirety of Argentina outside the Autonomous City of Buenos Aires.[4] The capital's cultural and political prominence, an integrated national economy, a quintessentially modern, centralized bureaucracy, and the positivistic progress of a mechanical view of the world: Retiro reproduced them all, as the nation expanded in the most literal sense through its rail lines.

If Retiro and Argentina as a whole were so symbolically and materially entwined, it is a cruel irony that this would be celebrated in 1997. Argentina had known by then six coups d'état and several economic crises, and the bulk of the railway network that Retiro had crowned and ruled over had been dismantled six years prior. By some trivial invocation of efficiency that amounted to an economic massacre for millions of Argentines, beginning in 1991 the system was shut down. For hundreds of miles in all directions railway sleepers were stolen, left to rot, or used as firewood; stations were demolished, abandoned, or vandalized; and hundreds of towns scattered around an area larger than France were left completely disconnected in an otherwise empty land. Similar oblations were expected of other middle- and low-income nations during the 1990s under the infamous Washington Consensus, including some of Argentina's immediate neighbors. But in Argentines' cultural memory, this decade of reforms and liberalized trade confirms, together with the economic collapse of 2001, a theme that has haunted the country since its inception, partly through the very role these railway lines were celebrated for: how Argentines are to understand, relate to, and position ourselves with respect to the world outside of us.[5] Retiro's anachronistic magnificence, built to symbolize and serve the monopoly of Buenos Aires over the expanding nation, at the time richer than many of the European nations its majolica and ironwork were imported from, stands today, architecturally restored and incongruously splendid, as a perfect embodiment of "the ruins of a stillborn great nation"—a politically and culturally peripheral one at that.[6]

Symbols like Retiro are slippery to think with, always tense with multiple meanings. By 2015 Retiro was terminal for two subway lines and served as Greater Buenos Aires's interurban train hub, a parochial destiny for its vaulted halls but attuned in other ways to what Argentina and Buenos Aires have since become. The station is the main daily gateway to the city proper for many of the ten million residing beyond city limits. Suburban trains are reliable and much faster than buses or cars; also, public transportation in Argentina is commonly used by all social strata, so those millions included lawyers and engineers as well as janitors and concierges. Adjacent to Retiro stands today a smaller train station, serving districts to the west; and next to this other station in the 1980s was built an international bus terminal where over one hundred companies serve every Argentine province, spanning vertically half the southern hemisphere, as well as Bolivia, Brazil, Uruguay, Paraguay, Chile, and Peru. Side to side, these stations occupy a quarter of a mile; Retiro, the original, has given its name to the entire area, now effectively an international transportation hub. About eighty of all two hundred bus lines serving the city of Buenos Aires begin, end, or pass through the dozens of bus stops arranged along the square opposite, adding millions of daily commuters to local and foreign tourists, immigrants and emigrants, office workers on their way from one neighborhood to the next, and people like Francisco, who takes the bus to his hometown in the province of Buenos Aires from here for holidays and special occasions.

These three stations empty on the same avenue, Avenida Ramos Mejía. A raised runway off this avenue links it to the bus station; Francisco had been instructing me since my arrival to sit at the window of a particular bar overlooking the mouth of this runway onto the sidewalk. From there I saw a line of no fewer than ten taxis bordering the sidewalk, bumper to bumper, as well as a second line of taxis double-parked into the avenue. None of this space was even marked as an official taxi stop. Some of the drivers stood outside their cars, smoking and chattering; only the drivers of the first two cars in the line nearest to the sidewalk were inside the car. Two young men offered taxis to dozens of suitcase-laden targets and the occasional passerby. Their success rate was extremely low, which did not seem to faze anyone but also meant the line moved very slowly and blocked access to a perpendicular street and a loading zone. They were so tightly parked that several buses had to triple-park to let people on and off at the official bus stop that these taxis completely blocked.

I later approached an official taxi stop, a few meters to the left of Retiro Station proper, where five taxis waited with their engines off. Tito, the young man trying to entice passengers, was nineteen; his uncle, a Buenos Aires taxista since the early 2000s and a regular user of that stop, had suggested he come from their native province of Mendoza to help them out. Tito's job was to ensure that only the taxis "allowed" to stop there did so, he explained to me; these drivers gave him a cut from every ride he secured, and this was all he could tell me before the drivers noticed that our conversation was extending beyond what would be expected of a potential passenger and hollered at him to get to work.

The Retiro area today once again reaches into the furthest provinces and even other parts of the world; but a century after securing the economic, political, infrastructural, and cultural monopolies that allegedly made Argentina what it was and Buenos Aires its gateway to the world, Retiro has now become the site, symbol, and rhetorical shorthand for another monopoly. The middle class did not know this other monopoly in any detail or from up close, but they spoke of it with unmitigated conviction as the taxis' "mafia"—some sort of shady arrangement that controlled movement, trajectories, people, and vehicles from a certain "inside": inside the trade, inside taxi relations, and inside Buenos Aires and Argentina's political and economic life. As we will see, this concept of an "inside," saturated with meanings and static, powerfully shaped residents' desire for, and expectations about, the possibility of some sort of irreducible, and irreducibly opposed, outside.

All in It Together

Used for decades to describe the taxi industry, *mafia* was a labile, imprecise descriptor, integrating past sensational crimes, exaggerated claims, concrete experiences of abuse, trade informality mythologies, and drivers' fiddling with the taximeter in an arc of entrapment, moral reprehension, and resentment. If *mafia*'s own unclear and opaque boundaries replicated the conception of cunning and elusive taxi drivers that we discussed in chapter 3, around Retiro the term evoked the strategic networks that residents presumed to sustain the brazenness and nonchalant effrontery of abuses carried out in broad daylight. Other such taxi congregations were at Ezeiza, the international airport twenty miles south of the city and federal territory, and thus the only fragment of Argentina outside of the city where these taxis can operate; Aeroparque, the city's own, smaller airport; and Buquebus, the maritime terminal where the ferries to Uruguay docked.

These gatherings were seen as culturally frustrating, crowding other urban dwellers out of roads and sidewalks; as economically abusive, inventing both captive markets and their stunted logics by limiting taxi access to strategic places and times, demanding inflated fares in spite of standardized fares across city jurisdiction, and engaging in other exchange practices based on making alternatives unavailable at the needed moment; and as plainly illegal, either by cartelizing access to an official taxi stop legally meant for any taxi to use, or by outright inventing a stop, disregarding public space and traffic laws. Within the industry, access to these stops was understood as a "privilege" to be acquired through a contribution, trade seniority, and/ or union belonging. In general anyone could drop off passengers at these hot spots, but only "authorized" drivers could pick up fares. Once, when learning the ropes of the trade, one of the drivers at Dionisio's picked up a passenger at Aeroparque right after dropping someone off; the following day three taxi drivers turned up at his house to discourage him from doing it again. He believed they had tracked him down by the car plate. I found an official stop by a hospital used only by propietarios, in agreement with a policeman patrolling the area and ensuring nobody else stopped there; but the union or its delegates control most such stops to "keep the trade free of abuses," as a delegate explained to me. Consistently, it was more often taxi choferes who used them, people driving for someone else and belonging to the union through this employment relation. In any case, this meant the union had a far larger say over who did what or not than the law would have anticipated and probably approved of. It also meant that hierarchies and exclusions internal to the industry, reviewed earlier in this book, extended their logics into spaces, times, and relations outside the trade, creating new hierarchies and exclusions in the image of the trade's inside.

These logics entrapped residents even when they knew better. Of course, Buenos Aires residents knew to avoid taking taxis in these hot spots: Retiro and Buquebus were both only yards away from main avenues where one merged with the general populace, escaping the captive dynamics these logics required. As for Ezeiza, the international airport, between the sliding doors at the arrivals gate and the stop where these taxis congregated there were usually no fewer than ten private car hires and rentals, buses, vans, and other forms of transportation. Aeroparque, however, was very poorly connected by anything other than taxis although it sat in the center of the city, and here Francisco had twice been refused service by taxis that had just dropped someone off. Although he imagined the hierarchies and exclusions the reader now understands, to passengers taxis were, after all, all the same: the fact that a particular car was not in on the arrangement was not his problem. Also, many of these taxis knew they could expect journeys from this airport into the wealthy metropolitan area several miles from Aeroparque; living within a relatively short distance of the airport, both Francisco and Valentina had been refused service, leaving them stranded at the airport unless they agreed to a far higher rate.

In a way, these abuses were indeed only possible because of the industry's political economy: as shown in chapter 1, the trade was defined by a monopoly, one much narrower and much more controlled that people imagined, but still centering on the exclusions of the taxi license. In other words, taxis' ability to effectively control movement in these ways rested on the fact that they already controlled the movement of strangers in other ways, by definition. This explains why, as explained in chapter 4, the taxi license gained such traction in the description of a monopoly robbing people of their choice.

Although they existed through those senses of monopoly, and resonated in the key of the same kind of moral outrage, these gatherings, as mafias, cartels, or whatever descriptor we choose, reflected and effected a logical shift from those original senses: put simply, this was a monopoly that had metastasized. An original control over a very particular kind of movement for very specific reasons and in very specific ways, which Uber's arrival rendered morally objectionable, had grown outwards, engulfing in its practices not only taxi transactions with actual and potential passengers but also pedestrians, buses, streets, merchandise transporters, and more. In popular reflection, this was understood to be possible and brazen only through the far more serious absorption and neutralization of other key actors within its logics. During my fieldwork a taxi stop suddenly appeared by Recoleta Cemetery, a prime tourist destination; from a given day onward, at least four taxis waited in line there. One of the drivers was emblazoned in the same black and yellow jacket I described in chapter 2. I showed the stop to Francisco, who without missing a beat pointed to a police officer within yards and to a city-run tourist office inches from the last car in the line. The problem was not the taxis: at the Ezeiza airport, he explained in resignation, there were national, provincial and city authorities, federal and provincial police forces, security cameras, toll booths, and the airport's own security systems. "Everybody knows. If they were not in it together something would have been done ages ago."

What "it" actually was and who was in "it" or not was never specified, but these gatherings passed for evidence and logical results of an established equilibrium that had even co-opted within its self-reproduction institutions whose probable job description would include the dismantling, or at least denunciation, of such abuses. This equilibrium was about the taxis in Retiro, but at the same time and through those same taxis it was also about something of a far greater magnitude and a more pervasive kind: self-reproducing orders often appear as if they can never change by themselves, or even be meaningfully disrupted from within.[7] If the image of a coherent, functional, and all-encompassing "inside" reproducing itself seems too clear-cut to be analytically productive, to a resident held for ransom in economic and logistic terms within the sight of police and other authorities in broad daylight in the heart of the national capital it seemed true beyond a doubt.

For people like Francisco, the flagrancy of the double parking and the selective refusal to drive further fed into the broad claim that taxis did not compete or sought to neutralize competition. If, as said earlier in this book, this was a misrepresentation of relations among different kinds of drivers and industrial hierarchies, and of relations between drivers, traffic, and passengers, this presumed lack of competition still sealed the notion of an order incapable of meaningful change by itself for political reasons. This idea is recurrent in developmental theories: local stasis, usually seen in exclusively political or even partisan or factional terms, legitimizes intervention by outsiders, more economically developed nations or supranational organizations promoting policies premised on transcending the local, the specific, and the partial.[8] In the streets of Buenos Aires from April 12, 2016, onward, Uber would play the outsider to this inside equilibrium in two senses that needed each other to be imagined as an effective disruption to a political problem. First, the company offered the same user base a service similar enough to that of taxis to be understood as a direct competitor, as an alternative for the same kind of relations. Second, it did so from a geographical, cultural, technological, and moral outside that the taxi industry, residents presumed, would never be able to engulf.

Competition: A Logical Machine

The middle classes celebrated Uber for its efficient convenience and stream-lined emancipation, as future chapters will show; they also saw in the conflict the materialization of particular ideas of popular choice as a kind of legiti-macy, as shown earlier. They downloaded Uber, requested cars, and drove for Uber and tweeted about it, adding to a public debate that even dragged in the newly elected president. But when Uber arrived, the taxi "mafias" came to occupy a particular rhetorical and logical space that deserves attention on its own: from April 12, 2016, in the throes of public excitement, residents discussed them in the tone one reserves for the terms and conditions of a death both longed for and foretold.

As chapter 6 will show, Uber rides are made of fundamentally different stuff than taxi rides; still, at the point of consumption, both were understood to be similar enough that residents, consumers, now had a choice. The avail-ability of choice, in and of itself a moral good as chapter 4 showed, would force providers to compete—so public debate told us with unquestionable certainty. Competition, one of the most intuitive and dynamic tropes of economic reasoning, is in fact a very abstract notion, encompassing more or less ritualized conflicts for resources: wars, public tenders, bazaar hag-gling, a company's HR selection process, or attempts by the capital city of a peripheral nation to ensure that infrastructure serves it first.[9] The crux of the conflict Uber triggered in Buenos Aires hinged precisely on different claims of what competition was and what it was made of. The taxi industry argued in courts that Uber was breaking the law because it was providing a taxi service as defined in the city's law without taking on the necessary fiscal and technical burdens (which, the industry emphasized, they themselves did take on). In this sense, Uber constituted an illegal taxi activity *in and of itself*, by the legal definition of the industry; its condition as competitor was here a logical conclusion.

The taxi industry also claimed that as a consequence of that tax and paperwork avoidance, the company was able to provide what they were alleging was the same service at a substantially lower price. This other sense of competition was seeking the frame of what Argentine law defines as *competencia desleal*—"unfair" competition. Competencia desleal is also illegal but for different reasons. It seeks to capture in law the distortion of engaging in a market through economically dishonest practices: sinking market prices by not incorporating certain costs, shouldering strategically lower revenues through resources external to that particular market, like cash reserves, or broadly speaking aiming less at participating in a market than at destroying the circumstances in which others can even be in that market. Crucially, across all these arguments, Uber and the taxi industry featured in the senses that mattered as equals. Uber's official stance in courts, press releases, and social media was to insist that it was a new service, a complement, not a competitor, arguably because to speak of competition would have amounted to accepting that the service was indeed sufficiently similar to that of taxis, and therefore likely to be affected by existing laws on urban transportation.

When people like Francisco spoke of competition, they portrayed Uber and the taxis as locked in a structural antagonism, held together by the fundamental similarities that allowed people to think them competitors in the first place.[10] Francisco had downloaded but never used Uber; his enthusiasm for it, however, verged on vindictive ecstasy: "Taxi drivers will now have to work, like I do, like you do, like everyone else does." They would have to at least actually hustle and cruise for clients, he added sardonically, telling a taxi driver on our way to dinner: "You'll have to compete now. I had to go through a selection process, compete with other candidates, and I have to work and be held accountable to ensure I keep my job." Valentina and Mariano spoke matter-of-factly of the virtues of a competition that, although none of us could concretely pin it down, we all understood had to do with opening up the transaction of giving someone a ride for money beyond the hierarchies and exclusions the taxi industry required to even exist at the expense of residents. Uber would dissolve the conditions in which clients could be limited by taxi drivers' practices, therefore doing away with the circumstances in which the "mafia" could thrive.

Competition worked less as a precise descriptor of economic relations than as a form of reasoning, a "logical machine" that did not depend on the concrete experiences it framed for the sense it could make.[11] Residents spoke of, and in terms of, competition to make sense of the macroeconomic process of Uber's arrival, referring to unfolding experiences involving them as consumers, spectators, and residents. Specific relations, individually or added up as a whole, could only be surmised, imagined, or extrapolated from a logical reservoir that was both positive and normative: competition would do away with the "mafia's" abuses, the hierarchies and exclusions that frustrated passengers and residents so much. Why would anyone choose abuse and opportunism if given the choice?

In structuring two mutually exclusive camps, taxis and Uber, the logical machine of competition evoked the early formulation of a problem that would only later be formalized as "the economy": the explicitly political concern with statecraft and the passions of the powerful.[12] Already Montesquieu and Steuart had argued that bills of exchange, foreign exchange arbitrage, and other forms of commerce, that is, of wealth unmoored, tradable and circulating around, would force rulers to behave and restrict themselves: if they tried to abuse their power, wealth would simply, in principle, change hands.[13] In other words, well before neoclassical economics and neoliberalism were fully developed, the inner workings of competition as a logical machine were already recommended as a solution to a political problem.

Uber was expressly welcomed and sought after as an economic solution, not a political one, or one that was not framed politically other than by its detractors. This is why, much to the scandal of social scientists, these residents cared less about Uber's precaritization of labor, bleached exploitation, and other alarms rung by the taxi industry, academics, and a small fraction of public figures. Within the logical machine of competition, Uber served as a functional bulwark against the abuses of the taxi industry even to people who did not use it. Three different buses could take Francisco to Retiro, and he had known for years to avoid taxis there. He welcomed Uber primarily as meaningful opposition to the hazy but powerful taxi industry mafia and the political order it reproduced, not as a consumer concerned about transportation.

In a similar sense, the intuitive virtue of competition is that it engages existing providers, in this case the taxi industry, in a reflective exercise if they want to stay in the trade; consumers, allegedly, benefit from this reflection as it allegedly leads to better service.[14] But Francisco did not care much whether taxis behaved themselves; what mattered was that there was an alternative. These last two statements could imply each other, but they meant different things. Uber opened a line of flight. Whether that line incorporated morally reformed taxi drivers was in a sense beside the point. One could now circumvent, slalom past, not engage with the mafias, in the most literal, physical sense. Before Uber, to avoid the taxis gathered next to her workplace Valentina had to walk two blocks to hail a taxi on a street away from the strategic intersection where her building sat. From the moment Uber became available, she requested vehicles to pick her up from the door of her building, meters from the waiting taxis. What drove most of the excitement around Uber as a competitor was not that the mafias would end because of the penitence and reflection of taxi drivers; rather, mafias would cease to matter because they were being fenced in by an algorithmic wall erected around them.

The taxi industry's self-reflectiveness was secondary, too, because the entire point of Uber as an economic solution to the taxi industry as a political problem was not having to engage the taxi industry on its terms—or indeed on any terms. This was a grand feat, for these terms were difficult to circumvent: the taxi industry had allegedly enfolded the police and other authorities in collusion with it. Uber's irruption and permanence in Buenos Aires outside the terms of the industry and the law, outside any terms other than those it set itself, reinforced its structural opposition to the taxi industry in a sense only implicit in this chapter so far: Uber was not only new to the trade in town, but it was coming into Buenos Aires's political, legal, and economic order, and opposing the taxi industry, from a perfect outside. It was, in fact, precisely because residents understood this outside to be inherently impervious to Argentina's political order, and impossible to subsume, that the taxi industry had *actually* met its match: the logics of opposition were as powerful as they were highly stylized.

A Stranger to Rule Us

"Of course it is a multinational company and of course it seeks to make money, that is what companies are for. Their business model is the same everywhere in the world; why would they care what the union of taxi drivers of Buenos Aires wants or does?" Francisco grilled me one afternoon, addressing, and in a way engulfing, the arguments that those opposed to Uber deployed. "What angers the union is that they cannot control Uber rides—it's in people's phones, it's already happening around us. Isn't your friend Mariano already driving for it?" He was, and Valentina was using it as a passenger. Uber was effectively setting the terms of public transportation with its rating systems and driver management practices, I argued; the union was no better, he replied, and "Even in that case, I would rather it was Uber than Viviani himself. Do you think the union cares about the trade or passengers?" Mariano echoed his point: Uber allowed people an alternative and was, to him, a more reliable mechanism of driver selection and control than the government's. With Uber there could be no inside contacts to grease your way in, or nepotism, exceptions, or pity; not so much because of any inherent virtue, but simply because of the platform's logics—and because it was set up elsewhere: "These people are not even here. This business is set up in this way precisely not to be drawn into conversations with local governments." Besides, Mariano argued, "Uber is already everywhere in the world. Objectively, it works—that's it. It's not my opinion, it's not about Argentina—it's a fact. If laws and politics have to change, then so be it. All innovations break the law, but it cannot be that because the union can't get its fingers onto it we must be stuck forever with these mafias and these bullies."

The technological determinism and disruption narratives of the conflict will occupy me in the last chapter. Noting the recurrence across time and space of rulers who are foreign in kind to the peoples that accept, or even desire, their rule, Marshall Sahlins developed the notion of the stranger king: a relation of authority based on alterity, on an insurmountable, in some way essential, otherness, of the ruler from the ruled.[15] This relation has a functional/utilitarian connotation: often peoples or groups within them seek the arbitration or intervention of an outsider with no preexisting links to internal political cleavages and free of moral duties to any fraction of insiders.[16] None of this means the outsider is, or is considered by anyone to be, morally pure or lacking self-interested intentions; rather, the stranger king's intentions, like the profit-maximizing goal of a private company, enter the logics of a practical problem the insiders have, like developing economic relations apart from an insider they cannot otherwise tame.[17] The seemingly uncontrollable multiplication of rides and the enthusiasm developing around Uber's function as an ally against the union reproduced Uber as a stranger that was wanted as such and as a ruler; a stranger that was here to stay as such, or so these residents hoped.[18]

Uber's alterity played out on several different fronts; all confirmed its technical and economic opposition to a political imagined as a static inside. As said earlier, it had broken into Buenos Aires with defiance, in spite of official and para-official warnings from the government, the union, and other taxi industry representatives. To the strikes, smashed cars and windows, vehicle seizures and police raids, Uber replied by deploying its platform, promotions, and discounts under the goadingly named social media campaign #UberLove and declaiming how much people wanted it. To its literal condition as an outsider this saga added a moral alterity: the sudden violence of its irruption in Buenos Aires and the audacity, and effective impunity, with which it paid no mind to any sanctions confirmed, as a trial by ordeal, that Uber was inside and among us but outside of the system of meanings we shared.[19] This was not a supernatural otherness, and of course, the company *chose* not to close down its services; the point is that despite legal, institutional, political, and plain street-level warnings, threats, and menaces, some of which would have deterred or broken many others, Uber prevailed.

The fact that residents understood and celebrated Uber as a competitor also enhanced its condition of otherness. Competitors are in themselves a challenge to the logics of an established market, particularly one as monitored and self-sustaining as that of the taxis. Uber's ability to provide a similar enough service without the material, legal, and cultural requisites making transportation happen in Buenos Aires worked as a discrete jump in quality, much like "introducing a new, devastating weapon into the arms race" that cannot be reduced to the logics of the other.[20] Effectively an authority over the transactions it created, Uber emerged as a de facto alternative jurisdiction to that of the law, the union, and the Argentine political, securing wealth by working around them.[21] As the above quotes from Francisco and Mariano evidence, it was because Uber managed to stay day after day outside the logics of the taxi industry and the Argentine political that it could actually be a competitor—which by definition reproduced its violence toward the transportation market.[22] It was not so much that the violence and snubs to the law were glorified in and of themselves, although out of exhausted vindictiveness they sometimes were. Rather, Uber's continued presence kept confirming not only that the people wanted it, as the middle classes knew, but that the taxi industry was unable to absorb the competition they saw in it, as we will see, even through violence.

Uber was not just any outsider, and it was not seen as such just because it came from outside; the company materialized also a cultural concern with something the inside lacked and could not give itself.[23] Uber's effective, unassailable opposition to the taxi industry and Buenos Aires's political and legal order could not be separated from the technical and cultural frontier it brought inside, crucial to the alliance the company established with residents. Uber was the first ride-sharing platform to arrive in Argentina, bringing from outside a technology viewed not only as superior to that of the taxi industry but as superior among innovations across the board. The company brought a different but also new way of organizing relations that Argentines knew from trips elsewhere, to that outside, or from news of what happened elsewhere, all of which confirmed its otherness with respect to us.

To a degree technological novelty was a desired otherness in and of itself, but it added a cultural complexity to the practical fact that Uber could not be absorbed by spatial co-optation. It also ensured that relations between drivers and passengers were irreducible to the logics of abuse and extortion associated to the taxi industry. This does not imply in the slightest that any ride-sharing economy platform is free from abuse, manipulation, cartelization, and other vices; the point is that to the extent that Uber was understood in opposition to the taxis, its otherness was to a great extent the reason it was preferable as a mechanism of organization, adjudication, and even sanction than any local institutions understood to be co-opted by a self-reproducing equilibrium. As Mariano and Francisco argued, "How could Uber be worse than what we already have?"

Uber's reception as creator and provider of a service understood in economic terms directs our attention to the "receiving insiders": locals who play a crucial role in supporting the stranger's king entrance or presence.[24] These were Uber users, whose transactions made the company economically viable; but people like Francisco supported Uber as an economic solution to a political problem, not necessarily as clients. Also, an even larger number supported its presence as a matter of an abstract but compelling principle of choice, as shown in chapter 4. These insiders were indispensable to legitimize and give rhetorical currency to Uber's moral, cultural, and economic alterity. Also, by endorsing and enabling the company's authority they shared in it themselves: Uber's authority as a stranger king, hinging on alterity, existed only in alliance with the authority of the people in the land, hinging on their condition as owners of the productive, immanent forces of that land that was theirs by right of autochthony and that they controlled.[25] In this sense, Uber's presence empowered citizens in ways other than those reviewed elsewhere in this book.

This argument brings us back to the previous chapter: Uber's presence legitimized these middle classes as sovereign citizen-consumers by opening a rhetorical battlefield that incorporated them, not the political that they rejected, as a legitimate site of authority. All consumers are autochthonous and immanent authorities in the ethereal land of market logics by virtue of existing as consumers. But Uber owned no cars or offices and barely employed any people in Buenos Aires: enabling residents like Mariano to use their own cars, time, bodies, energy and smartphones, as I show in chapter 6, reproduced the alterity that allowed Uber to compete and made Mariano an indispensable, empowered participant in the economies that were dismantling the political problem. In ways more literal than in political relations, the stranger king, economically speaking, activates the mechanisms of production within that land against the now-displaced local ruler.[26]

The World Outside Us

Nine days before Uber's effective arrival, the economically liberal, culturally conservative Argentine daily *La Nación* published a short editorial signed by a certain Mariano Otero, who was now CEO of Uber Argentina.[27] According to Otero, Buenos Aires in the twenty-first century could not neglect the disruptive power of technologies like Skype, WhatsApp, and Netflix, which were simplifying people's lives and creating alternatives. Technology opens doors to infinite opportunities, he added; Argentines were seeing the bourgeoning of sharing economies in transportation, apartment rentals, and workspaces, "the first glimpse of an era spearheaded by entrepreneurs who will transform urban spaces." Uber was here to stay and to smooth interaction between private parties; facilitating its expansion was "the first step of a path we must still walk as a society." He claimed Uber would create "economic opportunities" for more than thirty thousand people before the end of 2016 and would make life easier for Buenos Aires's residents, and then others in Argentina, just as it had "in more than four hundred cities around the world."

Otero was receiving a salary to place a product; also, although it is one of the most-read Spanish-speaking newspapers in the world, *La Nación* is produced by and for the Argentine middle class I discussed in the Introduction, one perennially anxious for a modernity, cosmopolitanism, and globalism that eludes it.[28] Therefore this statement interests me not as a site of truth but rather as a starting point for reflection on the logics of its possible persuasion. Otero's address to a middle class already elated by the news of Uber's arrival, his argument that four hundred cities in the world already had it, not only confirmed that as Mariano said, "it worked" but merged with a torrent of media coverage of Uber's conflicts in Uruguay, France, Chile, Great Britain, Brazil, and elsewhere, as well as with the experiences of the city's highly mobile middle class. Valentina had been for years submitting Uber receipts as expense claims to the local branch of the multinational company she worked for when working in Peru, Chile, and the US; she had already enquired about using Uber in Buenos Aires when it went live. Mariano had used Uber as a passenger during holidays in Brazil and Uruguay, and they both knew it was available in the UK, where I live. Everyone knew by now that not only most developed countries had some version of Uber or something similar, but most of Argentina's neighbors as well.

A fraction of this coverage, including well-established national newspapers like *Página/12* and articles in other mass media publications that other middle-class sectors also accessed, was highly critical of both the company's business model and its behavior in Buenos Aires. Yet more than nuanced public discussion around Uber, the sensational footage of cars ablaze in Paris and the hastily released editorials pontificating on the inevitability of modernity helped frame Uber's expansion in the mythical, apolitical sense, as a world saga whose logics appeared universal; eventually Uber had prevailed elsewhere as well. This chronicle, now a myth, expelled the taxi industry from history, as I show in chapter 8; but it also strengthened Uber's condition as a stranger king, doubling as a retelling of the company's travels and trials, "a tale of one marvelous victory after another" adding up to a single journey, verifying Uber's potency and its irreducible otherness beyond the political, the partial, the idiosyncrasies of all those places.[29] This epic story made it even harder to think about Uber politically, not only by further obscuring the company's internal hierarchies and exclusions, but also by reducing any nuance to a kind of bottom-line objectivity: "It works." This was not the alleged objectivity of its algorithms and maximizations, but objectivity as an economic force, "composed of distance and nearness, indifference and involvement."[30]

The quantification and evocation of these countries and places was equally irrelevant in terms of truth or descriptive precision. It mattered as a figurative, unstable, even whimsical, distribution of virtue and vice, right and wrong, insides and outsides. It invoked oppositions not between magnitudes but between types that come to be and to matter only when and in the way they are defined against each other. When both Valentina and Mariano mentioned with similar exasperation that "even Ecuador already has Uber," "the country-by-country taxonomy where each nation acquires its nimbus of transnational cultural resonance" worked to confirm that across a more or less conversational, ready-made cosmopolitanism of cultural idiosyncrasies, of various population and landmass sizes, of various developmental "stages," Uber had prevailed.[31] Working through a highly idiosyncratic sequence of association, distillation, and elimination, these arguments confirmed by their internal logics that the problem, or a problem, could only be inside. They were, in fact, imagined with that purpose even before they were uttered.

To many residents, Argentina's late arrival to the Uber saga was in itself exasperating. Yet that other exasperation, the one emanating from the disbelief that "even Ecuador" had Uber before Argentina and from the confirmation that, since "everyone" had Uber except us, the problem must be ours, reverberated with a well-documented anxiety concerning the economic, political, and even moral degradation of the national project.[32] The long-ago heyday that the plaque in Retiro evoked, exceptional even in international terms when it happened, ended shortly after the Great Recession in the 1930s. Back then, GDP per capita, health, nutrition, and literacy indexes ranked Argentina ahead of most of Europe.[33] But in the last ninety years, as Bass argues, "Argentina's decline from the ranks of the rich to those of the relatively poor, and from being politically developed to being politically unstable, steadily crept into the national consciousness. As the 20th century progressed, porteños were increasingly forced to confront certain realities; they had not lived up to their own self-image and lofty expectations, and the source of this failure seemed to be located within themselves."[34]

Uber's arrival activated these anxieties in the key of what Jansen calls "everyday geopolitics": the informal ranking and evocation of nations with the conviction that one's place in them matters.[35] Even today, in porteño everyday geopolitics Ecuador would be seen as less developed and modern than Argentina, and certainly less than the Argentina these residents knew in Buenos Aires. As a place of an allegedly undisputable lower rank, Ecuador completed the triangulation between these anxieties, Uber's epic story, and the taxi industry "mafia" in the key of the stranger king's bottom line: "All politics is local," outside things are otherwise.[36]

Taken literally, these triangulations were logically dubious, incomplete, contradictory, and sometimes outright nonsensical. Uber was not, strictly speaking, *everywhere* in the world, far from it. It had since its beginnings offered different services across the countries it operated in, even within regions and cities of certain countries, depending on the administrative level that regulated transportation. But Mariano knew this; Valentina did too, and they knew of the many conflicts the company was embroiled in around the world. Similarly, many residents blamed politicians or particular parties for Argentina's institutional decay, not themselves; others thought of this decay in terms of class, economic, or hierarchical asymmetries on a national scale, and so on (one would be hard pressed, though, to find an Argentine who did not agree with the notion that something really had gone very wrong).

Yet the contingencies proper to any individual life, process, or relation cannot logically sustain or challenge the terms of the opposition between Uber and taxis, between inside and outside, political and economic, vitiated and objective, the outside world and Argentines. They cannot even challenge the notion that at a certain level this logic might work as something other than a structural opposition. This is because *it is not through taxonomic precision that this opposition makes sense to begin with*; to dissect its logics, its claims, or its descriptions in search of internal inconsistencies is, in a fundamental way, to completely miss the point of how they persuade. As anthropologist Mary Douglas argued, these oppositions and their structures are not there to tell truth from lie, to read into the vagaries of microevents, but to frame social experience.[37] In fact, the very exasperation, hyperbole, and disproportion of the claim that Uber was everywhere in the world, strictly speaking an inaccuracy or a lie, was what *enhanced* Uber's condition as a stranger king, what confirmed that the vice was inside, and what, ultimately, led these people to embrace Uber more fully, consciously, and loudly. As competition, as a way out of the mafia's clutch, and as an economic logic: Uber's place in these structural oppositions made it exceptionally difficult to politicize the company and its actions in the academic and conversational senses of the term.

Not Exactly Strangers

In what I believe is the first extension of stranger king theory to eminently economic relations, Ivan Rajković shows how the workers of a Serbian car factory prefer foreigners (Italians) as directors and managers of the business.[38] While acknowledging abuses and vices similar to their own, Rajković's informants still see in the foreign trader, "supernumerary" to the saturated local space, an alternative of social relations that the inside cannot give itself or provide: an irreducible line of flight.[39]

Whereas many developing countries may recognize the patterns of stranger king relations, these Italian investors in Serbia and Uber in Buenos Aires sound the strings of a memory particular to former Yugoslavian nations and Argentina: to those workers and to these residents of Buenos Aires, these stranger kings bring with them the possibility of a return. Stranger kings are often understood as long-lost insiders who, after a symbolic or practical departure and exile, return to their former inside ready to assume authority.[40] In the cases of Serbia and Argentina, the terms of this return are reversed: Uber was never in Argentina, of course, but traces like the palatial disproportion of Retiro confirm to these residents that this is not a poor nation but an impoverished one. Its style, in turn, confirms that this era of grandeur was not ancient, tied to magnificent pre-Columbian civilizations or to Buenos Aires's stint as colonial backwater of the Spanish Empire; this wealth and economic promise, with its contradictions, exclusions, and exploitations, was recent and wholly Argentine.

Like the majority of Argentines in central Argentina, Francisco's grandparents had migrated after the Second World War from the French Basque country and Italy. His parents had added to a millions-strong emergent middle class of first-, second-, and third-generation descendants of Italians, French and Spanish Basques, Spaniards, Poles and Germans, peoples of the former Austro-Hungarian Empire (including the former Yugoslavia), Sephardic Jews, and Syrian-Lebanese immigrants. Up until the mid-twentieth century the country incorporated these migrants through land, jobs, unions, public universities, viable mortgage credits, a welfare system, and a plethora of institutions that the oldest among these people still remember as functioning. As Jansen has argued also for the former Yugoslavia, the anxiety and exasperation of such people is marked by this lived and cultural memory of possibilities in complete disproportion with their current status.[41] Jansen's Serbian and Bosnian informants know, as they subject themselves to ever-multiplying visa-related humiliations, that until recently their Yugoslavian passport was among the most powerful in the world. This experience of failure, which Bass identifies in Argentina with the Argentine self, works with Retiro's historical magnificence and Uber's irreducible competition toward an arc where the stranger's virtues are in fact confirmation that the distance between Argentina and the stranger works in reverse: it was Argentines who progressively became estranged through their own actions.

As a stranger that would always stay a stranger, competing against an industry and a "mafia" that would presumably never be able to subsume it within its logics, Uber represented to these residents the resumption of a path of progress. As I show in chapter 8, this was a time when Argentina's path and relationship with the world were understood in the processual logics of a regeneration; Uber would enter these logics too. Argentina would no longer be "the only place in the world" that did not have Uber, which it had "actually" never been, and the union, its taxis, and the "mafia" would be bypassed and neutralized. These two statements, the processual logics of a regeneration and the neutralization of the inside as a political problem epitomized by this "mafia," implied each other—they had to, in the terms of this reasoning.

The taxi industry fought the processes, temporalities, symbols, and rhetorical acrobatics unfolding in this conflict, anticipating, retreating, and advancing on several fronts at once. As they did so, the structural oppositions analyzed above resurfaced in disguise. At an anti-Uber protest, one of the taxi drivers who was haranguing us to resist symbolically linked Retiro and Uber one last time: "The company's argument is straight from the 1990s. These people come to countries like ours to sell people the fantasy of self-employment, they do not invest a single peso, they destroy our industry, and by the time those they have duped realize what happened they've already made millions and left." The 1990s, as said above, was the decade during which public services were privatized, trade was liberalized, and the Argentine industries that had employed all the children and grandchildren of those immigrants, including the railway, were dismantled. It was also the decade that Argentines remember for the one-to-one parity between the Argentine peso and the US dollar, evoked as a calamity even by the same middle classes that feasted on it, shopping their way through Miami and Cancun. When after the 2001 crash residents interpreted, or realized, that they had been living in a fantasy, the jobs that could have employed many of them had been destroyed.

I could not ask this protester what he meant by "countries like ours," which countries those were and what grouped them together. But "countries like ours" had been sold a fantasy in the past, during the 1990s, a con he claimed was repeating itself with Uber's arrival. He may well have known this, but most Argentines forget that the peso-dollar parity had been set up, much like Montesquieu's bills of exchange, to control an internal problem. By 1989 Argentina boasted one of the most severe hyperinflationary cycles of modern history; in neoclassical macroeconomic terms, inflation and hyperinflation are a political problem of managing currency production, issuance, and circulation. If a currency is mismanaged to the point of losing so much credibility that people literally hurry to pass it around, the only solution is to anchor it to an outside impervious to it and to that mismanagement. The plan worked, neutralizing inflation; it also did away with the possibility of sovereign, local—in the terms of this reasoning, political—monetary policy. The debt and privatizations that sustained the plan through the decade are deemed today far too high a cost.

The intensity of the tension between "countries like ours," as countries who benefit from intervention from the outside, and "countries like ours," as countries who keep falling for the fantasy of the stranger king, tells us nothing definitive about the opposition it reinforces. Some economists argue there were other ways to solve the 1980s hyperinflation, an alternative to solving the political problem with an economic solution from outside. For people like Mariano and Francisco, only Uber would ever disrupt the equilibrium the taxi industry had established for itself. The logical machine of competition told us casualties would be limited to one industry this time; besides, as with all economic readjustments in theory, even the most efficient ones, a stranger king's penetrative act is often by necessity one of violence, of *celeritas*: the initial moment when the stranger becomes supernumerary among us, different but inside. At the point of reconciliation, *gravitas*, often set in law, the stranger king has been accepted by the people, his people, as a legitimate ruler.[42] Uber looked for mechanisms to write itself into Argentine law, reiterating how ready it was to work with authorities on developing a legal framework "adapted" to its business; as of early 2021 this has happened in the province of Mendoza.

Four years on, taxis still gather outside Retiro. The station, Retiro proper, has been restored to its former splendor, although a multinational fast-food chain has taken over its formerly grand café and replaced its wooden, fin-de-siècle furniture with stackable chairs. So few passengers take taxis here that it is still unclear what they live on, exactly, or how they were "actually" affected by Uber's competition. But then again, the exact shape of the political problem was never too clear either, and the virtue of logical economic allies, here and always, is precisely not to have to think in terms of the political with any precision—not to have to engage it in any terms, much less so after decades of exasperation. The problem, of course, is that this makes it quite hard to determine what kind of country Argentina is, and on what grounds: one of dupes who get played by big corporations and bigger nations or one that has joined the world and is back on its former path to progress. Of course, even across mutually exclusive claims the question has replayed, structurally, variations on a theme, which is probably just as well, for the virtue and whole point of structural oppositions is precisely that they do not need to be literal, or exactly fitted to details, to make perfect sense of the experiences they come to frame.

6

A Copernican Phantasmagoria

UNLIKE TAXI RELATIONS, where institutions, laws, and spaces of negotiation render the transaction intelligible, Uber relations were intelligible through supply, demand, fare multipliers, and other logical formulations producing an experience my informants referred to as *ordenada*—an "ordered, orderly order." Revolutionizing how a certain kind of movement could be understood and inhabited in Buenos Aires, this order worked through unverifiable, indeterminate propositions that could not be engaged on the grounds of disagreement: they worked as portrayals one acted on or not, rather than as arguments one could take to task or disagree with.

This chapter examines this order generating relations and the means to engage in, and understand, these relations as a kind of phantasmagoria. Since the days when the term referred to a magic lantern used for entertainment, the trick of the phantasmagoria is to transform an objective problem of order, of knowledge, of shared epistemologies to make sense of what things are, or, in other words, a political problem, into an individual, subjective problem beyond interrogation in a modern world where the consumer, the audience, is the ultimate site of the truth that counts. This transference peaks when an undefinable "passenger experience" replaces meaningful questions arranging bodies with respect to some agreed-upon order. Uber's Copernican phantasmagoria ensures that the order it produces remains, paradoxically, impossible to order in any meaningful way, perpetuating the illusion that animated it in the first place: that an order that is not political is possible and within reach.

A Copernican Frame

During Uber's first week Mariano and I attended one of the company's training sessions in the upscale neighborhood of Belgrano. In an improvised antechamber up a flight of stairs several company representatives were assisting attendees and registering them as drivers on a row of laptops. Mariano, trained in business management, was working part time as a graphic designer at an advertising agency and looking for a full-time job when Uber arrived in Buenos Aires. He had signed up the day of Uber's launch, so we went straight into the conference room, where two young men hustled around, setting up a projector and helping people find a seat.

The lights went out, the presentation began, and these young men spoke in turns, cueing each other in a rehearsed casual tone and waltzing through the slides in the complicit register of informal River Plate Spanish. Save questions for the end, we were told as attendees raised their hands, but when we turned to requirements for becoming an Uber driver someone blurted out: "What happens if we have an accident?"

"Uber will not leave you alone . . . ," one of the presenters replied but was quickly interrupted by someone else asking, "But what insurance policy do we need?"

"All you need to drive for Uber is your regular policy," responded the other presenter.

"But that policy says explicitly it does not cover transportation for money."

"So long as you have your regular transportation policy Uber will cover you."

"But is Uber also an insurer? What kind of insurance would Uber offer us?" asked a third person.

"Look," the second presenter took charge again: the company was with us. Hadn't it been refunding the equivalent of thousands of dollars in fines to its new drivers?

The audience asked more questions, but this was not our time: "Let us finish telling you how this works and then we can take your specific questions individually." At the end attendees were encouraged to approach presenters one by one; Mariano asked practical questions about user support and we left.

To sign up Mariano had needed:

- His driver's license (it did not need to be the professional license required of taxi drivers), valid in all of Argentina;
- A current account in a bank in Argentina;
- A five-door car with air conditioning manufactured in 2009 or later, which included his Ford 2014;
- A personal driver's insurance policy, which he already had;
- His smartphone, running on Android 4.0; and
- A police-issued criminal record.

Criminal records were normally issued within forty-eight hours of placing a request on the police's website, but the latter collapsed under a surge of Uber-related requests. Unable to produce them on time, candidates like Mariano were manually cleared by Uber users' support in the meantime. Also, the first item of the terms and conditions of Mariano's private driver's insurance policy explicitly stated it would not cover any form of commercial transportation. Any Argentine insurance policy for the latter, such as what taxi drivers must have, would be much more expensive following actuarial estimates of exposition to traffic, likelihood of judicial action in case of accident, moral hazard, imperfect information considerations, and more. With a temporary blank space where his criminal record would have been and an insurance policy whose terms explicitly excluded the exact activity he was about to undertake, Mariano started driving right away.

Uber's activities had been declared illegal, taxi drivers were ambushing Uber cars, and city officials were towing them away; still, popular excitement fueled by Uber discounts and #UberLove, a social media campaign that chapter 7 tackles, kept Mariano quite busy. Uber had also launched a guaranteed-income policy whereby drivers who met a series of requirements (accepting seven out of ten trips at a rate of at least one per hour; being online for at least half the time slots designated as rush hour, Monday to Friday 7:00 to 10:00 a.m. and 5:00 to 11:00 p.m., and over weekends from midnight to six in the morning and from 5:00 to 11:00 p.m.; and retaining a 4.5 rating throughout) were guaranteed the equivalent of just over 800 USD per week.[1] Mariano never quite met these requirements but still attuned himself to the rush hours designated by Uber and quickly figured out how to chase Uber's famous fare multipliers, positioning his car with respect to the areas and times where demand for cars would likely be higher. He participated in an online forum where Uber users from around the world shared tips on how to avoid being spotted by taxi drivers: greet passengers with a hug as if they were friends, have them sit in front, et cetera (no cars driving for Uber carried any outward identification as such in Buenos Aires). Mariano was de facto living in his partner Pablo's apartment in the sprawling, hipster edges of the neighborhood of Palermo, but his trips took him mostly toward well-off Belgrano, the financial district, downtown Buenos Aires, and what porteños call Zona Norte. Outside of the city's jurisdiction and in the province of Buenos Aires, the latter was integrated with all the former in a continuous wealth, business, and culture and entertainment corridor. This integration would soon present a jurisdictional problem to the city's attempts to rein Uber in, as chapter 7 shows, but as far as Uber rides went it only grew tighter.

The ease of access to the platform doubled as what Uber's PR team and vast segments of Buenos Aires's middle class vaunted as democratizing empowerment: just about anyone could drive someone around for money. As chapter 4 argues, among the middle classes of late capitalism this was already a moral argument beyond, and running deeper than, the political: empowerment meant more *consumption* alternatives for passengers and the expansion of a *productive* frontier, channeling entrepreneurial citizen-consumers, both moral goods. Also, as we know from chapter 5, the middle class saw in Uber's platform a direct competitor to the taxi industry. This capacity to both compete and empower stemmed from a particular kind of framing where Uber's platform incorporated certain aspects of drivers' lives (car type, national ID, the fact of being insured) and deliberately or by default excluded others (type of insurance, type of driver's license).[2] The fact that Uber rides were effectively happening, and engaging virtually anyone so quickly and smoothly, confirmed to residents that as the framing of the emerging market of transportation relations sorted out the insides and outsides of the market, the factors that had been left out were not, in all evidence, inherently indispensable for moving people from A to B, but cultural or political accretions.[3] The taxi industry's political economy, which they already imagined as vitiated and corrupt, now sat outside this transaction as technically and infrastructurally redundant, excessive to the economic exchange they had until now brought to life.

The realpolitik success of Uber's framing created space for a question running through the arguments of earlier chapters and shaping the experience of this conflict: Why did "we" need thousands of taxis, their licenses, the union, the clinical verifications and professional licenses? Previous chapters have shown how the tropes of empowerment and competition provided depoliticizing answers that overwhelmed alternatives. Yet Uber's entry requirements, easily met by the upper layers of the working class and above, and its platform's workings, which drivers entered as inevitable equals, gave new life to the questions "What is a driver?" "What is a passenger?" and "What makes a ride?" I will characterize this impulse as Copernican: it offered an entirely new way of understanding how we can know a certain kind of movement and produced for those engaged in this movement a view from a very particular nowhere, exceptionally difficult to politicize from within.

Ways of Knowing

As chapters 1 and 2 showed, the taxi industry that porteños knew resulted from 150 years of cultural and institutional interventions into the encounter between two strangers who would never meet again. Categories ("taxi"), practices ("hailing on the street," "not tipping") abstractions ("taxi drivers' health"), standards ("taxi fare"), and laws ("law 3622 of the Autonomous City of Buenos Aires") rendered the taxi industry, its transactions, its bodies, and its organization knowable in specific ways. As chapters 3 and 5 showed, these interventions also shaped how residents understood the city's neighborhoods and seasonality, rush hours and traffic jams, but also local and national politics and government. Certainly, there were about two hundred "fake" taxis in the city; taxi rides beyond the limits of the city proper did happen; and some taxi drivers fiddled with the device calculating wheel revolutions in order to accelerate the taximeter. Still, those "fakes" had to look and function exactly like the real cars and practices to pass as such; interjurisdictional trips required some creative adjustments not to be seen with one's LED light on beyond the city border; and taximeters were not randomly altered but only deftly enhanced as a multiple of the original, state-endorsed fare, respectively. In other words, the spaces, norms, and practices of a whole way of moving around and understanding a certain kind of movement and transaction orbited around specific ways of knowing where government projects, union politics, legal requirements, passengers' expectations, and taxi driver practices converged.

Uber's arrival revolutionized residents' ways of understanding how things, their relations, and one's relation to them could be known logically and in practice. This was an epistemological revolution, of sorts: its grounds were certainly not exotic, unexpected, or unimaginable. Uber was the first proper ride-sharing platform to arrive in Argentina, but other platform, sharing, and "collaborative" economies already existed in Buenos Aires:

Airbnb, Craigslist, Couchsurfing, and coworking office spaces were only the more iconic examples in a country that since its 2001 crisis had been experimenting with sophisticated combinations of decentralized, deregulated, unregulated, or popularly regulated economies, consumers' "checks and balances," popular currencies, and parallel transactional networks on and offline. In terms of cultural reception of technologies, to that panoply Uber added a variation in degree, not in kind. Also, by April 2016 the middle classes had used Uber in other countries, and most people knew more or less how it worked: the excitement lay not in the novelty or the unknown but in the more or less known that was, finally, here.

Yet knowing more or less how Uber transactions work is not the same as experiencing these transactions and the knowledges they enable or hinder: to this particular form of movement, transaction, and practice Uber did bring a variation in kind. Certainly, to participate in the company's transactions (to even belong in Uber's platform), users provided information such as driver's licenses and insurance policy details (even if neither was of the legally suitable kind), car plates, and national IDs, produced by the same central authorities that brought the taxi industry to life. But from the moment Mariano fed that into Uber's system, processes of geolocation, pricing, communication, visualization, and time measuring written into Uber's script produced a driver that had not existed before, or outside, those one-off triangulations. A ride from, say, the wealthy neighborhood of Belgrano to the wealthy northern suburbs, of which Mariano did plenty, could not now effectively be separated from the fare, multiplier, geolocation, and maximizations written into that driver and that transaction: as he commented excitedly, he rarely received the same rate.

The taxi industry's legal argument hinged on a variation of this claim: Uber, they said, was an integral, inherent part of these relations, not a mere mediator between existing parties as the company argued in the legal conflict I retrace later in this book. As such, they insisted, it should be subjected to local laws both as a company and as a provider of transportation services. What Uber users experienced as the realpolitik of Uber rides, that is, rides happening around us regardless of permits and taxi licenses but also regardless of courts, street violence, and police intervention, was confirmation of the taxi industry's claim that the company resisted any order other than the one it created for itself, presumably one built around profit maximization strategies. To even enter the platform and belong in it and its relations was necessarily to be ordered by, and *only* according to, its terms.

Part of the taxi industry's frustration emanated from the fact that they were the main, or most visible, casualties of an order that resisted actual, genuine social engagement or disagreement—or, in other words, that resisted being politicized. Sure enough, one could decline a ride that was too expensive, wait it out until the price came down, or think that a price multiplier was a dodgy manipulation mechanism; but one could not actually *engage* the order that was already written into it, certainly not the way one could engage a taxi driver that was taking one for a ride. This was not only because the actual workings of these processes were inscrutable, inaccessible, and probably unintelligible to their users but fundamentally because the platform produced these relations as propositions: they could be accepted or refused, not debated or falsified.[4]

These propositions were not only a completely new way of understanding movement, transactions, and one's part in either. They were also produced for, uttered because of, and addressed to Mariano or Valentina as individuals at a particular point in time and space. How this ability passed for a kind of empowerment will be clearer later; what matters now is that when the company shattered the way of knowing that had orbited around the taxi industry it presented an alternative made of innumerable, nontransferrable, unique, ephemeral propositions. That the terms of these proposition were beyond a certain kind of engagement only meant that it was up to Uber's users to develop the reasons to make sense of them.

An Ordered, Orderly Experience

By Valentina's account of her first Uber ride as a passenger, her driver was a really sweet man in his forties working for an architecture firm and seeking extra money. The family-size car was immaculate, the conversation was interesting, and he had even offered her a bottle of water and chocolates. She had also been driven by a university student from the province of Córdoba trying Uber out of curiosity and by a mother of two who was at the time in between jobs. More than the fact that anyone could become a driver, which Mariano brought up as the platform's selling point, Valentina celebrated the platform for including these residents in an experience she defined as *ordenada*. People could fit driving for Uber around other tasks, both parties were linked by the platform, and passengers could see car plates, car types, and a pricing baseline for the ride, or, as Mariano summarized in his quotable if inexact manner, "*Ves todo*": you see everything.

Past participle of the transitive verb *ordenar*, to give an order to something, to be *ordenado* means to be ordered, as in having been subjected to an ordering, sorting act, and to be orderly, as in methodical, neat, and organized. Possibly stylized by enthusiasm about Uber's arrival, this ordered, orderly experience was to a great extent mediated by residents' understandings of how Uber worked. Valentina described the matching of passengers and drivers on the basis of minimized distances and the pinning down of everyone in the app through ratings. As chapter 2 showed, residents experienced taxistas as elusive tricksters, generating the economic, affective, and moral experience of being "taken for a ride" in an inherently unruly trade. Valentina reflected on these ratings as mechanisms of accountability helping produce reflexive selves, as we will see later; but these transactions left a trace and were a trace. She emphasized several times not only the possibility of retrieving objects forgotten in an Uber driver's car but the fact that the retrieval was mediated by the company, on its platform: everyone knew what belonged where. She did not drive for Uber but celebrated that residents could now strategize, time, plan, and map out their driving toward rush hour places and times—as defined by the app.

As a conversational term and as a pedestrian technological concept, algorithms featured prominently in residents' rationalizations of this ordered, orderly experience with the app and its workings. Mariano explained these algorithms to me on Pablo's phone, where a sign on his screen read that fares were slightly higher than a given rate set as normal: fares had been enhanced by a "multiplier." Where does this multiplier come from? I asked. "It's the factor by which the base rate is multiplied to factor in supply and demand so that they cancel out," he responded. Sure, I insisted—but *where* does it come from? A pesky tango commenced. "It comes from supply and demand." "But how do we know this?" "Because you can see it!" "I can only see a number on a screen, called 'multiplier.'" "And that number results from the convergence of supply and demand." "But how do we know that?" "Because the algorithm calculates them, it's there." A number was, indeed, there, linking a particular rate with potential drivers and passengers and their possible transactions over a given space at a point in time.

Uber's algorithms are famously secretive: Valentina herself directed me to a then-recently published academic paper on the subject.[5] More than a reflection of any knowledge of Uber's algorithms, Mariano and Valentina's arguments invoked a nonexpert, intuitive rationality of efficacy associated with the notion of algorithms.[6] What was interesting about this ordered, orderly experience that these algorithms were allegedly producing was that market clearing, efficiency, and excess of demand were all, strictly speaking, unverifiable to Mariano, Valentina, me, media reports, and quite possibly Uber employees themselves. They were unverifiable by definition because they all are highly stylized concepts developed by economists as abstractions. They exist to subtract the messiness of real life and make claims about exchange, value and production with a level of authority enhanced precisely by their distance from actual stuff. They do not transfer well to individual relations: Does my desire for a ride count as demand? If so when, for how long, and what are the means to capture it? Will a sufficiently low price convince me to take an Uber, embedding me into its relations and logics, making "demand" out of me? They are also unverifiable in particular: even if they could be transferred to singular relations or a concrete collective thereof, not a single one of these Uber users could "see" any of these relations other than through the information Uber processed to and for them.

In Mariano and Valentina's use of them, these concepts were less interesting as scientific descriptors than as evidence of a reflexive orientation enabled by Uber, a way of knowing these relations that was predominantly, if not exclusively, set in economic terms. Economics here was not a logical promise, as "competition" was in chapter 5, or a prescriptive vehicle for a moral claim, as "choice" was in chapter 4. Rather, this was economics as an epistemology, as a way of knowing these propositions, of imagining what they were made of and how they made sense, and of reflecting on one's position vis-à-vis them, not least since, as said earlier, they were aimed at the self.

Of course, the clinical authority of terms like *supply* and *efficiency* invisibilized the fact that Uber created these propositions as transactions and the terms in which they were set: in this sense, this economic way of knowing reinforces the arguments of previous chapters that economic tropes intuitively, strategically, and selectively reshape the distribution of the sensible in ways that can be harder to denounce or counteract.[7] But this economic reflexivity enhanced the logics, rhetoric, and affect of postpolitical reasoning in a more insidious way. As said above, these relations were born into a special nowhere, free from responding or even acknowledging the gravity and pull of hierarchies, exclusions, and frameworks examined earlier, pivoting on nothing other than the self's position with respect to that nowhere. Efficiency, scarcity, supply, multipliers, and their combinations, as economic descriptors, served here as "relational surfaces": they offered residents a rhetorical and logical purchase onto the constant triangulation of bodies, times, and spaces along an ever-changing frontier of possible propositions they could not really engage from outside this way of knowing.[8]

Beyond the broad intuition that rides were harder to find in rainy days, neither Mariano nor Valentina knew, or could know, what made movement and how, inside or outside of Uber's platform. The reader will recall from chapter 3 the highly idiosyncratic strategies taxi drivers deployed to maximize their chances in a vast lottery. These relational surfaces did not necessarily render "forces" more intelligible; but they allowed a rhetoric and disposition where Mariano responded to "scarcity" and Valentina waited out "demand surplus." In other words, in this ordered, orderly space, these propositions, as relations between these *individuals*, "assume[d] in their eyes the fantastic form of a relation between *things*."[9] Some readers may recognize here one of Marx's most famous quotes in the English language. Some among them will also know this translation is a betrayal, as Borges would say, because in the original version, the term Marx gave to the form of this relation was not *fantastic* but *phantasmagorical* (*die Phantasmagorische Form*). Overall the metaphor still works; yet the original, instead of emphasizing falsity, evoked a peculiar little device developed at the end of the eighteenth century to bring ghosts and other fabrications to life.

Uber, the Phantasmagorian

By the 1790s *phantasmagoria* was the name of a magic lantern that through lenses, screens, and carefully calibrated and distributed sources of light projected optical illusions onto strategically placed surfaces. By metonymy the spectacle organized around the lantern came to be known as a phantasmagoria as well.[10] There were at the time many other magic shows; the phantasmagoria's peculiarity was to conceal the lantern from the audience's view and to keep the rooms where the show took place in absolute darkness. Ghosts of beheaded revolutionaries and mythical kings made of pure light flickered in the empty depths as if self-produced and out of nowhere, "made to increase and decrease in size, to advance and retreat, dissolve, vanish, and pass into each other, in a manner then considered marvellous."[11] The sheets, screens, surface angles, and hidden panels populating the darkness offered a mysterious and invisible purchase to the ghosts, contributing to an experience at the threshold between science and superstition, objectivity and subjectivity, "between what we think we know and what we fear we might actually believe."[12]

Marx's original metaphor sought to capture this illusion: capitalist relations are made of the ghostly concreteness of prices, commodities, demand, supply, and other paraphernalia that, substituted for actual people and work, take on "a spectral reality of (their) own."[13] Uber did not bring capitalism to Buenos Aires, a city arguably born as a capitalist trading post not outside but on the edges of capitalist Western modernity: the subjectivities of twenty-first-century porteños were already cast in the framework of the phantasmagorical experience of capitalism. What Uber did bring, as said earlier, was the experience of an ordered, orderly order where Mariano, Valentina, and tens of thousands of others understood transportation relations through the contours and effects of such things as demand, supply, efficiency, and scarcity as produced by the light of Uber's app.

The phantasmagoria's view from nowhere emerges in the speed, quick succession, and continuous motion the act produces, constantly breaking down any point of reference a straggling ghost may allow spectators. This velocity propels the illusion forward and achieves the continuous effect of novelty proper to the commodity.[14] Uber's incessant recalculation of prices, distances, and times, as well as the spatialization and aggregation of bodies into the relations it created, was indispensable for these relations to actually work: it would be absurd in a disordered, disorderly way to offer Valentina a ride three hours after she needed it. In their restless quest for "phantasms of the most perfect delineation, clothed in real drapery, and displaying all the movements of life," phantasmagorias accelerate the production of their own ghosts, and their condition as a liminal experience propelled by technological disruption amplifies the total effect.[15] Just as iron, a functional material, collapsed the distance between purpose and aesthetics, function and art in the Parisian arcades, Uber's algorithms as these people understood them were perfect phantasmagorical material for the quick, slickly produced illusions of the kinds of order this Copernican phantasmagoria needed to put forward, with every proposition on the edge of the production frontier of a ride.[16] The aim was not only to dazzle and convince its audience, as it did, for by now the conflict's momentum among the middle class was definitely on Uber's side, but to ensure that the relations it promised, fully severed from any order other than the one it constantly recreated, would even exist.

In this experience, the hierarchies of the taxi industry, but crucially, of Argentine political and social life at large, were immaterial—literally. Uber's light pierced right through them, and they could form no relations and latch onto no purchase in and of themselves. Taxi drivers could download and use Uber as passenger or driver, and they would indeed do so as a means of "ambushing" Uber drivers or hemming them in to detain them; but they would enter this phantasmagoria only in a transmogrified state, as equals to thousands of others, forming relations only along the edges of the economic logics this order brought about. To the extent that Uber users would be able to differentiate themselves from the others, in itself another illusion I will turn to later, they would do so only on the terms that the Copernican phantasmagoria allowed.

With the analogy of the phantasmagoria, Marx was seeking to dispel the illusion, to recover the *real* relations concealed by the obscurity of the phantasmagoria's light. Indeed, to call those relations phantasmagorical was the indispensable first step to understanding how they shape the distribution of the sensible. This is what the taxi industry did in its legal claim: to call Uber a company, an intrinsic part of those relations of "scarcity" and "demand," was to try to create space for a reflection on how this view from nowhere worked. But as Walter Benjamin argued when faced with the heady, speeded-up days of fin-de-siècle capitalism, politicizing the phantasmagoria to audiences like Buenos Aires's residents would not be quite as simple.

Rhetorical Double-Plays

Keeping the term's confusion as to what it actually was—a means of production, a technology of representation, an objective reality, a subjective experience—Walter Benjamin saw in the phantasmagoria the key to the experience of capitalist modernity.[17] The phantasmagoria, he argued, never sought to test the credulousness of audiences or to effect literal belief in its fabrications (although some spectators reportedly flung their canes at the apparitions). Rather, it sought to generate a particular kind of experience *and* the means to engage in it. Phantasmagorians, runners and owners of the show, exploited the uncanny tension of their act with an expert rhetorical double-play, as in this reported preamble to a phantasmagoria in 1793: "I will not show you ghosts, because there are no such things; but I will produce before you enactments and images, which are imagined to be ghosts. . . . I am neither priest nor magician. I do not wish to deceive you, but I will astonish you."[18]

A particular feature of phantasmagorias, argued Benjamin, was that they were themselves demystifying acts: they desacralized the ghosts' aura by showing how easy it was to invent them, *which made them already a reflexive experience.*[19] Uber's empowerment worked by demystifying the taxi transaction, made of tricksters and charisma, rendering it now in terms a middle-class capitalist consciousness already intuited: anyone could drive someone else for money.

But phantasmagorias are also demystifying, reflexive experiences in a productive sense. By rendering ghosts as real as possible just as it rationalized them as fabrications, the phantasmagoria negated the very distance it was readily acknowledging: that between the rational, the objective, the what (of course, not ghosts!), and the means to understand it (What could it be and how to think about it, then?). Collapsing the tension it itself signaled between reality and perception, the phantasmagoria seized the senses, reasons, and dispositions of those it captivated, who now learned to inhabit and sort out the experience of a distance, a separation, that they knew was such but could no longer sense. This subjectivity developed a logical, rhetorical, and affective orientation that knew it was seeing fabrications: *the phantasmagoria's trick was never actually to lie, but to transfer the entire problem of the truth claim to the audience*. The uncanny effect of this displacement was sought and enhanced by the phantasmagorians' astuteness, for they never, ever, revealed *how* their act was actually produced.[20]

Here was the phantasmagoria's actual false bottom, and what made the phantasmagorical experience "complete," generating, from an obscure nowhere, the categories that *others* would have to develop to make sense of *its* propositions. This was why, Benjamin argued, to call the phantasmagoria by its name, as Marx suggested, or, in 2016 Buenos Aires, to call Uber a company and "scarcity" a manufactured purchase, was not enough to politicize anything. I asked Mariano where on Uber's map we could find all the platform's potential passengers. We could not. "They're not there, the system picks their requests up, you don't see them. You can, however, see the drivers nearest to you," and he showed me on Pablo's phone screen a flat map of Buenos Aires, centered on us and showing a couple of vehicles a number of streets away from where we were. A year prior to this conversation a researcher had claimed that Uber placed phantom cars on its maps to create the impression of business that would, in turn, create business in a hyperreal, cynical loop.[21] I told this to Mariano: Were these cars we were seeing even real? Did they represent actual drivers available then, or available regularly, or available ever? "Suppose they are all ghosts. The app will still look for a driver for you, even if it is not one of those."

Regardless of the truth value, Mariano's reflection shifted the grounds of the original question: from the veracity of a particular claim, that is, "Those are cars out there" our engagement shifted to Uber's capacity to find *some* car to drive us, that is, to work in the terms of the ordered orderly experience that those ghost cars stood for. This was what made the experience complete: the production, not of a mystified consumer who flung his cane at the ghosts, needed to be told he was looking at fabrications, or expected to get that very specific car, but of a subject working *with* the purchase of economic reasons to make sense of the experience. The original question, the one that took Uber to task, was now not answered but dismantled from within Uber's phantasmagoria.

The phantasmagoria was also harder to politicize because, in transferring the responsibility for a truth claim to the addressee of those propositions, reasons did not need to be commensurable or intelligible to anyone other than the user whose experience was discussed. I asked Valentina what kind of prices Uber was churning out. Were these "market prices"? What could "market price" mean for a transaction that did not exist outside the provider? Were these prices not designed to undercut taxi tariffs, which as it happened was illegal under Argentine law? Were these prices not completely unsustainable in the long run for Uber drivers? All of that could well be true, Valentina conceded, but if people wanted to drive or ride at a price they found convenient, even if they imagined it was generated by an algorithm seeking to maximize the company's income and not, for example, the availability of Uber rides or even market clearance, that was *their* prerogative. Similarly, when I pressed Mariano further on the ghost cars and other marketing strategies, I received an argument I have mentioned in the previous chapter: Uber's incentive was to sell rides and, in those early days, to build the user base that would create its business. Authorizing and encouraging the deployment of ghost cars as one among many strategies of inhabiting the market, this logic subsumed the particulars of these ghosts within the general production of the illusion without requiring any explanation from the phantasmagorian or its audience.

The tautology of a market price that suited the experience of the person who was engaged in that exchange, completing the exchange and making a certain price a *market* price, pointed to the third reason Uber's phantasmagoria was hard to politicize, even from the inside. I am concerned here with the kinds of truth claims economic reasoning can produce once political engagement has been displaced. Efficiency, supply, demand, and such economic reflections derive from the transposition of the laws of physics into economics in the nineteenth century, in a bid to naturalize the nascent discipline and its axioms.[22] These tropes carry the same intuitive traction and authority that gravity does to middle-class consciousness in late capitalism and *need not be verified or verifiable to produce an explanatory yet unfalsifiable truth claim*. As shown earlier, price multipliers were seen as evidence and as a tool of this efficiency. In fact, echoing the claims of Uber's representative Soledad Lago Rodríguez in the interview referenced in chapter 4, both Valentina and Mariano believed Uber brought about a more efficient use of all means of transportation, allowing consumers options varying in price, availability, convenience, and as many factors as the argument would need: efficiency spilled over.

Uber's PR blitz proclaimed the company's fares to be lower than taxis' on average, but more often than not Valentina paid more than a taxi would have cost. Also, the company ran out of drivers regularly during the first weeks, and more than once Uber had been unable to produce a driver to get her home, requiring her to take a taxi instead. When I pressed her on these points, she explained that with time more drivers would join the platform, or go online and act on the multipliers, and eventually supply and demand would clear; in the meantime, people had more options, which included of course taxis. A general, intuitive mechanics of efficiency could always find such a thing as a triangulation between fares, cars, and lack thereof to subsume seemingly contradictory evidence within the logics of its perpetuation. It also naturalized the difference between the unavailability of Uber cars during rush hour, proper to a self-clearing ordered, orderly order, and the unavailability of taxis in otherwise identical conditions, which normally frustrated people like Valentina.

This last point deserves further consideration. In producing both an order and the means to engage and reflect in it, Uber confirmed its otherness to other kinds of order, like the Argentine political. Its audience, Buenos Aires's residents, was not only fully aware it was inhabiting an experience of order created by someone else; as chapter 5 has shown, residents desired Uber partly precisely because of that unassailable otherness. But also, as previous chapters have shown, Buenos Aires's middle class was never a total stranger to the consciousness of late capitalism and the ways of inhabiting it. The taxi industry's strategy of shifting Uber relations onto political ground by saying out loud that they were fabrications, a variation of Marx's argument, could not domesticate the fact that this phantasmagoria, Uber's, may well have never been literally fooling anyone. People were ready, eager to depoliticize these relations and categories; now they had a culturally viable, unverifiable yet internally consistent epistemology to do so, an epistemology not only akin to postpolitical reasoning but extremely hard to counter outside of academic seminars and consonant with the economic intuitions of late capitalism.

The phantom cars flickering on Pablo's screen were also an ironic, uncanny reminder of the phantasmagoria's possible etymology, *phantasma agoreuein*: the ghosts of the public place or of the marketplace, "in the senses both of firmly located there and generated by it."[23] That marketplace was the ordered, orderly order where, as we have seen, the boundaries between reality and representation, inside and outside, objective reality and subjective experience were blurred.[24] Were the ghosts in the minds of those who saw them? Did they need to be there, or here, or anywhere to be "real"? In what sense did being "real" count, and to whom? Were they somewhere, out there, even if somewhere other than indicated? Were they a proxy reality, if not a literal one? Did, or could, the relations Uber channeled preexist it in some way as expectant demand, roaming the city as latent forces yearning to be materialized? Can there be a marketplace without the ghosts that generate and populate it?

Versions of these questions bedevil economic sociologists; as chapter 7 will show, they also haunted the city's judicial authorities trying to determine what kind of thing Uber was in terms of the relations happening through it. I have so far explored one side of the answer: in generating both the ghosts that populated this order and the categories that made sense of the experience, Uber's phantasmagoria shattered the framework in which these questions could be meaningfully asked, providing in return an order of propositions that reasons and intuitions could latch onto without being interrogated. I turn now to the other side of the answer, concerning the bottom line of Uber's, and any, phantasmagoria: the ghosts are as real as the audience want them to be.

Ghosts: From Public to Private

Around the 1900s these questions were at the forefront of the experience of modernity developing within the phantasmagoria's nowhere and outside it. Biologists, alchemists, philosophers, spiritists, and economists and their equations, seances, X-rays, and autopsies sought to give reasons to, and adjudicate between, the natural, the cultural, the human, the supernatural, the objective, and the phenomenological, locating each in its rightful place. In this sense, the phantasmagoria was a child of its times.

But the phantasmagoria was not adjudicating or helping develop consistent criteria for adjudication: as shown above, it did not engage these questions by exorcizing or defending ghosts and apparitions; rather, it evicted them. From the public realm and its order where the questions were asked, out there, it shuffled ghosts to the private and personal, reinterpreted as a particular kind of thought, affect, or intimate experience in the enclosed space of the self: the province of the nascent discipline of psychology and its kin.[25] As a result, ghosts were now no longer a public question, or one to make sense of through a shared order external to the individual. They seeped into the crevasses of the subjective experience of seeing, imagining, wanting to believe, and affording to conceive. Paradoxically, ghosts were now more real and unassailable than before, safely locked up in the inscrutable mental life of the individual, a space that modernity and its positivistic rules had explicitly defined as an order beyond the logics of the outside.

Uber's Copernican phantasmagoria mirrors an analogous shift at the height of late capitalism. Throughout her life, Valentina had lived in the neighborhoods of Belgrano, Palermo, Barrio Norte, and Congreso and had worked for different companies in downtown Buenos Aires, in the area around the Obelisk, or in the financial district about half a mile east. As well as taking Uber cars she biked and used public transportation, taxis, and her own car, so she knew how to circulate around Buenos Aires extremely well. When in an Uber car, however, she still often followed the route on Uber's app, visible to her and her driver simultaneously. Was it for reasons of safety, to ensure that she was not being cheated? Yes, to a degree, she said, but there was something else.

A street called Marcelo T. de Alvear, near her work, featured regularly on Uber's suggested route. Marcelo T. de Alvear is a narrow street, as are most in the financial district, and busy at all hours of the working day with motorcycle deliveries, security vans in and out of banks, tourists, taxis alighting and taking passengers, and the like. A few times her drivers had taken routes avoiding "Marcelo T," as porteños call it, that is, not following Uber's map. She once mentioned it politely, she told me, and the driver admitted that he had not even looked at the map and had avoided Marcelo T out of habit; in another case, the driver said he drove there daily and knew it was always busy; he suggested an alternative and Valentina agreed to it. Often she herself offered different routes.

Sure enough, in the background Uber's software would automatically reoptimize the journey, relocating that particular ride in the general order of circulation in the city and actualizing the unfolding transaction costs, estimated times of arrival, and other information making the transaction happen. But the route Uber calculated and showed both parties mattered to Valentina less in and of itself and more because it reflected the ordered, orderly transaction produced specifically for her. This was true in the sense of the triangulations mentioned earlier on, but also in a second sense: Valentina, the driver, the transaction, and the triangulations that made it pivot on her, as consumer of the ride, who would be asked to rate her driver in the terms of the phantasmagoria that created this relation.

Technical and algorithmic labor-management strategies often seek to frame the surveillance of workers as a project to develop their reflexive selves—to enable them to become better workers, however *better* is defined[26]. Uber's interface further naturalizes this management by replacing human interaction, middle managers, and other more intelligible HR encounters with the use of certain language, numerical methods, texting, and automatized communications.[27] Interestingly, just as this emergent "ethics of evaluation" passes for an objective grid, the only thing that actually matters is the experience of the individuals the phantasmagoria itself has created.[28] Valentina and her preferences were the ultimate judges of the entire order, in a trial structurally organized atop the question of how good the driver, or, as Mariano and I were told at the training session, the "passenger's experience," was. One could disagree with the app and avoid Marcelo T. de Alvear, but ultimately the only thing that mattered was how Valentina experienced or imagined or felt about that divergence, or any divergence—or anything else. How good the driver, the experience, or the ride was, was no longer a public question but a private one, in the same form of a proposition that could not be meaningfully debated or falsified.

In a sense this was precisely why residents celebrated Uber: it allowed them to redistribute the sensible along the lines of an ordered, orderly order that empowered passengers with a part and a voice in ways impossible until then. But to the extent that a subpar route choice actually and ever mattered only if it mattered to Valentina, this experience of order, out there, could be sustained and reproduced only by the audience's subjectivities. For over two centuries, phantasmagorias generated an experience where the truth claim that could count was transferred to an audience whose subjectivity was working through the uncanny experience of sorting out ghosts. Chapter 4 examined the matter of what the people, citizen-consumers in late capitalism, want, and how it constitutes a moral reservoir that supersedes

the legitimacy of a political question. We find now in this phantasmagoria's construction of its audience the site where economics trapped the
ghosts it conjured out of the political questions it colonized: the consumer's
preferences.

Echoing the relocation of ghosts from the public, shared sphere to the
private, subjective realm, the rise of neoclassical economics throughout the
twentieth century shifted the focus away from complex public questions
of social order and resource distribution and reproduction and toward a
watered-down psychology incarnated in individual preferences, or choice.[29]
The economic act of consumption was privatized to the extent that it mattered little why individuals consumed; what mattered was that they did, or
not, following their preferences, thoughts, aversions, and potentially infinite
considerations placed beyond the limits of public inquiry. In other words,
not only was it not my problem, or the phantasmagorian's, why or how
Valentina rated her ride, but the entire experience of this order was walled
off from interrogation from outside, and the matter of how "actually" efficient, empowering, or optimal Uber was crashed against this wall. "I think
it's efficient" was Mariano's invariable reply to my ramming on the wall.
We face now a magnified version of the personal relationship with pricing
I reviewed earlier, where if a certain price suits a particular user, that is the
end of it to the extent that, in a sense, that price can be nothing other than
the market price by definition.

In the phantasmagoria of late capitalism, consumers' preferences, desires,
and expectations are the gruesomely haunted house where political questions almost inevitably die. Mariano never changed his insurance policy.
Exhausted with my insistence that he was not insured in case of accident,
which on its own was not only sufficiently illegal but a potential financial
disaster, he told me that people did not care about insurance. They may not
care about it but it still matters, I replied; it does, hypothetically, but not
for the actual driving, he retorted. Besides, did I really think, given the PR
craze of #UberLove, #Righttochoose, discounts, and Uber's all-front media
offensive, that the company would run the risk of not covering one of its
drivers should an accident happen? Right after the first judge involved in
the Uber conflict ordered the immediate suspension of Uber's activities,
both he and I had received the email that opens the next chapter, where
Uber told us from Amsterdam it had our backs. Those were not the times
for questions; we would have to save them for later.

An Order Based on No Question at All

Users' preferences, in the form of ratings, were not per se factored into the construction of Uber transactions, but they were key to reproducing what Valentina experienced as an ordered, orderly order. She did believe that by tying drivers down to their performance, ratings would reward good service and hard work and foster accountability, in the sense of a method for keeping tabs and in the sense of bringing about a new sense of responsibility, which residents claimed taxis lacked, as chapter 3 showed.[30] With accountability allegedly came competition: I asked Valentina whether these drivers were really competing if Uber's interface was assigning rides on the basis of geographical proximity. She refined the point: "They compete in the sense that the better the experience, the most comfortable the passenger is likely to feel and the higher they're likely to rate."

This arguments points to a more logistical sense in which ratings reproduced Uber's Copernican phantasmagoria. Mariano and I were told at the training session that a minimum 4.5 star rating was required of all drivers to continue working. Transforming ratings into targets, the 4.5 threshold set by Uber was in itself a problem: the variety that indexes sought to represent and stand for was now compressed by drivers maximizing the likelihood to hit that threshold at the expense of things that mattered in other ways—like being properly insured.[31] Aware of this pressure, Valentina doled out the full five stars generously: only once did she rate a driver with four stars, because he took much longer than she thought he should have to pick her up.

Valentina's moral economy of feedback was only one particular case of the many generous, lazy, cruel, and meticulous passengers out there sustaining this order by sanctioning their experience. Gabriel, a friend of Mariano's, used Uber as a passenger, and all three of us met a few times; twice during those meetings Gabriel and Mariano disagreed openly on the matter of ratings. Gabriel had taken various rides and rated them all meticulously upon completion: twice he had rated his driver with four stars, once for being too chatty in an intrusive way and once one for being a slow driver. Mariano scolded him: his meticulousness could have cost drivers their work if it pushed them below the threshold. Besides, had he not made it home safe? Was he in such a hurry? The whole point was for drivers to improve their service through passengers' feedback, Gabriel retorted. Sure, and the driver being too chatty ruined your ride? Mariano baited. Did you at least leave any concrete feedback? Gabriel had not. Eventually people would learn how to use the rating system and what the stars meant, Mariano sighed.

Mariano might well hope that people would "learn" to use the ratings, but the lack of criteria as to what could, or should, count was precisely what fueled the perception of these ratings as an empowering device. A radical one, at that: anything in principle mattered if Gabriel said it did. Not only was there no longer a monopoly of knowing, but no monopoly of what was known, or could be known, or counted as knowable or worthy of being known: ghosts could take an infinity of forms. Chattiness, faulty breaks, functioning breaks, the right music selection, the performance of toler-ance, and an infinite, and infinitely detailed, string of experiences and their nuances could in principle constitute the good, bad, appropriate, or great passenger experience. Consistent rating, the elusive goal of all indicators, was now flipped upside down: inconsistency, or more precisely, a-consistency, the dilution of an epistemology, a frame of reference, that would guarantee that "experiences" were at least mutually intelligible or would judge them if they were not was the apex of democratic virtue.[32] All voices counted, irrespective of what they said at any point in time and with any intensity, and they all counted equally so long as they remained in a drivers' most recent five hundred ratings.

Because Uber's ratings were epistemologically void, they were impos-sible to *actually* rank or prioritize: a star subtracted today for chattiness and another one subtracted tomorrow for reckless driving were equalized, and neither could count more than the other. In his study of Wikipedia's project, Mirowski refers to this accumulation of voices whose very cacophony that cannot be ordered passes for democratic virtue as "radical populism."[33] But the semantic and semiotic nature of words, paragraphs, and grammatical sequences forces *some* order, even beyond the politics of knowledge, if a text is to be intelligible at all. Wikipedia voices need to share some epis-temological ground and to flow through it and into each other to at least make superficial sense.

Uber's ratings, in principle just five identical golden stars, double intui-tively as a graded scale from 1 to 5. Although they offer no intrinsic, universal (that is to say actual) gradation, differentials, or proportions framing what counts, the stars take on the arithmetic properties of natural numbers and their affective affordances as instruments, precisely, of order: an aura of se-riousness, a statistics-ready grammar, and the intuition of an ordinal, scalar experience of intensity and magnitude (5 is greater than 4 and both are better than 3). Like efficiency, demand, and supply, these stars have become a relational surface for such a thing as "the passenger experience." When Uber aggregates ratings, it piles verbosity, sexism, and mechanical malfunction on top of each other, "like icons" averaged out into the thinginess of an overall rating, a mosaic of broken ghosts that does not rank drivers in any epistemological sense, since ratings mean whatever one wants them to, but also does not in an economic sense: it only sorts them into two camps on either side of 4.5 stars.[34]

Most numerical indicators are somewhat linked to an institution that produces or uses them or to regimes of knowledge, political and economic interests, and so on. The very terms of their classification, their definitions, standardizations, scales, and proportions—that is, the hierarchies, the exclusions, and ultimately the order they put forward—can be disputed because they share an epistemological ground with alternative voices. This dispute may be profoundly unequal or ineffective, as in the case of a single Egyptian peasant resisting a government-led census classification of his land, or a taxi driver excluded from the trade's roster on the basis of a standardized visual acuity test, as chapter 2 showed; but there is someone or something to disagree with, and there are terms on which to do so.[35] Like the propositions reviewed earlier, Uber's ratings cannot be held to account for their relation to *any* truth; yet this infinitely indeterminate product is presented in an intuitive quality scale where ghosts are now so real that they have in fact become industrial policy, deciding who drives or not.[36]

These ghosts, however, have done more than dodge the question of the order they roam, and with far greater consequences in terms of postpolitical reasoning. As the problematization of taxi drivers' bodies detailed in chapter 2 showed, the deployment of techniques, regimes of knowledge, practices, and hierarchies sorted out bodies with respect to an intractable question: how to avoid another such accident, in itself a variation of how to know what we cannot know. As I argued then, on the premise of the likelihood of certain answers, an ensemble of hierarchies ranked and distributed bodies accordingly. To even ask the question, and of course to attempt to answer it, was a political act.

Perhaps the greatest illusion within Uber's phantasmagoria, the one consolidating its Copernican condition, is that its entire experience depends on it passing on to its audience the responsibility of providing an answer to a question it haunts and evokes but is actually refusing to ask. There is no question because there are as many questions as there are "experiences" and parts of experiences and approaches to experiences. The resulting order, a sort of false bottom in no box, is one made entirely of ghosts, which are by definition, as said above, impossible to order in any shared, meaningful, and consistent way, things, refractions flickering to the pace of ever-multiplying answers, all the more virtuous and meaningless for being so many and being so ghostly. This is why, although most calculative practices would normally open up new sites of disagreement, simply displacing the political to the grounds of calculation, this experience is inordinately difficult to politicize, in fact foreclosing the very possibility of disagreement.[37] The aggregate stars cannot mean anything, so there is nothing to disagree with. And the trick is that there is no trick, for this is exactly what these people understood and quite close to what they wanted, namely, an order made of no question at all, formed in the exact spot where what is, out there, collapses with our individual ways of understanding: the only place where an order made of no sorting question can be conceived of, not only as ordered and orderly, but also as anything other than a contradiction in terms.

7

The Political on Trial

LESS THAN TWENTY-FOUR HOURS after the taxi industry initiated legal action, the justice system called for an interruption of Uber's activities. In parallel, district attorneys had begun investigating the company's operations in Buenos Aires in late March, and had confirmed, independently, that Uber was breaching a series of laws and regulations. In refusing to interrupt its operations, the company turned an industrial conflict into a matter of contempt of court: the juridico-political order of the Autonomous City of Buenos Aires began a series of attempts to delineate, single out, and extirpate Uber from its jurisdiction. They all proved unsuccessful; whereas the justice system saw in these failures technical hurdles to its fundamental prerogative to determine what kinds of relations could legitimately take place in Buenos Aires and how, among the middle classes an alternative view gained traction. Highly publicized and disproportionately intrusive into banal activities of middle-class life, these failures worked as a "trial of strength," reinforcing the vaguely formulated but powerful proposition that Uber was beyond the juridico-political order attempting to stop it.[1] Trials of strength are not about truth, justice, or best-selling arguments but about endurance; although Buenos Aires's juridico-political order never ceased to view the company, its technologies, and its relations as a political problem, residents among the middle class found in this struggle evidence that these relations were irreducible to the political. In this view, legal and political action should work with the flows of these relations, rather than against or beside them, a conclusion that effectively neutralized the possibility of framing these relations differently.

Jurisdictions: A Matter of Speech, Speech Matters

As said in chapter 4, on April 12, hours after Uber's arrival, the taxi industry initiated legal action, accusing Uber of engaging in price dumping, promotion of uninsured transactions, and illegal use of public space, among other imputations. The following day a judge issued a precautionary measure: a set of temporary instructions until more was known about what was at stake or about the circumstances of a particular conflict. Referencing news reports of Uber's arrival; declarations by the minister for transportation of the City of Buenos Aires that the company was "illegal"; and the city's constitutional duty to protect the well-being, safety, and assets of consumers, ensure access to transparent, truthful, and timely information, and police the consumption of all goods and services within its borders, he instructed the city government to preventively interrupt "any activity carried out by the company Uber B.V., Uber Technologies Inc., or any legal or economic society operating under those or similar names." The judge refused, however, the taxi industry's request to block access to Uber's app, website, or any other publications bearing the name of the company. He claimed that plaintiffs' grounds for making such a request were insufficient and that such actions could amount to an invasion (literally, *invasión*) of jurisdictions beyond his. Also, the judge demanded that within five days:

- The Governmental Agency of Control "inform[] whether the company known as Uber has requested authorization to provide public transportation of passengers," and if so, since when, and that the agency forward all paperwork or certified copy;
- The Governmental Administration of Public Income "inform[] whether the company known as Uber, under any legal or corporate name, is registered for tax purposes," and if so, since when, and what its legal domicile is;
- The Autonomous City of Buenos Aires's secretary of transportation "inform[] whether the company known as Uber has initiated any processes to provide any kind of passenger transportation" and forward all paperwork or certified copy.

The judge threaten to sanction whoever did not comply.

Argentina is a federal country divided in twenty-three provinces plus the Autonomous City of Buenos Aires. At this juridico-political level, the city has its own executive, legislative, and judicial powers, enshrined in the national and city constitutions; this city as a juridico-political order contains the taxi industry. Although Uber's activities followed population dispersion and spilled over into the adjoining federal district, the province of Buenos Aires, it is unsurprising that the taxi industry addressed its grievances to the city's judicial power.

Uber's first twenty-four hours in Argentina triggered a frantic legal, technical, and narrative project of figuring out what, how, and where Uber was in terms of that order, an invitation to think about "the technical dimensions of law and the pragmatics of jurisdiction" that allow a juridico-political order to both speak and make sense.[2] More than challenging the righteousness of the order where such a thing as the Autonomous City of Buenos Aires exists, the point is to understand jurisdiction, as both the authority to speak the law and that which the law speaks, as an ongoing practical and performative process that frames and probes the limits of that order. Jurisdiction is "the performative labor through which courts presuppose the authority to speak law while simultaneously delimiting that authority . . . , [and] is also about the crafting of virtual and material spaces that determine the where and the when of this power."[3] Theoretically speaking, the judge's jurisdiction, the extent and scope of his authority's legitimacy to speak the law, coincides with the territory of the Autonomous City of Buenos Aires. In practice, thinking jurisdictionally about "the well-being, safety, and assets of consumers" (the forty-sixth article of the Constitution of the Autonomous City of Buenos Aires) requires disentangling the bodies, affects, matter, and processes that involve those consumers and whose boundaries rarely fit each other, let alone coincide with the territory of the jurisdiction at stake.

In other words, jurisdiction as work is about determining what belongs where, how, and in what terms. In principle, "entextualizing" tax records, company registries, and ministerial documents—that is, inserting all that paperwork from different entities into a single text of a purely legal genre—translates the administrative and political conflict into a matter of law, a dynamic examined in chapter 4.[4] Yet already by this time the judge and everyone else knew that a company, or something, called "Uber" had already launched a ride-sharing business in the city. This irrevocable fact would later fuel challenges to the judge's right to speak the law and to the righteousness of law's speech in this particular case; for now, the calling forth of those various texts incorporated into a single, rapidly growing file was part of the judge's work to determine whether such a thing as Uber, or

Uber Argentina, existed in fiscal, economic, legal, or statutory terms of any kind. In other words: What kind of entrance had Uber made in the city's juridico-political order?[5]

This file was enrolled in two problems: first, determining how to know and approach Uber and Uber transactions in juridico-political terms; second, deciding how to act on that knowledge. The tension between these two problems explains the hair-splitting decision to interrupt Uber's transactions yet refuse to block access to its interfaces. Jurisdiction is both a prerogative and a continuous emergence; it is deciding one knows enough to act in a certain way and the continuous metareflection on how much more one needs to know in order to act in a given sense.

As we know from chapter 4, many citizens disagreed on principle that the matter should be sorted out in the courts. We shall soon see, too, that the judge was not the only one thinking about the extension and intensity of his jurisdiction; and courts, summons, and legal files and arguments were not the only spaces, practices, and texts that would mobilize the notion of jurisdictions or their legitimacy. From the judge's perspective and at this stage, however, the fundamental possibilities of jurisdiction as defined by the city's political order were not at stake; in other words, the legitimacy of his authority as judge to even address this matter was not on the table, even if he were to choose to dismiss it later.[6]

Investigations

News that Uber's services were to be blocked less than a full day after arriving spread immediately. I had signed up as an Uber driver although I did not even own a car, and on April 14 I woke up to an email from "Uber Buenos Aires." On a white, black, and Uber-turquoise background, under the dramatically capitalized heading "Juan, YOU CAN DRIVE SAFELY," it read:

> Juan, we want to tell you that the precautionary measure that was news yesterday, dictated by a city judge, has NO effect on Uber. The judge simply ordered the authorities of the City of Buenos Aires to carry on with their usual controls around the city. Your activity is perfectly legal under the Civil and Commercial Code and no norm can forbid it. Our partners are very important to Uber, and remember, we are with you and will always have your back. Keep enjoying the experience of being your own boss generating income with Uber, driving when and as much as you want.

Written in River Plate Spanish morphology, the text was signed "Uber's Team." At the bottom right of the email was "UBER B.V., XXXXXstraat XX, XXXX HL Amsterdam."

That was certainly not what the judge had ordered, and to the extent that the whole point of the precautionary measure was to stop Uber's activities, this statement came quite close to committing, and inciting others to commit, contempt of court. Later that day the city's minister of transportation, Juan José Méndez, declared that the company had been "administratively" shut down and that if it ignored these orders penal and misdemeanor courts would intervene.[7] Also, the Governmental Agency of Control, which the judge had requested information from, had by now conducted its own investigation, presumably verifying that no company under any of Uber's known names had initiated any registration to provide any service. Also, it had already sent letters to two domiciles within the city boundaries found to be "linked to the company."[8]

These domiciles had been known to authorities for a while. In a move completely separate from the taxi industry's legal action, in late March two district attorneys from the Autonomous City of Buenos Aires had initiated ex officio an investigation into Uber's then-future arrival to the city. They had discovered the existence of a limited liability company named Uber Argentina, domiciled in the eighth floor of a building in the financial district. This company was apparently formed by the association of Uber International Holding BV and Uber International BV, both foreign and both declaring as legal domicile that same eighth floor; these premises were the address of a law firm. The attorneys' investigation also showed that no firm under any of the names above had been registered with the secretary of transportation or had requested any permits to conduct any business. Also, they identified Argentine citizen Mariano Xavier Otero as Uber's "general manager," and his domicile as being in the city center.

By April 14 everyone in Buenos Aires knew who Mariano Otero was, as he appeared on national media declaring that the company's support for its drivers was "total," that it would reimburse all fines incurred by its "partners," and that "if necessary we will take this matter to the justice."[9] "The justice" had by now sent letters to Otero's home address and to that office in the financial district, eager to engage him and the company on this very subject, but an Uber spokesperson declared "having no knowledge of what is going on at courts" as the conflict widened by the hour. They added that the company's operations "carried on as normal. We will stay in Buenos

Aires so people can enjoy their right to move around the city, and we are committed to creating economic opportunities for more than thirty-five thousand Argentines before the end of the year."[10]

On April 15, in a press release–cum–blog entry titled "Defend your #RightToChoose, travel with Uber and all your rides will be free!" the company shared how "unbelievably excited" they were to be in Buenos Aires.[11] "Our users and partners' welcome was all we expected of the Argentine capital. . . . So everyone has the chance to get to know Uber, free rides from now until Wednesday, April 20."[12] Uber was part of a new history, the text added, enthusiastically explaining how demand for Uber had been extremely high and asking its users to be patient and not to forget to share their experiences on social media with the hashtag #UberLove. Already by now the city's three hundred traffic wardens had been charged with identifying Uber rides as they happened in the traffic, which they were managing to do at a rate of three per day. These drivers were fined the equivalent of 4,130 USD; Uber took care of the fines.[13]

That day just after midday, another city judge, Claudia Alvarado, mandated police raids at Uber's two addresses, to be carried out that same evening. She grounded her order in the investigation led by the two attorneys I mentioned above and the fact "known to the public" that Uber rides were already occurring and continued to take place after judicial instructions to cease. Progressing through metadiscursive reflections on her own prerogatives as a judge, like a reference to the article of the city's Code of Penal Procedure explaining when the laws of private property could be overridden and a private domicile searched, this work of jurisdiction took on a different momentum: if the other judge's precautionary measure gave preliminary orders until more was known, Judge Alvarado's instructions worked on the basis that the juridico-political order she embodied could already verify it had been violated, presumably willfully so.

The judge requested from both raids the seizure of documents, printed or digital, pertaining to Uber's company structure, full-time employees, lists of drivers, and information about their cars; balances of payments and any information describing the mechanism of the transactions; documents, printed or digital, resulting from or pointing to bank accounts being used by Uber or on its behalf and details of transactions; passenger database and details of all trips up to that day; and documentation linking Uber to any of its drivers in any form, as well as the seizure of any information in hard drives, pen drives, and magnetic or optical storage devices containing any information related to Uber. In the case of the law firm, the judge mandated the intervention of appropriate technicians to extract this information from any physical support (computers, servers, etc.) while leaving the objects themselves in place. She also requested the presence of a witness from Buenos Aires's bar association "given the kinds of confidential information a law firm handles" and the potential entanglement of information pertaining to Uber with information of other kinds, beyond the scope of this unfolding case. In the case of Mariano Otero's domicile, the police were to remove anything that could be linked to the company's activities or his involvement in them.

Circumscribing, separating, and adjudicating between Uber and non-Uber transactions, Uber employees, objects, sites, and matters: jurisdiction as work is a labor of purification, in the latter's most modern sense.[14] This work takes these subjects as separate, or at least separable, from each other, to isolate and figure out the nature of the relations they entertain with each other, but fundamentally, with the juridico-political order the judge represents. Jurisdiction presupposes the possible existence of those legal subjects: in other words, after however cumbersome a labor of distillation there is, or will be, such a thing as Uber, Uber relations, Uber users, Uber prices in the Autonomous City of Buenos Aires, to speak of in some sort of consistent, bounded way. This is to say, jurisdiction presupposes that such a separation is ontologically given, that it is in the very nature of these processes to be separable in some way.

Tragicomic Encounters

This was only Uber's third day in the city; now that newly elected president Mauricio Macri had declared that Buenos Aires's taxis were a symbol of the city and the nation, the conflict had taken on a literally spectacular character.[15] Accordingly, most television channels offered live coverage of police raiding the law firm's offices in the financial district, on Leandro Alem Avenue. The building's glass doors had been locked from the inside; behind the doors were guards, and behind the guards were turnstiles, themselves guarding access to the elevators leading to the offices being searched on the seventh and eighth floors. Several taxi drivers gathered outside to protest. As bewildered yuppies scurried out of the building, a young man appeared before the cameras, on the blond side and with a scruffy beard, telling the crowds we should all welcome the freedom to choose. He was taken for an Uber employee, which he said he was not, and an Uber driver, which

he also denied; he clarified he was a fellow citizen and "potential" user of
Uber. Uber was not there to steal their jobs but to bring more options, he
insisted. Uber was "where," exactly? What about taxi licenses, what about
Uber dodging taxes? He was asked. He said it was wrong, too, that taxi
drivers should pay; the state should refund their license and we all should
compete freely. His tone was messianic, and it seemed as if he actually
believed his own words, but in the context it passed for a provocation. A
protester pushed him to the ground, someone kicked him, someone else
quickly stopped the fight, screaming that violence was not the way, and he
was helped up. As the building's security personnel watched from across the
marble foyer, behind the tightly shut glass doors, some protesters escorted
the mysterious man to the other side of the avenue.

Leandro Alem Avenue is very wide: now on the other side, eight lanes
away from the building, the protesters trying to calm things down hailed a
taxi that happened to be actually cruising for clients, and helped the man in.
But the cameramen had followed, and along with the reporters came some
taxi drivers as well. Upon seeing the blond man with the scruffy beard enter
the taxi, the latter began insulting the taxi driver that had just been hailed,
assuming he was somehow in cahoots with this man. Gesticulating furiously,
the driver lowered his window to scream that *he* was working and had no
clue who this man they had just shoved into his car was. Upon hearing all
this racket, more protesters now came to this side of the avenue, presumably
thinking someone had figured out who the man with the beard was. They
had missed the beginning of the explanation, so the insults recommenced
with a larger and growing crowd. By now there were few protesters left by
the building with the offices where some local trace about Uber might be
found, and many more protesters standing in front of the taxi that was trying to work. Eventually things were explained; the taxi drove off into the
emptiness of the business district after rush hour, taking the young man,
now just another taxi passenger, away. The cameras worked their way back
to the building and protests resumed, for the police were still searching the
premises. Under the headline "Uber Defender Takes a Taxi," in the news
studio the journalists scoffed—somewhere else, far away, wherever "Mr.
Uber" was, "he had probably just died laughing."[16]

At the time, Uber's PR strategy was the same as its address to the juridico-
political order that interpellated it: carry on as unconcernedly as the guards
behind the glass doors. Uber was not breaking the law but was unregulated,
its spokespeople and lawyers argued to cameras and judges respectively,

adding that by its very nature as an innovative disruption it exceeded the tools of the law. Uber's communications manager Soledad Lago Rodríguez said in an interview that Uber was "proregulation" and "eager" to help local regulators develop legal frameworks adapted to the twenty-first century.[17] In the email I had been sent on April 14 and in its legal presentations the company argued that article 1280 of the National Civil and Commercial Code allowed for any two private parties to enter a private transportation agreement with each other; Uber was, they said, only a "mediator" between such two parties. Being an app, Uber did not occupy any public space but only "virtual" space, and in driving through it, its partners and users were only exercising their constitutional right to circulate freely in the nation.

The nature and texture of the opposition between public and private, between "real" and virtual, as deployed by lawyers, judges, Uber users, and the company's rhetoric, deserve an analysis beyond this book's purpose. What matters for us is that those arguments were rebutted, first, on the grounds that all rights enshrined by any legal document in Argentina, including the national constitution, are to be enjoyed in conformity with all laws regulating their exercise. For example, two private parties have the right to agree to a transportation service that suits them both, but this right can never override, and is bound by, laws requiring that private transportation of any kind be accordingly insured, which as we know from chapter 6 was not the case with Uber at the time. Second, in Argentine legal doctrine Uber cannot be understood as simply a "mediator" or "facilitator" because it is setting the terms of the very contract at stake, with the price or value of the ride being only the most salient. Uber is integral to that transaction, and irreducible to individual desires or preferences as far as this juridico-political order defines individuals and their interactions within its jurisdiction. On these grounds, the justice proceeded with the more contentious arguments that I revise in the coming sections.

But that Friday evening it was not the rhetorical solidity or judiciousness of Uber's legal defense that was being tested, or the efficacy of its marketing strategy. The tragicomedy of the raids affirmed among the middle classes the image of the taxi industry as a recalcitrant, active obstacle against what was passing for economic and technological progress, individual empowerment, and freedom to choose, as I discuss in chapters 4, 6, and 8. Also, the fact that as these places were being searched and the police, the law, judges, and other city authorities were trying to pin Uber down, the company's services continued undeterred legitimized and enhanced the conviction that Uber was in key ways external and impervious to the city's order of things, as chapter 5 argues. However, the fact that like thousands of Uber drivers, Mariano drove through the evening into the early night as passengers requested his service through the app doubled as evidence for a different kind of trial gathering enormous momentum. This trial was not legal but spoke to the city's juridico-political order; it was not conducted by the judge but came to concern her jurisdiction directly as a kind of work, as a prerogative, and its limits in both senses. This trial concerned Uber directly, almost by accident lending credence to the company's official stance: the multiplication of Uber rides in the heat of #UberLove and the failure of jurisdictional work to stop it began to pass for verification that something about these relations exceeded the juridico-political order that was trying to pin them down.

Jurisdictional Pragmatics: Internet

Uber's app never stopped working and people carried on using it, so on April 22, the company's tenth day in Buenos Aires, the judge issued further orders. Binding facts and norms in a text "presuppos[ing] and constitut[ing] the broader narrative of law as a force of social ordering more generally," the judge retraced a temporal-logical sequence, from the company's arrival, to its persistence in its activities, to Mr. Otero's defense's arguments.[18] Dismissing the latter, she then considered the attorney general's exhortation: to immediately block all interfaces that might allow the hiring or any other use of Uber's services.

On the eleventh page the judge engaged in the most literal exploration of her jurisdictional prerogatives so far. The attorney framed his request through a law allowing authorities to *clausurar*, shut down, a *lugar*, a place, if it was verified that violations of the law were occurring there. The question was, the judge says, to determine whether the law invoked by the district attorney could apply to an app—whether there was a there "there," and if so of what kind. The twenty-second edition of the Royal Spanish Academy's dictionary, she continued, "defines the verb *clausurar* as: 1) to close, bring to an end; 2) to close, temporally or permanently bar access to, a building, a premise, etc. But in turn, the verb *to close* has several meanings that extend beyond physical property, as the *etc.* at the end of the definition mentioned above indicates." *Clausurar* was a transitive verb; according to the law she was referencing, she said, one shut down a *lugar*, some place.

The question was now to determine what counted, or not, as a place, the judge continued: the fifth accepted meaning of the term *lugar* in the same dictionary is "passage, text, or sentence; expression or assemblage thereof from an author or a written book." Therefore, she concluded, "Both a webpage and an app, as text or code inserted into the internet that can be assigned to an author, in this case the company Uber, are, according to Spanish language etymology, susceptible of being shut down or otherwise barred from access." On this basis, the judge ordered the National Body of Communications (ENACOM) to design the necessary measures so that all nine internet providers across Argentina would block the site http://drive.uber.com/argentina, related digital platforms, apps, and any other technological support enabling the hiring of cars under the services offered by Uber, in any of its names, "within the strict territory of the Autonomous City of Buenos Aires."

Jurisdictions are about sovereignty and power, but crucially, they are about contingency, as actors ponder through language the extent and nature of their authority over matters presented to them.[19] This is because the legal authority that jurisdiction presupposes and produces is always potentially set against other sources of authority, a caveat that, as we shall soon see, would prove premonitory. Precisely because of the reflections that make it, "Sovereign power imagined through legal language is always pointing to its limits."[20] As fabric of legal narrative, then, both legal language in particular and language in general serve as hermeneutical tools, as the prods that test those limits. The recourse to etymology, ultimately just the intimate history of a term, works here as much more than argumentative preciousness. Uber, its relations, whatever its stuff was, was proving hard to locate and purify, to even stabilize as any single thing, site, or person: as Richland shows with a similar discussion around the term *income*, at stake was whether through association and similarity/synonymy the terms of this specific case could be framed as a particular instance, the latest iteration, of a more general form addressed by other texts, written in previous times.[21] Simply put, at stake was whether the law that made jurisdiction happen, based on historical cases, bodies, and matter, could meaningfully and legitimately apply to this case.

We must remember that this work was happening alongside the company's argument and description of itself as a virtual mediator, an innovation, and a technological frontier, strategically deploying a language that resisted circumscription to law and casuistry. The judge's conclusion that Uber was, indeed, a *lugar* that could be *clausurado*, a place that could be shut down, was thus an insistence on the part of the juridico-political order on the stakes of the case as it had mapped them out. Whether Uber or anything by that name should or "actually" could be separated or circumscribed through specific forensic technicalities was completely secondary for this particular aspect of the argument. From the judge's perspective, the Uber case and the company remained knowable and to be known through, and subjected to, the jurisdictional pragmatics of the juridico-political order as it existed.

The ENACOM replied almost immediately that these orders were technically impossible to follow, for reasons older than the city itself. What was now the City of Buenos Aires had been founded in 1536 as a port on the southernmost edges of the Spanish Empire in South America to serve as point of departure for silver extracted from present-day Bolivia for passage to Europe. After the expulsion of Spain from the area in 1810 a confederacy of thirteen shire-like provinces emerged. The province of Buenos Aires was one of them but inherited the confederacy's only international port. As the country inserted itself into the commercial patterns of nineteenth-century capitalism as an agricultural exporter, the province of Buenos Aires quickly consolidated its hegemony over the others.[22] Decades of internecine conflict would follow until in 1880 the federal government took the city, the port, and its revenue from the province. With a line inscribed onto then-empty pampa the Argentine government created the Autonomous City of Buenos Aires as a federal entity on its own, and the province of Buenos Aires was given a new capital twenty-five miles south.

Since that day, the Autonomous City of Buenos Aires and the province of Buenos Aires had been two adjacent but different jurisdictions in Argentina's juridico-political order. All national internal borders were constitutionally constructed as nonborders, forbidding any restrictions in the circulation of infrastructure, capital, goods, and people within the nation. Today, Greater Buenos Aires is a concentration of thirteen million people, centered in the city and spilling over into the province for miles in all directions, integrated by railway lines, mail, banking, highways, electricity, sewage, and internet infrastructures piercing the border above and below ground. The border between both jurisdictions, originally a road, is today the busiest highway in Argentina, counting four lanes in each direction at its narrowest.

Days later I interviewed Gabriel, an ENACOM technician, a lawyer who had retrained as a computer forensic engineer. Uber's IP, its internet address, was in the United States, he explained, certainly beyond the judge's jurisdiction; there was no such thing as "Uber Argentina." Additionally, the integration of antennae, subterranean cables, and other internet infrastructures between "the strict territory of the Autonomous City of Buenos Aires" and the province on the other side of the road was such that in technical terms the whole area worked as one. Theoretically speaking, it would have been easier to block access to Uber's IP for the whole of Argentina: internet travels the world mostly by cables, and at the points of entry into Argentine territory, when the nine local internet providers took over, the IP could be blocked. "But that would violate the other twenty-three jurisdictions," he explained, "because you would be carrying out this judge's orders in territories well beyond her prerogatives." At the level of Argentina's juridico-political order there was nothing to object to, and the ENACOM would be misplaced to present an objection on those grounds. Technically, "It is just absolutely impracticable."

A Proposition

Uber's entrance and presence in Buenos Aires remained throughout a violation of the City's juridico-political order. From the judges' end, the difficulties of purifying and extricating Uber relations to align them with the limits of their jurisdiction constituted a technical problem in the rightful and legitimate exercise of their authority. Nothing across the files they ever produced up to 2020 would imply that they understood the properties of internet infrastructure or anything about Uber's practices as an ontological affront, or as events or forces of an irreducibly different nature and order.

But legal process is never solely a matter of courts in times when "media and the cameras have entered the courtroom."[23] Uber's strategy in Buenos Aires had always been to ostentatiously dismiss the domain of the courts, advancing its position through social media campaigns, press releases, and promotions. Besides, the conflict had begun on the streets, with pickets, blockades, and smashed windows, ambushes to Uber drivers, and a whole mobilization of public officials. The stakes were public in the most literal and theatrical sense of the term, bursting out of the same court documents that residents kept a watchful eye on. Even when, as chapter 4 showed, the private experience of consumers was enshrined as a *site* of moral legitimacy, the *arena* of adjudication remained the public in its carnivalesque stakes. Besides, these residents already understood Argentine legal process as permeable to political pressure, the taxi industry's or the government's, so in their reasoning the case had never, really, been confined to courts.

"The judge wants to *clausurar* the internet," scoffed Pablo, Mariano's partner, purposefully selecting the most absurd possible wording during a coffee. "Not internet—just Uber transactions," I replied, but he was not budging: "You can't stop Wi-Fi like that." Why? I asked. He flipped his palms up: you cannot just interrupt information traveling through electromagnetic waves—air, matter, and vibrations won't follow the trace of an avenue. Besides, he added, what about people traveling from one side of the avenue to another—or *on* the avenue? The absurdity of the case evidenced to him the properties and distributions inherent to transportation relations had to be understood together with wireless internet coverage. A filmmaker in his midforties, Pablo had two smartphones, two laptops, and a desk computer; Mariano added a smartphone, a laptop, and a tablet to the household's electronic menagerie, and both crossed the border regularly and unreflexively several times a week for work, leisure, or just any casual reason. Neither had any expert knowledge of physics, infrastructure, or legal process, at least not in the canonical sense of expertise. Their claim to the logics of the unfolding conflict was one premised on a sort of common sense.

By *common sense* I mean a relatively organized yet disparate "body of considered thought" whose authoritative, practical, and immethodical accounts claim to strike at the heart of the matter as immediate deliverances of experience.[24] Like jurisdiction, common sense is a way of knowing and of organizing knowledge, distributing causes, effects, logics, and senses. Like other ways of knowing and of relating to knowledge, common sense is also marked by hierarchies, exclusions, and the socioeconomic affordances of those who speak it.[25] Vast segments of Argentina may lack running water and any kind of internet, but for middle-class lives in what remains a comparatively quite rich and culturally liberal city, the very notion of "*clausurar* the internet" to begin with, never mind the fact that it was suggested as a way to stop Uber's activities, amounted to an absurdity in the key of disproportion and excess. Technologies and their materialities have a way of embodying the cultural identities and promises of a given era; if, as Barry shows, "the malleability of metals was once viewed as an index of the transformative capacities of capitalism," the dispersed yet integrated territorial experience of internet relations qualifies the late capitalism that a self-consciously cosmopolitan middle class inhabits.[26]

Experiencing the failed ban with smug exasperation, these residents would find in this common sense the purchase for a nonexpert affront to the juridico-political order as a valid way of knowing and of sorting that knowledge out. The key to understanding this affront is to remember that the technical difficulties of engaging Uber could not be reduced to an alternative political claim—by the company or by the middle class. They resulted from historical, institutional, and material entwinements between the city and the province, not from an agenda countering, or even addressing, the juridico-political order of the city and the nation in political terms. Of course, the technical difficulties did benefit Uber's agenda, since the company could effectively continue undeterred and since its self-description as immaterial mediator gained it a legitimacy it did not deserve. Also, after all, the company could have cooperated with the justice and switched off its platform. But when it did not, it was the entirely accidental misalignment between jurisdictions and internet infrastructures that obstructed the judge's determination. Had history played out differently, the whole of Greater Buenos Aires could have been contained in a single jurisdiction and Uber relations could have been easily interrupted.

As the conflict played out, however, among the middle class the proposition crystallized that these technologies and materialities were irreducible to the terms of Buenos Aires' juridico-political order; and this irreducibility had less to do with Uber as a company than with the nature of the relations at stake. If the juridico-political order exists and becomes effective through the work of jurisdiction, then the cinematic failure of this work evidenced that these kinds of relations exceeded in some fundamental way the terms of this order. I use *proposition* in Stengers's sense: a claim that affronts the order it addresses directly by putting forward an argument rejecting the terms of that order.[27] Preliminary forms of this proposition were already floating around: Uber's spokespeople insisted that innovation could not be subsumed in the logics of arrangements based on past experiences, and as shown in chapter 5, the middle class was already understanding Uber as external and impervious to the local order in key ways. Also, as chapter 8 shows, the nation had just elected a technocratic government: the language of the necessity of a profound economic, political, and social upheaval, including an institutional "catching up," had persuasive traction among residents already associating the company with a symbolic and structural otherness to Argentina and its political life.

Echoing and bouncing off of these various claims and characterizations, this proposition did not categorize what, where, or how Uber was, certainly not in any taxonomic sense; it also did not attempt to grow into a full-fledged agenda or to seek any intellectual consistency. This proposition did not need to think of borders or internet infrastructure, law or physics in the epistemology of the juridico-political order, in spite of the despairing irony that the relations at stake came to life through them. In other words, the idea that these relations exceeded the juridico-political order of the city held "no obligation to the great narrative" of the order it opposed or that order's regimes of knowledge: it did not need to make sense of the sense that the judge was making of the issue.[28] It worked less by offering a fully formed alternative engagement with these relations and more by pointing, in unmethodical, intuitive terms, to the growing gaps between the clear-cut lines of the juridico-political order: "this" is excessive, "this" is irrational, "this" is absurd. The tone of the proposition was set by the infrastructural, economic, connective, and "natural" immanence and dispersion of Uber relations as these people lived them. By *natural* I mean the biophysical phenomena that this common sense took as objective, like the undulations and dispersion of electromagnetism, as inseparable from the request for an Uber ride coded in them as a smoke signal is from the aggregation of smoke particles.

But after centuries steeped in certain forms of economic thinking, *natural* also implies the propensities, desires, potentialities, and preferences through which people interact with their surroundings, crisscrossing the human, the technical, and the biophysical—like calling an Uber when one feels like it.[29] In this sense, the proposition's claim to the natural gained traction less through ethical deliberation and more from the concrete experiences of rides that continued to happen, undeterred, by the tens of thousands. For centuries, too, this sense of the "natural" has led to an ethical-managerial orientation: to be righteous, rightful, and productive, any intervention must work with and toward natural forces rather than against or in spite of them. A famously researched example is the re-creation of the city of Nantes in the eighteenth century, where "the flows of water, islands, air, and so forth" inspired existing and projected economic activities: the notion that geographies, topographies, and demographics define human activity is a powerful one, and its pull on alternatives greater in the face of the perceived absurdity of going against nature.[30]

Hardening increasingly "from within" the relations these residents engaged in, this proposition shaped the experience of the conflict and the possibility of retorting from the juridico-political order's perspective—or indeed, from anywhere.[31] First, the proposition subordinated what could be known and how, as well as the legitimacy of that knowledge, to logics it took as irreducible and anterior to that juridico-political order: flows trumped borders. Second, it circumscribed the operational possibilities of any knowledge to technical management: work with, not against, the flow. Third, it merged these "natural" transactions with the people's economic nature—and with the company enabling them. As the proposition hardened around the issue of internet infrastructures refusing to give in to a juridico-political order based on the historical vagaries of a border, the company using those infrastructures to produce the relations that were passing for a natural phenomenon became harder to visibilize *as such*, and thus to speak back to.

Jurisdictional Pragmatics: People Move Around
The proposition that these relations exceeded the city's juridico-political order could have remained such, unacknowledged beyond residents' exasperation. Irrespective of its truth value, the proposition consolidated its claim to the stakes through a progressive sequence of what Latour calls trials of strength: challenges, conflicts, and encounters where alternative claims test the resistance of a particular claim.[32] As judges, attorneys, union leaders, protesters, laws, infrastructures, and an increasing and increasingly complex array of actors failed to stop or even engage Uber in the terms of the juridico-political order of the city (or in any order other than the company's own), it became increasingly difficult to counter the notion that these relations were of a different order, and that any engagement would have to work from the premise of their inevitability to be successful. Trials of strength are not about truth, popularity, or commitment in conviction but about concrete, no-nonsense endurance, as the next episode in the saga shows.

By late April, Uber's app was approaching half a million downloads, between passengers and drivers, and the judge now requested technicians to retrace the circuits of the transaction and identify possible routes to disrupt them. The ENACOM informed her that Uber BV processed payments from platform users through Raicer Operations BV, a company based in the Netherlands receiving the money for each ride, retaining 20 percent and depositing the remainder in each driver's current account in Argentina. On April 28, just over two weeks after Uber's first ride in Argentina, the judge instructed all six credit card providers operating in Argentina to abstain from enabling sales points for any of the companies under the various legal names listed above and associated with Uber, as well as to interrupt any money transfers or other activities facilitating Uber transactions—again, for the territory of the Autonomous City of Buenos Aires.

This ban was put in place. Credit cards stopped transactions through Uber's app, but people quickly found ways to circumvent these restrictions.

Websites showing how to pretend to be abroad, thus outside the judge's jurisdiction, and how to deal with the ban when being really abroad proliferated, some even recreating verbatim conversations with credit card operators.[33] Some cards did allow for the transactions; Valentina, formerly employed by the Buenos Aires branch of one of the largest credit card companies in the world, explained the confusion as follows:

> Credit card companies can block transactions only under certain conditions. The first n numbers of a credit card number locate clients at a country level; you cannot tell apart cards issued in the city and cards issued past the avenue. Worse, this has nothing to do with where the card holder is at the time or where the transaction is taking place. If Uber doesn't inform the card company where the charges are coming from the card issuer cannot know. Last, implementing the ban, dealing with phone calls to approve individual transactions, is costly. The ones who did not implement the ban might prefer to pay whatever they were fined rather than to engage in these costs.

For many years an economic consultant, Valentina explained the above with clinical, ludic detachment, like a seasoned chess player reviewing potential strategies halfway through a game. As soon as I laid down my pen she threw herself back in the chair, sighing, "It's just all so stupid." Chasing Uber was stupid, but also even the thought of trying to block the cards, the many ways in which this ban was already gearing up to not ever work, and how obvious this should be to everyone. Of course people would find a way around the ban. Were there other ways of interrupting the logistics of Uber payments in particular, or Uber's operations in general, given the jurisdictional and technological circumstances of the conflict? Not that she could think of. She was much more conversant in the grammars of law and legality than most of my other informants. What was the solution? The solution was to leave people in peace, she advised. "There's no way to ever do this right. People move around."

The ban continued for a long time, but eventually most users found a way to dodge it. Mariano's enthusiasm for circulating instructions on how to get around it verged on a middle-class form of political resistance: he wanted to do whatever he wanted with his car. Echoing Valentina's exasperation, he saw in the failure of the ban not a political victory, which he could have claimed for himself, but a defeat of recalcitrance by common sense. People and their cars, cards, and internet cables had been moving around well before Uber's arrival, crisscrossing the border between city and province unimpeded (even if, ironically, it was the philosophical principles of the juridico-political order now under popular siege that allowed them to). Uber relations were not only mounted onto the cultural practices and economic interlocking of these circulations between Uruguay and Buenos Aires, between city and province, but effectively merging with them as a single whole. After rides to Zona Norte, Mariano went round to visit friends living in the area, or stopped for food or shopping, and often returned to the city without switching Uber on. In an amusing turn of events, the very fact that the judge's orders necessitated the practical disintegration of relations formally constructed to be integrated for almost 150 years, lest the country fall victim to internecine battle, rendered the area's juridico-political order as an evident social construction just as it naturalized many of the direct consequences of that same social construction. In other words, this was just an "artificial" border, but people "obviously" and "naturally" moved across it, because "that's what people do." "Next they will come for the cars," exaggerated Pablo to evoke the absurd, irrational connotation implicit in the partition.

That this ban was so easy to boycott therefore reinforced the trial of strength against the juridico-political order's aptness and jurisdiction over Uber relations: everyone was a phone call away from rendering it inefficacious. But it did something more than that. In the terms of the city's order, one single resident dodging the ban was as much of a violation of the judge's jurisdiction as a hundred or ten thousand. The latter cases were more visible or evidenced a technical shortcoming; but conceptually they did not, in and of themselves, constitute in principle anything other than the sum of equal parts. In the rhetoric of the proposition that the juridico-political order's logics were not the appropriate route to know and engage these relations, however, the generalized boycott of the ban passed for evidence of a collective—of an economic mass.

This is a similar collective to the one we encountered in chapter 4, who, reasoning about legitimacy, made a political problem into a moral one. Here, however, the casual, effective behavior of these people, minimally coordinated on social media, linked them to other behaviors also being naturalized, like "moving around." The actions of these people, in their spontaneity and aggregation, amounted to a "natural" way of acting on one's propensities and inclinations in neoclassical economic intuitions. When people want something, they go for it, or in Valentina's terms, the fact that not one or two passengers but "people" would find a way around the ban confirmed the nature of these aggregate behaviors as irrevocable "forces" more than the ban's shortcomings.

The rhetorical aggregation of thousands of self-managed, individual boycotts into a force of its own and the credit card companies' cost-benefit decision to ignore judicial orders and pay the fines instead were different problems, but both reflected the core of neoclassical reason where actors act out their natures.[34] That the juridico-political order went against those natures not only was a problem in itself but evidenced that it either did not understand those natures or did not know how to assess them appropriately, or worse—did not know how to work with them, as one works with gravity, temperature, or water currents. From the perspective of the proposition that these relations transcended the juridico-political order's capacity to know, these judicial attempts amounted to a violation of an order that was both moral and natural, evidencing both a hubristic recalcitrance and a miscategorization of what was "really" at stake.[35] These natures did not need to play out as such, or to be salient in the way they were; but the sequence of governmental failures lent them collective cohesion and hardened the links between Uber's PR strategy and electromagnetism in Greater Buenos Aires, between the middle class's interjurisdictional dispersion and the international dispersion of Uber's financial infrastructure.

Hetherington refers to Latour's trials of strength as "trials of force": the capacity to endure is not a property inherent to the claim, in itself, or to the parts that support it, but lies in the relationships between the claims and their parts.[36] Uber was not only now entangled with economic forces, and its relations were not only cast in the moral language of choice and empowerment, as said in chapters 4 and 6 respectively. Its alignment with the behaviors and relations of the people who used its services, with the dispersion of population and infrastructure in the Greater Buenos Aires area, enhanced the difficulty of formulating an alternative and discredited those who attempted to do so on any terms. Whatever the "actual" nature of Uber and its relations was, hiding in between the natural, the normal, and the commonsensical, it was not, for these residents, one that the government was prepared to understand. A fortunate coincidence for the company and its supporters, one would think, if one did not think that this had been Uber's strategy from the beginning and that history and geography had dealt the government and the taxi industry a terribly unfortunate hand.

Allies and Claims

If the exact content of this proposition varied across specific utterances, after a month of trials of strength this middle class took as fact the need to find the "appropriate" way of relating to Uber relations.[37] Reading about Uber conflicts elsewhere, Francisco supported Mexico City's approach: 1.5 percent of the value of each ride should go to the state in taxes. For others, like Mariano, the justice should simply drop the case; and for still others, like Valentina and Uber's CEO, the justice should develop regulation suitable to platform economies, conflated with sharing economies in River Plate Spanish as *economías colaborativas*, "collaborative economies." Aside from the laissez-faire enthusiasm of Mariano's approach, these are variations of the foreclosing of disagreement through a technical grammar for the management of flows of commerce and electromagnetic waves.

Social scientists would of course agree that all of these solutions are profoundly political, and that all they do is change the ground of contention. The premise that the juridico-political order was of a nature inherently unfit to deal with the Uber conflict (and would, consequently, produce only inappropriate, absurd, or irrational strategies and policies) was in itself a huge disruption of the distribution of the sensible: infrastructure, electromagnetism, and the properties of matter were key sites of power relations.[38] Indeed, for Minister for Transportation Juan José Méndez, these power relations were of a known and familiar kind, just presented in a materially contorted way. Two years after these events, in the candid interview mentioned in previous chapters, he declared to national daily *La Nación* that during his meetings with Uber employees he felt as if he were negotiating with the Colombian terrorist group FARC.[39] Uber used the technological innovation argument around the world, he said, but the company seemed to be differentially aware of and responsive to jurisdictions and juridico-political orders: "With Uber there seems to be one kind of discussion for developed countries and another one for Latin American countries. Or they are more afraid of the French justice than of Argentina's justice."[40]

In this sense, the point here is the effective subordination of the common experience to economic relations so narrowly defined as forces and natures. As Latour would say, trials of strength are all about allies: the more a claim recruits and the thicker the network that joins them, the more enduring the claim will be.[41] Méndez embodied the executive power of a technocratic government more anxious to modernize Buenos Aires and Argentina than to determine what modernity could mean; it is ironic that he, of all people, was one of the most salient and possibly genuinely committed allies the taxi industry and Buenos Aires' juridico-political order had throughout this conflict. But Uber, a company seeking to expand its business, found in residents' frustrations and expectations an unusually unswerving ally.[42] Together with borders drawn in the late nineteenth century and the practices of credit card companies, what these middle classes understood as commensurate, ridiculous, or pertinent ways of understanding relations in late capitalism advanced the proposition on the company's behalf and preemptively pathologized genuine alternatives. Made of what passed for facts, not of what could count as knowledge, this proposition flew in the face of the law, the constitution, and a whole panoply of institutions many of these residents had just voted to respect, as the next chapter will show. As Méndez and the taxi industry learned, though porteños as they were they already probably intuited, it was not about whether technologies were, or were not, political, but about their contextual capacity to solder together the claim that they were simply beyond, or of a kind that required the distribution of the sensible to be purposefully subjugated to them.

8

The Scarlet P

AFTER WHAT SEGMENTS of Buenos Aires's middle class lived as twelve years of "hyperpoliticization," Macri's coalition presented the electorate with a canonically technocratic agenda premised on the refounding of the Republic, the resumption of trade, the "normalization" of international relations, and respect for law and institutions. This chapter shows how this narrative helped an exhausted middle class to understand present, past, and future experiences through technical, economic, and moral categories: power cuts, skyrocketing currency exchange rates, and various other processes and events were now intelligible not in political terms but as a sort of purge, indispensable punctuation marks on the path toward betterment.

This narrative also provided the means to write off those who resisted its categories, including, after Uber's arrival, the taxi industry. The latter's resistance, the protests and the fights, were taken as a matter of course and explained away as such, semicolons we had to put up with as the industry faded out. Aware that they were being written out of history, several actors in the industry engaged in what I call indexical reflexivity: an active, strategic performative work, visible and intelligible to, and aimed at, those whose categories organize the distribution of the sensible that explains one's disagreement away. This work involved performing a particular kind of civility during protests, insisting on the legal routes of the case, on the fact that the judicial power largely agreed with them and on exposing the incongruent position that middle class put itself in, validating in its popular support for Uber the company's assault on the institutional order they sought to protect. It was a labor, ultimately, aimed at removing a mark they were carrying by someone else's design: that of the Political, that of Peronism, and that of the Past.

People of Their Times

In 2015, the international press portrayed Mauricio Macri as an outsider to Argentine politics, but in most senses of these terms this was not really true. Through his father, Italian-born multimillionaire Franco Macri, the extended family had been involved in logistical and cultural industries and public services in Argentina for decades. In 1995 Mauricio became president of the world-famous Argentine soccer club Boca Juniors, developing his public persona from within the fungible, Gatsby-esque iconicity of jet-setters, politicians, *vedettes*, and high-flying businesspeople proper to late capitalism. Argentines understood this aesthetic prematurely: Perón, charismatic military and political leader, and his wife Eva, trained actress whose dramatic gravitas emerging technologies of mass political communication would reward, naturalized in the 1940s the borrowings between show business, business, and national politics that Macri's techno-pop slickness would fit with ease.[1] His "formal" entrance into the circuits of party democracy in 2003 was neither surprising nor historically unintelligible, and, as far as Argentines are concerned, he had always been some sort of insider.[2]

On June 24, 2003, Mauricio Macri founded in Buenos Aires the political "front" Commitment for Change, "a pluralistic militancy behind Macri's leadership, focused on serving the people and solving their problems."[3] Drawing from across the party spectrum, including of course Peronist variations, its members committed themselves not to negotiating across conflicting stakes but to performing and capitalizing on the premise that political allegiances, fragmented interests, and electoral strategizing were an atavistic hindrance to Argentina's progress. This may or may not have really been the extent of these "statesmen's" political imaginations, but the time was ripe to market themselves in these terms to Argentina's electorate, battered by the 2001 debt default and resentful of traditional parties and political institutions. Participation in business and the world outside partisan politics not only was not frowned upon but confirmed that one was not "in it for the money"; it symbolized one's distance from ideological passions and one's first-degree kinship with the bleached realpolitik of problem solving. Macri would remain president of the multimillion Boca Juniors brand for four more years.

On May 25, 2003, days before this organization was founded, Argentines had elected Néstor Kirchner, Peronist governor of the province of Santa

Cruz, as president. His wife and lifelong political ally Cristina Fernández de Kirchner had been national senator for that province since 2001. Amid the economic and political rubble of 2001, Kirchner was a leap of faith: faith in Peronism, its mediation machine, and its mythical capacities to save Argentines in the last hour, but also faith in someone most Argentines outside his largely unpopulated province had never even heard of.[4] Charismatic, cynical, astute, intelligent, Kirchner launched a heterodox model of fiscal and monetary expansionism that, depending on one's interlocutor, promoted economic growth at fabulous rates and alleviated poverty or overheated the economy toward its precrisis levels.[5]

His style was memorably confrontational in the friend-foe logics of populism, and these years were rife with conflicts with the historically powerful agricultural sector, with mainstream media and with anyone questioning Kirchner's particular kind of historical revisionism.[6] Militant organizations entered as such several governmental administrations. As said in earlier chapters, Argentines broke into two camps: the Ks, or Kirchner supporters, and the anti-Ks. There were Peronists on both sides, but Kirchner relied heavily and spontaneously on Peronist iconography, as would his wife later on, and his political ways were historically intelligible through the impassioned dichotomies that Peronism reproduced. In 2007 Cristina Fernández de Kirchner ran for president and Macri ran for the office of chief of government of the city of Buenos Aires. They both won; Fernández de Kirchner took over from her husband and, resigning from the presidency of Boca Juniors seven days before being sworn in, Macri began his political career in institutional terms. Perennially anti-Peronist and then anti-K, the city became a natural electoral stronghold for Macri; "anti-K" and "Macri" began to converge. By the time both Macri and Fernández de Kirchner were reelected to their respective positions in 2011, their actively political supporters saw in the other side the exact negation of their convictions.

Intensified by his wife, Néstor Kirchner's expansionist, protectionist, and confrontational model was by now showing signs of exhaustion well known to Argentines from crises past: inflation spiraled into trimestral double digits, national reserves dwindled, and international transactions were restricted and then effectively banned in 2012. Birthed as a capitalist country within the patterns of nineteenth-century world trade, Argentina never attained economic self-reliance in several key sectors; entire industries and vast swathes of small and medium companies went bust for lack of anything from certain nonferrous metals to books in foreign languages to some kinds of ink.[7] By early 2015, forty-three fellow World Trade Organization members were threatening retaliation.[8] Trivial transactions had become absurdly convoluted: to buy earplugs from abroad, Francisco had to register as an importer and fill in enhanced tax declarations. Valentina's oven, in her own kitchen, was wholly manufactured in Argentina except for a part that ensured the knobs stayed in place, as she found out when it broke and the retailer could not replace it. Mariano asked me to bring him a book, as Amazon did not deliver in Argentina. For a trip to neighboring Brazil, where Pablo was organizing a small film festival, Mariano had to purchase Brazilian currency illegally, in the unlit basement of a travel agent.

Meanwhile, as the national bureau for census and statistics redefined the rate of inflation, Fernández de Kirchner's opponents decried what they defined as the manipulation of national numbers for political gain. The government outlawed the private production of inflation indexes, accusing its opponents of sabotage by a "coup de market," and halted the production of poverty indexes, arguing that they were "stigmatizing."[9] Months later, one of Kirchner's ministers declared that Argentina had fewer people in poverty than Germany; boasting on her CV of a master's-level degree she had not finished, at twenty-six years of age Delfina Rossi, daughter of another of Fernández de Kirchner's ministers, was made director of Argentina's National Bank.[10]

The sense that politics had taken over residents' lives intensified during the austral summer of 2014–15. During a heat wave, whole areas of Buenos Aires, the second-wealthiest city in South America, spent days, even weeks, without electricity. As melted ice cream and rotten milk streamed from small businesses in the sweltering heat, government officials blamed the avarice of utility companies who wanted the national project to fail. Companies replied that with frozen tariffs amid spiraling inflation it was impossible to repair infrastructure, never mind invest. Shortly afterward, on January 18, 2015, federal prosecutor Alberto Nisman was found dead in his apartment. The following day he was due to testify against Fernández de Kirchner in a case concerning collusion with Iran around the terrorist attacks against the Argentine Jewish community in 1994. The case made world headlines, as did the government's insistence that Nisman had committed suicide; for anyone who disagreed with the K project, as Argentine intellectual Beatriz Sarlo put it to the national senate, Nisman's death "marks us forever. . . . I see a people realizing that forces have been unleashed, forces it does not understand and that maybe nobody will ever be able to dominate."[11]

Amid other forms of institutional disintegration, the General Confederation of Labor broke into two; as said in chapter 1, taxi union leader Viviani remained loyal to the president, helping run the half that was on her side and securing his name on the ballot for the city parliament under her wing. Fernández de Kirchner could not run again for president in 2015; her husband Néstor had died in 2010. Lifelong Peronist and governor of the province of Buenos Aires, Daniel Scioli was put forward as the K candidate. Mauricio Macri did run, his first presidential attempt, spearheading a broad national coalition called Cambiemos, Let's Change. Alliances with older and regional parties offered his technocratic "front" the capacity to penetrate the vastness of Argentina beyond his natural stronghold in metropolitan Buenos Aires.

During this campaign, as I said in chapter 1, Macri tried to seduce the Peronist electorate by erecting a statue of Perón in Buenos Aires. The scale of the gaffe only confirmed the one sense in which Macri was perhaps truly an outsider: aside from some misinformed PR assistant, nobody in Argentina would have believed Macri to have the political imagination or the statecraft character to believably harness the forest of symbols of any political party, much less those of the strongest political myth in Argentine life. But in late 2015, when ovens did not work and inflation calculators were called traitors, his incapacity for depth of ritual was framed as an innate virtue and vaunted as such. Elocution lessons filed his posh cadence away without affecting his propensity to aseptic banality, and more than ever Macri could carry with exceptionally natural ease the burden of being the ultimate icon: that of the idea that icons should be no more.

Past and Future in terms of the Present

Argentina is a federalist country whose provincial, municipal, and national electoral cycles for legislative and executive powers sometimes overlap. They did in late 2015. Let's Change put candidates forward at all these levels. It promised a "re-founding of the Republic," including the "normalization" of financial and commercial transactions; a geopolitical realignment away from Venezuela, Bolivia, and Iran and toward a broadly defined community of nations; megainvestments in transportation and energy infrastructures to "reactivate" the nation and its regional economies; a technical meritocracy to "reinstitutionalize" the nation; and the "reconstruction" of national indexes.

Macri's coalition won not only the national presidency but also the positions of governor of the province of Buenos Aires and chief of government of the Autonomous City of Buenos Aires, a trifecta beyond its supporters' wildest dreams. The province of Buenos Aires had been governed by Peronism since 1987, and the millions in its industrial belts right outside the city of Buenos Aires were imagined as its unshakable bastion. Let's Change's candidate, María Eugenia Vidal, was a technocrat, a non-Peronist, and a woman, in a nation and a province where space for women in politics was still mediated by Eva Perón's figure.[12] For the first time since the position of chief of government of the Autonomous City of Buenos Aires had been created in the mid-1990s, these three executives, by far the wealthiest and most powerful in the nation, were joined under the same political banner. The tone was one of wild expectation, and the grammar was superlative throughout, across detractors and supporters alike.

This unimaginable success was openly qualified even by Macri's electorate. Among my informants, only Mariano and Francisco had voted for him with some conviction. To many residents in the middle of the middle class, Macri appeared on the ballot, and also affectively, as the only alternative to a rapidly rotting Potemkin village propped up by rabid and rather sloppy ideologues. His coalition exploited this polarization, framing the Ks as an excess of politics, which is probably one of the reasons Macri never spoke of his party: during his first address to the nation, upon being sworn in on December 10, 2015, he mentioned his "team" eleven times. A presidential speech is not there to be examined for truth value, but its writers captured sublimely the political imagination of a depleted and resigned electorate, running out of ink and electricity, whose experience was ripe to be framed in ways where political ritual and calculation converged:

> To me, politics is not a competition between leaders to see who has the largest ego. It is the work of modern leaders who work as a team to serve others. Politics is not the stage for lying and cheating the people and the world with fake data. . . . I see this country as one large team of millions. In the last century our society privileged individual leaders . . . ; in the twenty-first century we have understood that things work when we work as a team, joining efforts, professionalism, experience, and the good intentions of many. . . . I have put together great teams who created concrete solutions to people's problems. We want everyone in, Right, Left, Peronists and anti-Peronists . . . ; this is what millions of Argentines asked for, tired of bullying and years of pointless confrontation, . . . fanaticism and violence. We will work to

inspire among Argentines an ethics of progress and self-development. We cannot think and manage our work, health, or security through old ideas. We must tackle our problems with new resources and boldness in ideas . . . . We tell the world: we are the children of this time, and we try to understand it without prejudice or resentment. . . . I want to promise, finally, to always be sincere with you. Part of this sincerity is to say, now, that the challenges ahead are enormous and we will not be able to solve our problems from one day to the next. But great transformations happen step by step, and thus, I assure you, we will be every day a little better.[13]

Celebrated as ideologically flat, the "team" was composed of PhDs in economics, political science, and finance from LSE, CUNY, and the Universities of Buenos Aires, Chicago, and Michigan; and CEOs and board members of the Argentine and regional branches of JP Morgan, PriceWaterhouse Coopers, and General Motors, among others. Some lacked prior political or partisan affiliation; others had circulated around the party landscape, such as Lino Barañao, minister of science, technology, and innovative production, who was working under Fernández de Kirchner's cabinet. His continuation under the Macri administration was presented as an example of postpolitical, sensible, expert-driven consensus beyond ideological allegiances.

This speech belongs in the genre of standardized closure a winner gives to a recurrent rite of passage in democracies: the contained, temporary antagonistic contest of election cycles. But with epochal sagacity, out of a modular frame its writers stylized, and capitalized on, a process that was already under way in residents' imagination. This was the process that Koselleck defines as temporalization: a framing of experience by linking it to past and future, generating the experiences, categories, and rationalities to explain the times we were living in, the ones we had lived in, and the ones that would come.[14] Economists and industrial leaders of various political allegiances had been warning that it would take years to reconstruct national indexes, lower inflation, and recreate international commerce arrangements obliterated by hastily set blanket bans. "Do you have any idea what it is going to take to rebuild this country? To lower inflation, to create jobs for people chronically dependent on state aid, to rehire and train technicians to reconstruct inflation indexes, to populate national administrations with people who are prepared for the job, instead of the son or cousin of someone in power?" Pablo asked during dinner with him and Mariano before Macri was sworn in.

The speech framed the electoral result as a victory over *years* of "pointless confrontation," vaguely equalized with obsolescence, fanaticism, and an insincerity whose time, as we shall soon see, was literally up. These millions of bodies had now been separated from their passions and partisan allegiances and asked to work together in the project of a nation emancipated from political time. The time of infighting and competing dissolved into developmental days, weeks, and months adding up to a horizon of expectation heralded by hard work and expert knowledge rhetorically depoliticized. This was, we were to believe from the mathematics of the electoral cycle, what the majority of Argentines wanted, least disliked, or believed in. As we will see, the terms of this temporalization offered the incoming administration a sizable margin of action—not necessarily because it was taken literally or as an unquestionable truth, but because it met the middle class halfway, enhancing the experience of a purge with a temporal grammar whose technical, economic, and moral categories could write off the political as excess and any excesses as political, including bodies and claims legitimate in the strict order of things.

Macroeconomic Salvation

Temporalization works as a strategy for a government and as a frame for experience for residents because single processes need not be addressed, or even imagined, individually. It opens the way to various rationalities that punctuate the experience of the present and give it a sense and direction with respect to the distribution of the sensible emerging from a purge.[15] Pablo and Mariano had been waiting for years to buy US dollars, a common strategy among Argentine middle classes to flee the vagaries of the Argentine peso.[16] Although the government reestablished currency exchanges a week after taking office as per one of their most spoken-of electoral promises, Pablo and Mariano decided to wait until the exchange rate was "normalized." For several days they still had no US dollars, but this was now an economic decision guided by economic, technical, and historical reasons, since they knew, as most Argentines do, that after stifled demand exchange rates often overshoot. Thus, in their disposition and in the government's narrative, the categories and rationalities that punctuated the experience of the present were explicitly nonpolitical and were explicitly discussed and mobilized as corrective of problems emerging from political categories and rationalities. The "normalization" of currency exchanges was celebrated less as a triumph of free commerce philosophy and more as a return to a path that had been interrupted for "political" reasons.

"Normalization" as a trope lends a moral character to the parts and rationalities it doles out. As chapter 4 shows, postpolitical reasoning often takes on a moral authority by association with objective, natural, technical, or other reasons understood to precede or supersede the political. The government exploited this moral momentum through the category of *sinceramiento*: a neologism from the verb *sincerar*, to render sincere, transparent, raw, and honest, evoking the opposition between what is true and naked, or sincere, and what is veiled and clothed, invoking a recurrent moral allegory for progress since the nineteenth century.[17] A particularly contentious policy during the K years had been to heavily subsidize electricity bills across metropolitan Buenos Aires. Defenders of the policy argued that a welfare state should engage in such redistributive action to ensure that the poor could access basic services. Its detractors retorted that the blanket subsidy was hardly "redistributive," since it benefited districts whose GDP was closer to that of inner London than that of marginal Argentine districts, where electricity was three times as costly and where residents were among the poorest in the nation. Constituting a third of Argentina's population, metropolitan Buenos Aires's electorate swung any national election, which lent traction to the latter's argument that the subsidy was a rhetorical veil hiding a political intention.

In one of the first press conferences of the decade, in itself framed as an act of brave sincerity, the government explained that because of the labyrinth of ad hoc policies, subsidies, and differentially frozen tariffs, electricity infrastructure had not been updated in years. Works would begin soon, but we had to be aware that they would take years, that in the meantime further power cuts would be likely, and also, that in order to invest in this infrastructure, utility bills would have to rise. *Sinceramiento* was thus an economic, technical, and moral category: it made joint sense of a present process to leave behind the insincere, political rationality of subsidies and of future price hikes and power cuts. Like most of my informants, Valentina expressly agreed with what was to her a matter of common sense. She participated in a government-led scheme to swap older lightbulbs for LEDs, which were more expensive but cheaper to run, thus paying off in the long term, and convinced her parents to do so too. She kept a stack of candles just in case, but electricity provision, like currency exchanges, was now removed from political temporalities and inserted into a processual horizon whose hiccups were already accounted for. If the lights worked, great; if not, we had all been warned, and we could give ourselves a reason so that *both* light and no light were "anchored retrospectively from that futuristic point."[18] Like many other temporalizing rationalities, *sinceramiento* did not just displace the political but colonized its processes, times, and categories from within, helping temporalization assign the parts and arguments for a new distribution of the sensible unfurling before our eyes.

Uber's platform and the national project of a late capitalist technocrat were too obviously aligned for anyone to reflect too much on the causal sequence of events. But as we know from previous chapters, most porteños, including taxi drivers, assumed that the absence of Uber in Argentina was due to the union's connivance with Fernández de Kirchner. The exact reason the company arrived only in 2016 we may never know, but in any case Uber transactions cleared in international currencies, blocked by Fernández de Kirchner for reasons of magnitude far greater than Viviani's loyalty. Only when Macri's government "normalized" currency exchanges on December 17, 2015, were the international flows of capital set for Uber to arrive. The capacity of this detail to fly under the radar of most residents, while they still believed Macri's presidency and Uber belonged together, in fact reinforced the experiential, logical, and affective fertility of temporalization as a process. Currency exchanges, price hikes, infrastructural investments, and renewed press conferences condensed into a historical "collective singular": their specific causalities could remain wholly unknown yet be imagined as collectively entwined with the postpolitical future they punctuated and were to bring about.[19]

This is, of course, not a coincidence. Guyer's notion of punctuation draws directly from notions of time in neoclassical macroeconomics, a rich rhetorical quarry for a processual imagination of the future as an all-round economic optimum where deviations are technically overcome. As she shows, this is also the temporalization of religious salvation, punctuating and creating present experiences with respect to a long-term future of grace. For those who believe in either, that is, in salvation or in a macroeconomic order beyond deviance, the site and nature of the teleological horizon ahead, never back, are not up for debate: they will come in due course through hard work, efficient tariffs, and painful but sincere introspection. One either accepts them or not, but in the distribution of the sensible emerging from December 2015 this was not a symmetrical choice, or one between remotely comparable parts. In an exceptional partisan configuration, under the promise of overhauling the national economy toward that salvation after years of vice, to fight the purge, the punctuation, and their categories was to be damned.

Those Who Refuse to Let Go

Two weeks before Uber launched its platform, Jorge Lanata, one of Argentina's most famous journalists, interviewed Soledad Lago Rodríguez, Uber's communications manager for the Southern Cone, for the radio show I referenced earlier in the book.[20] In this show's broad audience converged the middle classes that would constitute Uber's market and much of the electorate that had spent the summer throwing rotten food away and considered itself sovereignly gaslighted on the matter of the murder of a federal prosecutor. As Lago Rodríguez vaunted Uber's efficiency and reassured audiences that the launch was on, no matter what, one of the show's interviewers asked: "In Argentina there's a particular context. . . . Two weeks ago the Central Bank announced it would switch from paper to digital bank statements, which as a technological development simplifies several things, is environment-friendly, et cetera; and [a truck drivers' union prominent figure] and his men organized a strike outside the bank. No person, no truck would leave or enter the bank until paper statements were reestablished so that no jobs would be lost. In such a unionized context, do you think it will be easy for Uber to launch its operations in Argentina?"

She answered evasively, but example and allegory had set the tone. "Only in this country could this ever happen," Lanata exclaimed. "Anywhere else in the world they would send you your bank statement via email. Paper! Why not send it on a stone, engraved? Where are newspaper correctors? Linotype setters? Why stop something which is better for everyone?" As they framed experience, economic, technical, and other-than-political categories refused to allow themselves to be read as political: they replaced actual disagreement, genuinely competing stakes, with the moral register of right and wrong that Lanata's exasperation was steeped in.[21] They also shored up the sorting out of parts and their respective participation in the experience of temporalization by delineating what could be rightfully and righteously debated, how and by whom: in other words, they provided the reasoning that foreclosed the political.

Of course, these other-than-political categories could themselves become the site of disagreement—could themselves become political.[22] For example, a particular paperless strategy could be shown to be less environmentally friendly than another because of server space or other considerations and this could generate disagreement. Also, someone could, in fact, make a compelling moral case for saving jobs. But what this affair outside the bank shows, and what Uber's conflict would go on to magnify, was first that temporalization categorized (and depoliticized) at a larger and looser scale without losing in precision or intensity. This was the scale of "everyone," which included, for example, Valentina's reasoning about lightbulbs, within a logic greater than those of the process at stake. Second, temporalization categorized by triangulating *already existing relations*, processes, and bodies. Just as electricity infrastructure was temporalized on the basis of what was at the time when this reasoning became salient, and not on the basis of a presumed time zero, a union leader, particularly one openly opposed to the incoming government, did not enter the temporalization unmarked. The political and that which had to be depoliticized were quite marked from the start, and several orders of magnitude away from, and more urgent than, the microprocesses of going paperless.

In this sense, Buenos Aires in effective lockdown over what the middle class saw as a technically, economically, and environmentally optimal decision "better for everyone" reminded those residents that the Political their temporalization was confining to the Past was not letting go. It also confirmed that whatever symbolic, material, processual, or affective triangulations between Peronism as a mediation machine, the Political, and the Past Let's Change had sought to entomb in that infamous statue still haunted the shared experience where this middle class was reassigning parts.

The protests outside the bank were, in their concrete materiality and in their claim, a competing stake in the emerging hierarchies to the technocratic distribution of the sensible that assigned innovations, sustainability, and progress a specific place, however oversimplified that place might be upon reflection, and that shut out others with respect to it, like workers that would presumably lose their jobs. They were a political intervention, in the most concrete, institutional sense of the political embodied by unions like this one, and in the more general sense of a resistance to a temporalization where the political was being not only displaced but written off. Much to the exasperation of Lanata and millions of residents, paper statements were reinstated, exacerbating everyone's conviction that the impact of Uber's arrival, by then "imminent," would be spectacular. Consistently, far more than moral dismissal awaited those on the wrong side of the temporalization frontier.

The very day that Lanata interviewed Lago Rodríguez, Uber conducted an induction seminar at the historic hotel Castelar, built in the Beaux Arts style proper to 1920s Buenos Aires at the 1152 of Avenida de Mayo. Local pied-à-terre of poets Federico García Lorca and Norah Lange, the hotel is architecturally protected as part of the avenue's heritage ensemble, but during the hours of the induction taxi drivers smashed every single window on the building's facade, confirming that the conflict would play out in domains other than courts and Twitter. "They are showing themselves to be what we always said they were—savages. They will not stop until someone's killed," said Pablo, urging Mariano not to use Uber until things settled down. Mariano refused: "This does not change anything. It was obvious they would react like this, and complain to politicians and trigger a legal case, and this will not stop until the government clears Uber. People will start to use it anyway, eventually it will be legalized; what do taxi drivers think will happen? The sooner they get used to it the better it will be for them."

Mariano had started driving for Uber right away. His resolve probably stemmed more from a cocky sense of carelessness than from a fully reasoned strategy, but from the outset in his reasoning the union's resistance, like power outages while the government sorted out infrastructure, was already accounted for and explained away as punctuation along a path of *sinceramiento*. It was an inevitable semicolon marking the way to somewhere else. Although only the most daring among the victorious read in Peronism's electoral defeat the actual demise of whatever Peronism was, many among Macri's electorate wanted to see the entire overhauling of the national economy, the social contract, the body politic of the nation— they discussed these things in these very terms. Resistance to this technocratic, postpolitical project was not "just" morally sanctioned: blockades and smashed windows represented the factionalism, privileges, and vested interests this temporalization pathologized, all encrypted in what Macri called "the challenges ahead."

Many other actors and voices were explained away, shut down, sidelined as white noise; but for all the reasons explored throughout this book, not one of them was written off in as literal *and* symbolic a way as the taxi industry even before the first window was smashed. Uber embodied the rationalities of technological innovation and economic development, both of which already explained away frictions as teething problems in logics of evolutionary or continuous improvement. As chapter 5 shows, Uber's was a world saga, local conflicts foretold sensationally as iterations of each other and naturalized to the point of appearing as beyond politics.[23] The public visibility of taxi drivers' union leader Omar Viviani during the conflict only confirmed its cultural association to these residents' low opinion of unions, of Peronism's mediation machine, and of the just-defeated K project. Uber's rhetoric of individual empowerment and freedom had not only succeeded in equating the taxi industry with an unfair, almost irrational monopoly, and its members with Luddites withholding progress from everyone else; it was teasing Argentines at a time where several other bans and restrictions were being lifted in a general spirit of resumption of an alleged normality that now, retrospectively, seemed to have been withheld.

Indexing What They Are

As seen above in Mariano's reasoning, even utterances legitimate in Argentina's institutional order, such as pleading for one's rights or protesting in public space, were preemptively subsumed in the temporalization of experience in ways that effectively wrote them off as white noise. *Of course* they would start a legal case; *of course* they would complain; *of course* they would fight competitors away. This "ofcourseness" meant that in many ways the case, the complaints, and the strike *were* part of that experience but *had* no part it. Valentina took taxi drivers' violence with resignation, but as matter-of-factly as Mariano did. She felt for them, as a collective, but just as we were all bracing for violence, we would all end up accommodating to the reality of Uber. She knew there was a legal case, Valentina retorted to my insistence, "but the reality is after all that the law is not fit for technological innovations, here or anywhere in the world. They should sit down with Viviani and find a way out, as they did everywhere else in the world where now Uber is running." She was the one that brought to my attention the case I mentioned in chapter 4 of the Peronist and Kirchnerist parliamentarian who ended up driving for Uber: "For you, now that you've Peronized yourself!"

On April 13, twenty-four hours after Uber's arrival, taxi drivers simultaneously blockaded twenty-five intersections for an entire hour. The bus system was paralyzed and the subway could not cope. Hundreds of thousands were stranded as police forces, newscast vans, and journalists monitored the protesters and the unfolding chaos. I was at one of the protests, surrounded by news vehicles and by reporters armed with cameras on shoulders, on tripods, and atop cars; microphones, smartphones, and all sorts of paraphernalia occasionally teased out statements from the protesters and kept watch on their most minute actions. A reporter approached a young driver to my right to ask whether they were ready to compete with Uber, which was being downloaded at a dizzying pace and "becoming the new reality." The driver pleaded for reasonability: "These people don't pay taxes, don't invest anything, don't have professional driving permits or commercial transportation insurance; it's not just unfair competition, it's illegal. . . ." Cutting him off midphrase, the reporter asked whether he did not think it was time they modernized and improved their service; as the driver stammered out that the average life of a taxi car was just four years, a snarky voice in the crowd asked whether they were not hurting their very own cause by showing themselves to be against progress and people's freedom to choose. Noticing this interaction, a union representative hurried to us as the cameras closed in on the now visibly anxious young driver and explained in a rehearsed clinical tone that the union and other representatives had channeled the industry's complaints legally. Meanwhile a motorcycle rider meandered between the taxis, swearing against the union, the "taxi mafia," yelling that if they really cared about their job they would be actually working and providing a better service instead of preventing others from going about their days and de facto resorting to disrupting everyone else's life. "Band of thieves!" he screamed as he navigated the last cars, and sped off yelling "Viva Uber," middle finger raised at us.

The swift reaction from the union delegate and the aseptic response to what was in fact a provocation are clues to how these people understood the problem they faced. The industrial and economic conflict where their very livelihood was at stake, never mind other considerations like legality and urban order, was entrapped in a tautology. Licenses, union prerogatives, opportunism, monopolies, Viviani, an alleged refusal to let people choose: as of April 12, 2016, in the experience of the temporalization we were living they began to pass for each other—and crucially, for taxi drivers themselves. Several in the taxi industry realized immediately that they were entangled in the particular logics that according to Bill Maurer certain financial derivatives follow. This conflict had been written for them in terms such that they had become that which they indexed, and they were indexing that which they were: all those excesses passed for the taxi industry, and the taxi industry passed for them.[24] Not only were Uber itself and the conflict depoliticized and explained away, but the shadow of the Political denouncing specific bodies, materials, or actions had expanded to a perfect mark the size of whatever they were or did.

This tautology shaped the sheer possibility to react or reply, whether as a collective or as individuals, in ways that transcended numbers, relative strength, or arguments: it blocked every possible avenue for talking back, for effectively reclaiming a part of the experience in ways that prevented others from shutting them out. Sometimes this is possible: as Abélès and Badaró show, four cotton-producing African nations fought to set an extremely unequal tariff conflict with developed nations in the terms of fair trade, a foundational WTO principle, instead of its treatment as a developmental affair, which set the scales against them. These countries expressly attempted to reshuffle the terms in which the conversation would be had in the first place, removing themselves from a position where by definition they were at a disadvantage, as underdeveloped players who needed to be led by others, and constituting themselves through the properties had by those who denied them a part: equals around the same table, where fair was fair.[25] In other words, this was a repoliticization of the conflict.

The taxi industry's problem was different: How to resist being written off by others without confirming, *in the very rhetorical and material act of challenging them*, the reasons those others were writing one off in the first place? How to challenge being dismissed and the grounds for the dismissal when the very act of challenging the dismissal had already been explained away as the reason why one was being dismissed? In other words, in protesting, initiating legal action, and mobilizing bodies, cars, institutions—in fact, in the very act of driving around and picking up passengers with a license now reframed as an unfair monopoly—the taxi industry and any of them were confirming their part as a semicolon already accounted for. The Political that belonged in the Past had collapsed onto them.

Indexical Reflexivity

After months of near-daily strikes, Macri's administration issued a "protest protocol" requiring that all street protests allow a whole lane for vehicles to circulate. Some protests abided by it, some were forced to abide by it, some went under the radar; but during the three protests against Uber I attended, blocking major intersections, someone always took on the task of ensuring that a lane was kept clear at all times. During the protest referenced above, a taxi driver instructed our small group: "Do not react to the provocation, do not touch any cars, keep the lane clear, do not overflow into the sidewalk. We stay for exactly one hour." This anxiously managed orderliness is extremely uncommon in protests in Buenos Aires, where all too often the deliberate testing of certain boundaries is in itself part of the political message. Protesters engaged pedestrians in conversation, some apologizing and explaining that this was the first time in years that the taxi industry had blocked the streets (to the best of my knowledge this was indeed the case), for as workers in transit they knew personally how disruptive it was, but that given the circumstances they had no choice. Someone even helped an elderly resident cross the street. An experience that the middle classes usually understand in terms of bravado and excess was playing out like a boys' choir gathering on a Sunday afternoon.

Soon after the first ride on April 12, ambushes began: taxi drivers or their friends and families would download Uber's passenger interface, request a car, and direct the driver somewhere near a police station, where other taxi drivers would surround the car until the police arrived. Later that week, one of the drivers I met at Dionisio's returned from taking part in the ambushes; they had also been instructing each other to avoid touching the car or even addressing the driver. The government had warned that Uber activities broke city laws, and city authorities were towing Uber cars away; these taxi drivers became vigilante bailiffs, as it were, rather than executioners, working with city authorities and the police in what was effectively playing out as an impromptu, slightly surreal, yet impeccably integrated governmental exercise. Ambushers chanted, recorded the event, and circulated the footage to the media and among themselves and their WhatsApp and Facebook groups.

This monitoring, curating, and choreographing of actions, spaces, and interventions of self and others aimed less at the "actual" stakes (the industrial, legal, and economic conflict reviewed throughout this book) than at the terms of the tautology that foreclosed the conflict and silenced their part, writing their reasons off as unworthy of being genuinely discussed. I will refer to the awareness of the difficulties of this tautology and to the acting on them as *indexical reflexivity*: an active, strategic performative work, visible and intelligible to, and aimed at, those whose categories organize the distribution of the sensible that explains away one's condition of disagreement. Indexical reflexivity is the work the industry had to engage in in order to avoid being written off, to try to be actually heard, to even attempt to participate in the emerging distribution of the sensible, regardless of success, if only to later be dismissed again.

Indexical reflexivity took different material, discursive, and affective forms. To a great degree it was of an adverbial quality: in the literal sense of the grammar, tone, and modifiers making a point; in the figurative sense of *how* one protested, stood with respect to a lane and chose discursive outlets; and in the broader sense that one's approach to the stakes needed to work through the circumstances, the conditions of those stakes. Several of these senses I have illustrated above. Early on in the conflict I met the leader of a taxi propietarios' chamber who was being interviewed by dozens of radio and TV shows as well as national and regional dailies. Having studied social sciences at university, he was articulate, well-spoken, and quick to think on his feet and could handle the legal and rhetorical detail of the case in front of cameras and audiences with clinical detachment. He also had that intuitive astuteness indispensable to identify, and resist provocation by, reporters seeking to bait him into any comment, action, or voice inflexion to be passed as proof of the taxi industry's opposition to "what is good for everyone."

His bottom line was *Tenemos que desmarcarnos*. The verb *desmarcar* translates literally as "to remove a mark." Its reflexive version, *desmarcarse*, to remove a mark from oneself, evokes in River Plate Spanish what soccer players do to wriggle out of the opposite team's man-marking. The bottom line thus translates literally as "We have to remove the mark from ourselves." The strategy agreed on with other industry leaders was to emphasize that the taxi industry was not alone in insisting on Uber's illegality: city authorities and judges had explicitly pronounced on Uber in these terms, thus making it more difficult to isolate and pathologize the taxi drivers and their cause. As he put it to me, "Even Juan José Méndez [minister of transportation for the city of Buenos Aires] agrees, and he is on Macri's side!" Not only did the minister insist that the company was ostentatiously breaking local laws; he was already making the point I referenced in chapter 7, that "Uber seems to have one kind of discussion with developed countries and another one with Latin American countries," comparing Uber with the FARC.[26]

Taxi industry leaders also harnessed the very terms of residents' temporalization to "dismark" the cause, and with it the trade and its arguments. The more militant among them spoke of "resistance" and used other such explicitly political terminology, but the general and concerted strategy was to perform impeccable civility intelligible as such to the middle class, and a calm, procedural reasonability full of technical, economic, and legal details and void of inflamed language. They also enrolled technocratic authorities and middle-class aspirations to that technocratic horizon to remove the mark upon themselves. Macri's campaign had explicitly promised a middle class "sick" of corruption and nepotism a return to the rule of law and respect to the institutions. Was a judge's decision that Uber was flouting the law not an institution to respect? The industry leader I mentioned above pushed this point publicly, performing both the coherence and respect of law of the taxi industry and the unfair inconsistency of these middle classes, who claimed to support the universal rule of law and bandied about the term *taxi mafia*, but asked that the law be reinvented so that it did not stand in Uber's way. He collected evidence from Frankfurt, France, and several US states, learning dates, cities, and conflict-specific information by heart. He made the point tirelessly: either Uber worked with professional drivers and obeyed judicial instructions, or in most countries of that developed world that Uber supporters sought to emulate the company had already been banned, fined, or forced to adjust itself to local laws, not the other way round. Indexical reflexivity was constantly seeking to manage two sides of the same coin: to demonstrate that the taxistas' claim did, in fact, belong in this reasonable, technical order, as this evidence showed, and that it could not be written off as the political, not so long as the political was equated to vice.

The Razor's Edge

To call indexical reflexivity a work of performance is not to dismiss it as contrived, staged, or any less "real," but to emphasize that those who engage in it know that to be effective it must be seen and understood by others in specific ways. This book has shown postpolitical reasoning worked through technical, moral, natural, economic, and affective categories; this particular leader made a point to try to touch on them all, as he explained during one of my interviews: "We are in favor of competition, and we are the first to admit we must improve as an industry. We are not even asking for Uber to leave the city outright; we are asking for it to abide by laws and, if it is going to take a cut of each trip and create work relations, then it should pay taxes and social charges, call its drivers 'employees' and their remuneration 'salaries,' and obey the law that should hold for everyone. If not, why are we accepting a rule breaker with such open arms?" The industry was working hard to "modernize" itself, the term on everyone's lips, and several taxi associations had been developing apps. Soon after, the city government launched BA Taxi, its own taxi app for the city.

Aside from all the effort that can go into it, as with most performative work, the effectiveness of indexical reflexivity depends to a great extent on its audience, and on its capacity to reframe and negotiate the categories that organize the dismissal. One polite and well-spoken taxi driver before the cameras would not accomplish this. Interviewers pressed taxi representatives on the matter of safety by evoking Miguel Lecuna's murder in 2001, detailed in chapter 1, after a decade and a half and hundreds of millions of uneventful taxi rides. Residents skeptical that the industry was effectively controlled, as shown in chapters 1 and 3, and convinced that it operated like a mafia, as explained in chapter 5, did not receive well the insistence that the taxi industry was far more controlled than anyone believed, and much more *en blanco* than most industries in the city. They took it mostly as defensive and exaggerated lies, furthering the dismissal of the taxistas' cause—irrespective of which kind of transportation was "better" or "safer."

These categories were particularly difficult to reframe because they were encased in the logics of residents' temporalization of several processes, relations, and bodies at stake in this conflict. The fact that the taxi industry refused to acknowledge the gladiatorial truth of popular support as the ultimate site of a legitimate moral order, as chapter 4 explains, passed in itself for evidence that they knew they were benefiting from the unfair monopoly that supported them at the expense of everyone else. Besides, the very act of blocking one of the busiest corners of the city to protest what the middle classes saw as an inevitable technological innovation was in itself an affront to the premise of order. The launch of the city's app was received sardonically by many Uber supporters—not least since it verified their argument that the logics of a competition whose intricacies one did not really need to understand had forced the industry to "improve" their service, as shown in chapter 5. This could be a sensible assessment, to the extent that had Uber not arrived, BA Taxi would perhaps not have been developed; but the launch of the city's app did not change in the slightest Uber's business model in Argentina, its approach to local laws and authorities, or the legal case that had never stopped trying to pin it down. The emergence of this local app confirmed in the experience of this present that Uber was a stranger king, whose logics remained impervious to the chaos it provoked, and that as such it did work as a market weapon against the political order the taxi industry epitomized. As a result, the very development of BA Taxi, even if it was an "honest" effort to participate and belong in this future of innovation alongside the "team of millions" of Argentines, passed for confirmation of the logics that denied a part to the industry in the first place, however flawed those logics may have been.

Indexical reflexivity offered great scope for personal intervention, like deciding to help an elderly lady cross the street one was blocking; but because it was as a collective that the taxi industry was temporalized and written off, work to break the terms of the tautology would have to be streamlined at a similarly collective scale.[27] This collective was unmanageable, not least because in some sense it did not even exist: the postpolitical categories could, and did, circumscribe the taxi industry as a single undifferentiated whole, but as I have shown throughout this book it was made of extremely different actors, often antagonistic to each other, and in some strict senses it would have to include governmental administrations dealing with the industry, public notaries overseeing the taxi license market, and dozens more. Still, working with an intuitively circumscribed collective of people driving taxis around, it would have been unthinkable to streamline and choreograph the behavior of dozens of thousands of bodies, scared of losing their jobs, taunted by reporters, and otherwise managing their march along a razor's edge. This much was clear early on: one evening the driver engaged in the ambushes arrived at Dionisio's in a terrible mood. During the ambush some passersby had insulted the taxi drivers, the Uber driver had joined them in chorus, and in frustration one of the taxi drivers had kicked the Uber car, denting the door and scratching the paint. He was restrained by the others, but pedestrians gathered, and the situation degenerated into a tiny urban drama magnified by thousands of retweets, reposts, and reports marking the taxi industry, again, as the Past to leave behind.

Histories, Myths, and Other Argentine Times

Weeks, months, years passed; street protests dwindled, flaring up intermittently as spinoffs of the original legal case made their way through courts and government officials made statements. By July 2016, three months after that initial Uber ride on Argentine soil, the topic of the company still haunted most taxi rides. Mauro smiled blithely and carried on, but Andrés lost it twice, first with a lady trying to explain how important it was to accept progress and adapt ourselves, and then with a young couple who disagreed with the route he chose and declared to him that "this is why people don't like you all." Andrés stopped the car and demanded they got out and hail an Uber right there, if it was so fantastic, and that they leave him alone.

Neither Mauro nor Andrés ever joined the protests. Both thought it would only increase resentment toward them, but the jaded tone of their refusal evoked a view over a horizon beyond the postpolitical reasoning that was writing them off—so far beyond, in fact, that it could not have been intelligible as a temporal, or even logical, sequence to that future, as if it were of an order greater than what the authors and characters of the present experience could understand. As I prepared to leave Buenos Aires a few months later, the taxi license had not yet lost value. It would not, according to Mauro: "People will always take taxis." Andrés nodded. For a while he had a sign on his taxi window, spelling "Uber = Tax Evader" in black letters over a yellow background. Right underneath it read, "Sindicato de Peones de Taxis": the union had financed several versions in banners, stickers, and flyers. Andrés still despised Viviani and his union, and he had always suspected the union, the government, and Uber to be in on something, "but Uber evades taxes all the same, so I don't care who paid for the sign."

Mauro had voted for Macri. Andrés had voted for a minority party in the first round, and when Macri and Scioli, Fernández de Kirchner's candidate, made it to the second round, he decided they were all the same. "All" as in these two, but also "all" as in everyone, Macri, Kirchner, and the Peronists, and he did not go to vote. Mauro was calmly hopeful for the country. "I think Peronism will rally behind Macri—that's what they do, rally behind the winner. Or they might dissolve into a sort of social democratic socialism?" he pondered. "Mauro—don't be an idiot," Andrés replied. "You left Uruguay a million years ago. This is Argentina. Peronism will never go. After Macri, in four years, Peronism returns." The year 2019 came and Peronism did return, so history proved him right; then again, for eighty years now the myth of Peronism's perennial return is always somehow verified, and a good follower of the 'ethic of fortune' would know to take myths seriously, if not literally. As it became obvious during my fieldwork on the taxi industry, and later on the Uber conflict, that I would have to grapple, not with Peronism itself, but with what my informants made of it, and render some of its aspects to audiences completely unfamiliar with it, I asked Andrés point blank several times "What is Peronism?," if only to get a sense of what exactly that which always returned was.

Vos sabés lo que es el Peronismo—you know what Peronism is, he dismissed me with a knowing grin as if I had been trying to catch him unaware or otherwise trick him. I was, and he was right, for I understood it intuitively in a glance, in a gait, in a stance, but had the authorial duty to figure it out as an ontology, a way of understanding an ontology, an aesthetic turn, a party, or something else. My informants outside the taxi trade, Francisco, Valentina, Ariadna, Mariano, and Pablo, were none the wiser, although they offered variously trenchant replies: a mob, a charismatic movement, a way of doing politics, a lie. Novaro's characterization of Peronism as a mediation machine had some traction among the segment of the middle class that for eighty years had been voting it out, or ridding itself of it by other means, only to see it always return.[28]

Viviani was the key to understanding Peronism, argued Mauro, and indeed, although one could probably not reduce Peronism to Viviani's audacity and calculation without losing some crucial part, one would be really hard pressed to find a more perfect example for it in the terms of this ethnography and how its main actors understood these times. Argentine political philosopher Ernesto Laclau saw in Peronism what he would characterize as the essence of the Political: an ensemble of demands inherently irreducible to each other or to technique, propelled forward by an affect that onlookers and intellectuals dismiss as irrational or atavistic at their own loss.[29] In a way, if we take these residents' enthusiasm seriously and trace the contours of the parts it distributed or disallowed, to these people, in this moment in time, Peronism and the Political were surely not the same on an analytical plane, but ethnographically speaking they were quite difficult to tell apart. This may well be why Macri, the technocrat seeking to transcend the political, built that statue to Perón, after all: to pin it down, put it in a place, and keep it at bay. The statue still stands, next to Buenos Aires's Customs House. Macri lost the 2019 election to Peronist Alberto Fernández, whose vice president is Cristina Fernández de Kirchner.

Less than a week after Uber's arrival, union officials told the press that taxi drivers' work had decreased by 30 percent. Was this the case? I asked Mauro and Andrés at Dionisio's. There was maybe a bit less work, Mauro conceded, but Andrés snapped: "There sure is, for those lazy bums at the union, expecting work to come to them, clustering by the airports and Retiro, sponging off union charges from the people who actually work. Our friend the anthropologist had not yet been born, but you should know better, Mauro, this is not new. It's the same as the hyperinflation of 1989, then the neoliberal 1990s, then the crisis of 2001, then Kirchner, there's always something. This is what Argentina has always been. You want to work? Work is there. Hop in the car and go find it." And it was so that in this horizon beyond the postpolitical, not in the sense of temporal or logical sequence but in the sense of a magnitude by far greater, another temporalization never stopped happening. These just-under thirty-seven thousand taxis had been carrying for decades another mark, top half yellow, lower half black, indispensable to punctuate the experience of transactions in a perennial present with no future and no past. In this horizon neither Peronism nor the Political was a mark, or if they were it was irrelevant to tell them apart from each other or from what there was: come Macri, Kirchner, Peronism, or Uber, Buenos Aires would always be open to the smart among those hustling for a fare that could be just further up the road, if they knew what to seek and how to find, a LED light spelling "LIBRE" on the top right.

CONCLUSION

AS OF JANUARY 2021, Uber continues its operation in Buenos Aires and has already expanded into the cities of Mendoza and Mar del Plata. Authorities in Córdoba and Rosario, the second- and third-largest cities in the country respectively, have succeeded in blocking the service or suspending the company's operations. In the years since my fieldwork the legal conflict and the company adapted to each other: authorities managed to severely hinder Uber's capacity to process card payments, so the company launched a cash-only modality it already had in other countries. Legal actions proliferated against Uber drivers at several civil, penal, and commercial courts, but no univocal jurisprudence emerged: in some cases it was deemed that professional licenses were not needed for the "new" service that Uber was, while in others vehicles were seized and Uber drivers' licenses to drive were revoked. In the meantime, Uber appealed legal action against it at every single instance; a national case was launched, then repealed, then launched again. On February 10, 2018, the attorney who had been chasing Uber since the beginning, Martín Lapadú, secured a national ban from a city tribunal, after "strenuous work," finally cornering telecommunications companies.[1] Uber appealed the ban, and in June of that year a chamber of appeals admitted this appeal, stating that blocking Uber "would unnecessarily and disproportionately harm rights such as that to access and distribute information; the gathering and circulation of knowledge through apps, tools, and online contents; and the possibility of [internet] users to freely communicate and develop."[2]

We must also be aware that in late capitalism, and especially in peripheral countries like Argentina, these conflicts are never completely domestic, or at least not in any straightforward sense of the term. Between early 2017 and the weeks prior to the chamber of appeals' decision, international NGO Access Now and the Inter American Association of Telecommunication Companies (IAATC) criticized the judicial action as an "arbitrary," "excessive," and "damaging" sanction that would not solve the problem and that sent "worrying signals" to markets about the rule of law in Argentina.[3] Whereas IAATC is directly implicated in the provision of telecom services, and thus is effectively a business lobbying group defending its interests, as of January 2021 Access Now described its mission as "[to defend and extend] the digital rights of users at risk around the world. By combining direct technical support, comprehensive policy engagement, global advocacy, . . . we fight for human rights in the digital age."[4] Incidentally, part of Access Now's "global team" is based in Córdoba, Argentina's second-largest city.

Along even grander lines, on March 22, 2018, the American Convention of Human Rights released its 2017 report on human rights in the continent, where it analyzed the issue of "freedom of speech on the internet in Argentina," pointing in particular to the judicial orders to block Uber's website and app.[5] Edison Lanza, the organization's rapporteur for freedom of speech, declared: "The internet is a disruptive technology that has amplified freedom of speech. . . . It is of the utmost importance that judges take this into account whenever they take a decision concerning the internet. . . . In my view it is disproportionate for a municipal judge to censure an app, as in the case of Uber. If there are issues in the market of transportation, then it is a matter of transportation policy, but not an issue about the internet. What is the purpose of blocking a transportation app if its contents are not illegal?" The report identified by full name the judges of the Autonomous City of Buenos Aires who had ordered the ban.

Virtually everyone in Buenos Aires suspected that conversations in upper governmental circles had influenced the formal trajectory of this conflict, a suspicion I shared but cannot responsibly endorse here as those spheres were by orders of magnitude beyond the reach of my project's means. It is also unclear how it is "disproportionate" for a "municipal judge" to rule according to the laws and arguments within the judge's jurisdiction that a particular transportation relation is harmful to residents' civic integrity; it is equally unclear why Mr. Lanza argues that the contents of the app were not illegal, or what exactly the contents are other than the stuff that produces rides that violate the city's rules. Of course, framing this conflict as "a matter of transportation policy" and Uber itself as "the internet," an "app," and "freedom of speech" is a cunning way to depoliticize the conflict, provincializing both the concern with the app's impact and the arguments against it. Yet most importantly, what matters for the purposes of this book is less whether Uber relations "actually" are a matter of free speech than the fact that invoking free speech triggers a moral legerdemain that has swapped the ground of this debate and that in contemporary capitalism makes it very hard to argue back. "Freedom of speech" enhances the asymmetry between a "municipal judge" and the rapporteur of an international organization with a moral injunction.

Examining the logics, rhetoric, and affects implied in these grand declarations, supported by grand agendas and large funds, we find that the American Convention of Human Rights and Francisco, in his shop in middle-class Buenos Aires, are both appealing to a particular, intuitive register of universals that neutralize, displace, or pathologize a certain kind of disagreement. "Excess," "arbitrariness," "censure," and "disproportion" are writing off the very sophisticated reasons the taxi industry presented to claim its stakes in the conflict, as well as the legal arguments presented by the judges of the case. If anything, the fact that Francisco and Mr. Lanza could probably understand each other intuitively and reflect in uncannily similar terms would confirm to them the irrevocability and righteous universality of their cause: the former would see himself endorsed by a global political authority and the latter by the conviction that he was speaking for the voiceless little man in some southern metropolis.

In spite of this convergence, I have written this book in the conviction that there is something fundamental about how people understand and inhabit disagreement in late capitalism that we can only learn ethnographically. International businesses may have deep pockets, hire shrewd lobbyists, deploy what we could describe as predatory or vicious practices, and find ways to persuade international organizations' rapporteurs; also, technocratic governments in developing nations may swing between naïveté and complicity with these practices and the political actors that enable them. Yet to explain how the middle class desired, turned to, and argued for Uber through these reasons would be to give the company, these governments, and these lobbyists a power that I do not think they had (or deserve to be granted) and to make Uber into a more intractable fetish than the one its best lobbyists could ever evoke. This conflict was not, strictly speaking, even about Uber: it was about how algorithms, a history of decay, borders, currency exchange restrictions, internet cables, and a myriad other props served as purchase for a way to reflect on that which we disagree with and the possibility to foreclose it.

I have tried throughout this book to unravel the logics, rhetoric, and affects of this reasoning, which I have called postpolitical. This was not the first time middle-class Argentines reasoned in this way about disagreement; also, the conflict could have stayed contained to a very specific struggle over different ways of moving around. Those logics, rhetorics, and affects that made it such a pivotal event for the middle class made it an excellent case study into the particulars of an orientation toward reasoning about disagreement that has become increasingly common around the world. The "near-fanatical obsession" with popular participation in politics, the convergence between the questions experts and nonexperts are asking about economics, pandemics, or immigration policies, and a broad academic, political, and societal turn to the glorification of the experience of the average person's life require that we trace this kind of reasoning outside of governmental structures, international circulations of money, or the managerial mindset of business practices.[6]

As I said in the Introduction, the logics, rhetoric, and affects traced in this book fold into and point to each other and to the broader intuition they stand for. The reader will have realized that the trope of competition extends the logics of gladiatorial truths every single time it is deployed; gladiatorial truths imply in their framing a jurisdictional battle, where the People, as a notion or as a collective, speaks a law for itself, rejecting ipso facto competing jurisdictional claims. To remain a stranger in Buenos Aires was in itself, necessarily, to constitute oneself as an alternative jurisdiction that resisted, by the gladiatorial truth of consumption, the logics of the juridico-political order. All these tropes thickened and entrenched the temporalization that the taxi industry had to fight off by engaging in indexical reflexivity. And so forth.

I sought to capture this cacophonic variety by thinking about the postpolitical as a kind of *reasoning*: a development and organization of knowledge that reshuffles the common experience. Whereas in some linguistic or cultural traditions the term *reasoning* implies a core of methodical clarity and logical consistency, as every single chapter of this book has shown, we reason and learn how to know through affects, intensity, rhetorical borrowings, and trans-genre grammars that often contradict each other, diverge, or are simply false. Their combinations may be unprogrammatic or hard to model in econometric projections, but this does not mean they are entirely random, erratic, or unpredictable. We would be mistaken, I think, to call this reasoning anything other than that (aside from the fact that denying it that name on the grounds of its lack of system would amount to the positivistic narrowmindedness the social sciences often claim to have superseded), not least because the sense it makes frames the experiences of the lives we study.

Many of these inconsistencies and stylizations derive from the crystallization, about a century and a half ago, of a series of wildly different notions that were taken to be self-evident and organized as such, through equations and axioms, to support the edifice that would tower over the science and practice of order: neoclassical economics. But I did not take the scenic route through these tropes to present the inconsistencies they lead to as evidence of their inherent unsuitability or fault. Academics, and much of the world outside academia since the subprime crisis, already know or intuit that. The point is that these notions, today, are intuitive, are readily available, and persuade of their legitimacy and of the legitimacy of the causes they attach themselves to in spite of their flagrant inconsistencies. To be sure, among academics, in our seminars, we agree that the political always returns, or is never fully foreclosed, and that algorithmic management, economic competition, and freedom of choice are "actually" just as political as institutional guardianship, state-endorsed monopolies, or barriers to trade. We spend an ever-growing amount of time, energy, and paper in an increasingly esoteric, endogamic literalism while we are missing the fact that we have no *effective*, no-nonsense, persuasive grammar to, for example, argue to people like Buenos Aires's middle class against the bottom line of gladiatorial truths. We can argue alongside it, campaigning against Uber and decrying labor precaritization, but none of this even begins to counter the ever-more-intractable traction popular legitimacy has across partisan and class lines. In fact, in so doing we are possibly entrenching that legitimacy, as going at it sideways passes for evidence that one has no direct way of speaking back to it—in turn evidence of its alleged unassailability.

As I said in the Introduction, taxis are still there, the "mafias," taxi licenses, and labor relations remain the same, and aside from Viviani's retirement, Buenos Aires's taxi industry has not changed in any structural sense since Uber arrived. But postpolitical reasoning matters less for an accurate or effective description or prognosis of a particular conflict or social situation, and more for how it shapes the public sphere around that conflict, and in particular how it affects the possibility of meaningful disagreement. This means disagreement as political equals, as a part with a part in the whole, without being pathologized, morally disallowed, or written off. In the case of Uber's conflict in Buenos Aires, in the terms that mattered to how the company's arrival affected the city, that the conflict was beyond the political and not something one could meaningfully disagree about was to a certain segment of the middle class plain common sense. For academics in particular and for societies at large this is a problem, in itself, of a wholly different and more insidious kind than how "neoliberal" or "actually" political Uber was.

Notes

Introduction

1. "The Southern Cone" is a cultural, historical, and economic denomination for the southernmost nations of South America, always including Argentina, Uruguay, and Chile and including in certain uses Paraguay and southern Brazil as well. The interview was part of the radio show *Lanata sin filtro*, aired March 28, 2016. The relevant extract was uploaded to YouTube on the same date: https://www.youtube.com/watch?v=UkgWtW9oZaU.

2. "Los taxistas se oponen a Uber: 'No lo vamos a permitir bajo ningún concepto,'" *La Nación*, March 28, 2016, https://www.lanacion.com.ar/buenos-aires/los-taxistas-se-oponen-a-uber-no-lo-vamos-a-permitir-bajo-ningun-concepto-nid1883806.

3. Uber Argentina, tweet, March 27, 2016, https://twitter.com/Uber_ARG/status/714105410689638400.

4. Uber Argentina, tweet, March 29, 2016, https://twitter.com/Uber_ARG/status/714826354676658176.

5. "Uber comenzará a operar esta tarde en Buenos Aires," *Revista Fibra*, April 12, 2016, http://revistafibra.info/uber-comenzara-operar-esta-tarde-buenos-aires/.

6. Guillermo Tomoyose, "Los números de Uber en Buenos Aires: 90 mil descargas de la aplicación y 20 mil pedidos de viajes en 24 horas," *La Nación*, April 14, 2016, http://www.lanacion.com.ar/1889277-los-numeros-de-uber-90-mil-descargas-de-la-aplicacion-y-20-mil-pedidos-de-viajes-en-24-horas.

7. Uber Argentina, tweet, "Conocenos y defendé tu derecho a elegir. Hasta el miércoles tendrás 15 viajes gratis hasta $200. #DerechoAElegir https://newsroom.uber.com/argentina/es/defende-tu-derechoaelegir-viaja-en-uber-y-todos-tus-viajes-seran-gratis/ . . . ," April 15, 2016, https://twitter.com/Uber_ARG/status/721048455632842753. See also "Defendé tu #DerechoAElegir, ¡Viajá en Uber y todos tus viajes serán gratis!" Uber Blog, April 15, 2016, https://www.uber.com/es-AR/blog/defende-tu-derechoaelegir-viaja-en-uber-y-todos-tus-viajes-seran-gratis/.

8. "La batalla por la calle está en la ley," *Página/12*, March 30, 2016, https://www.pagina12.com.ar/diario/sociedad/3-295709-2016-03-30.html; and "Uber: Macri defendió a taxistas y dijo que son 'un símbolo,'" *Perfil*, April 14, 2016, https://www.perfil.com/noticias/politica/uber-macri-defendio-a-los-taxistas-dijo-que-son-un-simbolo-20160414-0026.phtml, respectively.

9. Hansen and Verkaaik (2009) originally developed the concept of urban charisma.

10. "Uber sigue en la mira, pero no se detiene: Tuvo 500 mil descargas y ya cuenta con 37 mil choferes," *La Nación*, May 19, 2016, http://www.lanacion.com.ar/1900153-uber-sigue-en-la-mira.

11. Rancière (2011).

12. Rancière (2011: 13), my emphasis.

13. He approaches the depoliticization of the distribution of the sensible through the notions of archipolitics, metapolitics, and parapolitics and the emergence of "consensus democracy." See Rancière (1999: 61–93).

14. Wilson and Swyngedouw (2014: 6). On the postpolitical more broadly, see Mouffe (1993, 2005), Žižek (2009), and Crouch (2004).

15. For the inclusion of nonexperts in social studies of knowledge, see Callon, Lascoumes, and Barthe (2009) and Barry and Slater (2005).

16. See Reeves (2011), Demetriou (2007), Navaro-Yashin (2002, 2012), Nuijten (2004), Aretxaga (1999), Thiranagama and Kelly (2010), Laszczkowski and Reeves (2017), Stafford (2019), and Shiller (2019). Jansen (2016) discusses the difference between theorizing from affect and taking affect ethnographically seriously.

17. See Mirowski (1989) and Wasserman (2019).

18. Whyte (2019) and Slobodian (2018) examine the emergence of neoliberalism as an institutional and political project.

19. Carrier (1997: 14); see also Carrier (2012).

20. See Venugopal (2015) and Ferguson (2009); Eriksen et al. (2015) debate whether social sciences, specifically anthropology, should even use the concept of neoliberalism at all.

21. Evans-Pritchard (1965: 63).

22. For example, Ferguson (1990), Whyte (2019), and Barry (2005).

23. Maybury-Lewis (1991: 214) and Rock (1985).

24. Rock (1985: 118–249) and Halperín Donghi (1992).

25. For immigration statistics, see Archetti (1999: 2; 2003: 11), Bass (2006: 437), and Schneider (1996: 175). For state infrastructure, see Plotkin and Zimmerman (2012a, 2012b).

26. Hobsbawm (1994) examines these themes in depth.

27. Rock (1985) and Waisman (1987: 5–6).

28. Nouzeilles and Montaldo (2002: 3). Garguin (2007: 163) examines the link between Argentineness and upward mobility.

29. Gorelik (2004: 15–68) and Garguin (2007: 166) discuss the preeminence of Buenos Aires; Halperín Donghi (1992), its irreversibility.

30. Martínez Estrada (2017).

31. Scobie (1964, 2002); also Archetti (1999) and Sarlo (1988).

32. See, for example, O'Donnell (2002), Sarlo (2001), Soriano (2002), and Joseph (2000).

33. Murmis and Portantiero (2011) and Amaral (2014).

34. This characterization belongs to Argentine intellectual Beatriz Sarlo (2001: 38–40).

35. On Peronism, see Brennan (1998a, 1998b), James (2010), Sidicaro (2003), Mustapic (2002), and Novaro (2014b).

36. Lazar (2017) makes this point.

37. Savigliano (1995: 20).

38. Hansen (1999) and Chhotray (2011) examine this conflation.

39. On the middle class's strategies to protect their savings, see D'Avella (2014).

40. López-Pedreros (2019: 226) discusses the normative legitimacy of such a middle class.

41. On the issue of social media as a public and political arena, see Sarlo (2011).

42. This is a variation of López-Pedreros's argument (2019: 81).

43. See Gupta and Ferguson (1997) and Strathern (1987) for a discussion of anthropology at home.

44. On these tensions, see J. Taylor (2002), Scalabrini Ortiz (2001), and Wright (1974).

45. Marcus (1997); see also Abélès and Badaró (2015: 116–21).

46. Strathern (1987: 16–37).

Chapter 1

1. I avoid the word *barrio* in this book. In River Plate Spanish, *barrio* is the exact equivalent of *neighborhood* and has none of the sociocultural connotations it has carried from northern South America and Spanish-speaking Central and North America into English parlance. It is an official and conversational term used to refer to neighborhoods with a per capita GDP similar to that of inner London or New York City. *Cafés de barrio* are independently run cafés with wooden, marble, or Formica tables and usually older waiters. As spaces of ritualized socializing they are very similar to western, southern, and central European and North African cafés.

2. Scott (1998); also Roitman (2005).

3. Parapugna (1980: 27).

4. Parapugna (1980: 30).

5. Parapugna (1980: 78).

6. Parapugna (1980: 44).

7. Domergue and Cabrera (2010; 7, 15, 27 respectively).

8. Parapugna (1980: 313).

9. Cassagne (2002) and Gordillo (2013).

10. "La ola de inseguridad: Asesinan en un taxi en Palermo al marido de Georgina Barbarossa," *La Nación*, November 3, 2001, https://www.lanacion.com.ar/348353-asesinan-en-un-taxi-en-palermo-al-marido-de-georgina-barbarossa.

11. Roitman (2005: 22). Hart (1973) first developed the notion of informal economy.

12. See Elyachar (2013), Roitman (2005), and Gandolfo (2013).

13. Goldstein (2016: 18–24).

14. Castells and Portes (1989: 120) discuss this kind of informality.

15. See Lazar (2012) and Usami (2004).

16. Trial periods exist in Argentine labor law for up to three months after the beginning of the employment relationship. As there were no records of this date, there was no way to prove this was not a trial period.

17. "Juicio oral por un crimen en un taxi," *Clarín*, March 14, 2003, http://edant.clarin.com/diario/2003/03/14/s-04201.htm.

18. Strictly speaking, the radio taxi modality existed already, but it concerned mostly corporate bookings until then. Jansen (2014) coins the term *gridding* to refer to people's attempt to create ordering and administrative structures when central authorities do not.

19. Brennan (1998a), Plotkin and Zimmerman (2012a), and Stawski (2012: 94–97) analyze the relationship between unions, state practices, and Peronism at the time of the latter's emergence.

20. Lazar (2012: 20).

21. Wolf (1990: 586).

22. "El gobierno porteño retirará licencias por alquilar taxis," *La Prensa*, November 7, 2001. http://www.laprensa.com.ar/257857-El-Gobierno-porteno-retirara-licencias-por-alquilar-taxis.note.aspx.

23. Ibid.

24. See Lazar (2012: 21).

25. Bähre (2014) develops the notion of trickle-up economies.

26. Beatriz Sarlo, "Entrevista con Beatriz Sarlo: 'El peronismo es tan indispensable como Borges,'" interview by Ricardo Carpena, *La Nación*, April 30, 2011, https://www.lanacion.com.ar/1369124-el-Peronism-es-tan-indispensable-como-borges.

27. Sarlo (2001: 40).

28. Plotkin (1998: 30) examines this reasoning.

29. See Novaro (2014b) and Brennan (1998b) for problematizations of Peronism.

30. Buchrucker (1998: 3) argues that Argentines intuitively understand Peronism.

31. I use here Sahlins's (1963) characterization of Big Men.

32. Sarlo (2011).

33. See Healey (2012).

34. Novaro (2014a: 36).

35. See Lazar (2017) for negative perceptions of unions in Argentina.

36. "Viviani: 'Néstor y Cristina nunca sacaron una ley en contra de los trabajadores,'" *Minuto Uno*, October 19, 2015, https://www.minutouno.com/notas/1298081-viviani-nestor-y-cristina-nunca-sacaron-una-ley-contra-los-trabajadores.

37. "Omar Viviani: 'Cristina ya está, cumplió una etapa,'" *Télam*, July 22, 2016, http://www.telam.com.ar/notas/201607/156203-viviani-cristina.php.

Chapter 2

1. "El desgarrador relato de la madre de Leonela Noble," *Minuto Uno*, February 3, 2013, https://www.minutouno.com/notas/276674-el-desgarrador-relato-la-madre-leonela-noble.

2. "Taxista atropelló a cinco personas y mató a una joven," *Diario Popular*, January 29, 2013, https://www.diariopopular.com.ar/general/taxista-atropello-cinco-personas-y-mato -una-joven-n145041.

3. "La madre de Leonela aseguró que el taxista tiene 50 multas por alta velocidad," *Infobae*, January 31, 2013, https://www.infobae.com/2013/01/31/694275-la-madre-leonela-aseguro-que-el-taxista-tiene-50-multas-alta-velocidad/.

4. Foucault (1985: 115); see also Padovan-Özdemir (2016) and Padovan-Özdemir and Ydesen (2016).

5. Haidar (2013), García Fanlo (2014), Torre (1989, 2012).

6. Foucault (1994: 237).

7. Ibid.

8. Oksala (2013).

9. See Crampton (2013) for a Foucauldian analysis of the spatialization of disease.

10. Foucault (2003: 249).

11. The literal translation of *potrero* is "paddock," but in River Plate Spanish the term refers to vacant lots in cities or semiurban areas where football is played following its conventional rules but in improvised conditions. For tango dancers' *tener adoquín*, see Taylor (1998), and for football players' *tener potrero*, see Archetti (1999).

12. See Swidler (1979) for these strategies and Oyler (1996) for the distinction between being in/an authority.

13. A canonical reflexion on Foucault's sense of spatiality is Foucault's own with respect to Nantes (2009: 17–18).

14. Foucault (1995: 66).

15. I follow Lipsky's (1980) formulation of street-level burocrats.

16. Foucault (1991: 75).

17. Du Gay (1999: 581).

18. I follow here Lazar's analysis of *contención* (2017: 109–11).

Chapter 3

1. Hansen and Verkaaik (2009) call this "urban charisma."

2. On (auto)mobility, modernity, and urbanity, see Thrift (2004), Sheller and Urry (2000), and Seiler (2008); on mobility as freedom, see Spragens (1973), Humphrey (2007), and Cresswell (2006). For a critique of the romanticism of freedom in terms of spatial movement, see Cresswell (2006: 55; 1997: 377) and Urry (2000: 28), Adey (2010: 70), and Wolff (1993).

3. See Granovetter (1985).

4. See Granovetter (1985: 489–90).

5. On relationships between market actors, see Carrier (1997), Garcia (1986), Block (1990), and Dore (1983).

6. See Block (1990: 46).

7. Bauman (2014: 140).

8. Rancière (2011: 13).

9. All of them use oil marginally, however; otherwise GNC dries up the engine.

10. Taxis in Buenos Aires do not accept credit or debit card payments.

11. See Rancière (2011).

12. Appadurai (1986: 51).

13. On commodity mythologies, see Appadurai (1986: 48).

14. The full lyrics are available on Todo Tango's website (last accessed January 16, 2021): http://www.todotango.com/musica/tema/1052/Taxi-mio/.

15. Olivia Sohr, "Protestas sociales: Qué se propone en la Argentina y cómo se regulan en otras partes del mundo," *Chequeado*, April 17, 2014, https://chequeado.com/el-explicador/protestas-sociales-que-se-propone-en-la-argentina-y-como-se-regulan-en-otras-partes-del-mundo/.

16. Lears (2003).

17. Appadurai (1986: 50).

18. See Herzfeld (1988).

19. Appadurai (1986: 51).

20. See Corcoran (2010: 1–4).

21. Lears (2003: 15).

22. Ibid.

23. See Figueiro (2016a, 2016b) for an analysis of the ethics of small-scale gambling in Buenos Aires.

Chapter 4

1. Guillermo Tomoyose, "Inminente llegada de Uber a la Argentina: Comenzó la selección de conductores particulares," *La Nación*, March 27, 2016, http://www.lanacion.com.ar/1883036-inminente-llegada-de-uber-a-la-argentina-comenzo-la-seleccion-de-conductores-particulares.

2. Uber Argentina, tweet, March 27, 2016, https://twitter.com/Uber_ARG/status/714105410689638400.

3. Evangelina Himitian, "En medio de una polémica, Uber empezó a capacitar choferes," *La Nación*, March 29, 2016, https://www.lanacion.com.ar/1883967-en-medio-de-una-polemica-uber-empezo-a-capacitar-choferes.

4. "Para autoridades de Uber, 'Lo existente en materia regulatoria no comprende un servicio innovador como el nuestro,'" *Télam*, March 29, 2016, http://www.telam.com.ar/notas/201603/141248-uber-regulaciones-transporte.php.

5. Soledad Vallejos, "Entre la novedad y la ilegalidad," *Página/12*, March 29, 2016, https://www.pagina12.com.ar/diario/sociedad/3-295651-2016-03-29.html.

6. "La batalla por la calle está en la ley," *Página/12*, March 30, 2016, https://www.pagina12.com.ar/diario/sociedad/3-295709-2016-03-30.html.

7. Uber Argentina, tweet, April 8, 2016, https://twitter.com/Uber_ARG/status/718432305468043268.

8. "Video: Uber comienza a operar en Buenos Aires; taxistas trancan calles," *La Prensa*, April 13, 2016, https://www.prensa.com/mundo/Uber-Buenos-Aires-taxistas-principales_0_4459054193.html.

9. Nacho Viale, tweet, April 12, 2016, https://twitter.com/nachoviale/status/719962408408719361.

10. Soledad Vallejos, "Debut callejero con protesta y advertencia legal," *Página/12*, April 13, 2016, https://www.pagina12.com.ar/diario/sociedad/3-296832-2016-04-13.html.

11. Latour (2010: 226).

12. Yablon (1990), Shannon (2007: 235), Riles (2006: 21), and Brenneis (2006) discuss how documents organize subjects.

13. Bourdieu (1987: 831).

14. "Uber: Macri defendió a taxistas y dijo que son 'un símbolo,'" *Perfil*, April 14, 2016, https://www.perfil.com/noticias/politica/uber-macri-defendio-a-los-taxistas-dijo-que-son-un-simbolo-20160414-0026.phtml.

15. del Nido (2019) analyzes this anxiety for modernity.

16. "Rodríguez Larreta adelantó que si Uber 'cumple con la ley' podrá operar en la Ciudad," *El Cronista*, March 29, 2016, https://www.cronista.com/economiapolitica/Rodriguez-Larreta-adelanto-que-si-Uber-cumple-con-la-ley-podra-operar-en-la-Ciudad-20160329-0081.html.

17. Sarlo (2011: 228).

18. See Nuijten (2004).

19. See Helmke (2004).

20. "Taxis vs. Uber," *La Nación*, March 28, 2016, http://www.lanacion.com.ar/1884034-taxis-vs-uber.

21. See Carrier (1997).

22. Berman (1983: 111).

23. C. Taylor (2003: 2–5).

24. Locke would later pick up this argument to frame the notions of government and consent as an ongoing process where these equal people agree to give themselves a hierarchy to rule and tax them. See C. Taylor (2003: 2–5).

25. C. Taylor (2003: 15; 74).

26. C. Taylor (2003: 20–21).

27. C. Taylor (2003: 15–17).

28. C. Taylor (2003: 5). For the obsession with popular participation in politics, see Chhotray (2011).

29. See Kazin (2017).

30. See Mirowski (2009).

31. Uber Argentina, tweet, "Conocenos y defendé tu derecho a elegir. Hasta el miércoles tendrás 15 viajes gratis hasta $200. #DerechoAElegir https://newsroom.uber.com/argentina/es/defende-tu-derechoaelegir-viaja-en-uber-y-todos-tus-viajes-seran-gratis/ . . . ," April 15, 2016, https://twitter.com/Uber_ARG/status/721048455632842753.

32. See Mouffe (2005).

33. "Uber sigue en la mira, pero no se detiene: Tuvo 500 mil descargas y ya cuenta con 37 mil choferes," *La Nación*, May 19, 2016, http://www.lanacion.com.ar/1900153-uber-sigue-en-la-mira; Mariano Otero, "Opinión: Una alternativa de transporte útil y viable," *La Nación*,

April 3, 2016, https://www.lanacion.com.ar/economia/una-alternativa-de-transporte-util-y-viable-nid1885396; and the relevant extract of Jorge Lanata's radio show *Lanata sin filtro*, "Sobre Uber y los taxistas: *Lanata sin filtro*," uploaded to YouTube March 28, 2016, https://www.youtube.com/watch?v=UkgWtW9oZaU, respectively.

34. Rosenblat and Stark (2016) challenge the "choose when to drive" rhetoric.

35. See Carrier (1997: 52).

36. See C. Taylor (2003: 122).

37. Ormerod (1994: 65), in Carrier (1997: 52).

38. See "Sobre Uber y los taxistas."

39. Latour (2010: 165).

40. See Gago (2017).

41. see Frank (2002).

42. see Carrier (1997: 50).

43. "Un ex diputado santafesino trabaja en Buenos Aires como chofer de Uber," *Perfil*, June 5, 2016, https://www.perfil.com/noticias/sociedad/un-ex-diputado-santafesino-trabaja-en-buenos-aires-como-chofer-de-uber-20160605-0040.phtml.

44. Koselleck (2004: 184).

45. C. Taylor (2003: 131–33).

Chapter 5

1. Sahlins (2008).

2. This is a fragment of the rationale behind Retiro's inclusion in the Registry of National Monuments as offered in Executive Decree 262/1997, March 20, 1997, https://web.archive.org/web/20080619074442/http://www.monumentosysitios.gov.ar/catalogo/index.php?table_name=monumentos&function=details&where_field=indice&where_value=546.

3. Rock (1985).

4. For immigration statistics, see Schneider (1996: 174–75).

5. J. Taylor (1998).

6. Nouzeilles and Montaldo (2002: 4).

7. Mitchell (2002: 210–23).

8. Mitchell (2002), Ferguson (1990).

9. Colloredo-Mansfeld (2002).

10. Colloredo-Mansfeld (2002) develops the notion of competition as structural antagonism.

11. Bourdieu (1998: 96) defines competition as a "logical machine."

12. Hirschman (1977: 69).

13. Hirschman (1977: 70–77).

14. Carrier (1997).

15. Sahlins (2008, 2014).

16. Caldwell and Henley (2008: 167); also Li (2001: 50).

17. Henley and Caldwell (2008: 270); also Kian (2008).

18. See Simmel (1908) for the importance of the stranger's remaining a stranger.

19. On strangers and moral alterity, see (Sahlins 2014: 147); also Henley (2004).

20. Sahlins (2008: 188).

21. De Heusch (1991: 114) discusses the stranger king's ability to work around existing arrangements.

22. On staying outside the established order while inside and reproducing the interruption of the political, see Caldwell and Henley (2008: 165).

23. Sahlins (2014).

24. Argyle (2008).

25. Sahlins (2014: 139).

26. Sahlins (2014: 154).

27. Mariano Otero, "Opinión: Una alternativa de transporte útil y viable," *La Nación*, April 3, 2016, http://www.lanacion.com.ar/1885396-una-alternativa-de-transporte-util-y-viable.

28. del Nido (2019).

29. Sahlins (2014: 147–51).

30. Simmel (1908: 2).

31. Malkki (1994: 48).

32. Muir (2016); also J. Taylor (1998, 2002).

33. Waisman (1987).

34. Bass (2006: 439).

35. Jansen (2009).

36. Jansen (2009); the quote is from Sahlins (2008: 184).

37. Douglas (2002).

38. Rajković (2019).

39. Simmel (1908).

40. Caldwell and Henley (2008: 166).

41. Jansen (2009).

42. Sahlins (2014: 148).

Chapter 6

1. "Cuáles son las razones por las que Uber afirma que su servicio es legal en el país," *La Nación*, April 7, 2016. https://www.lanacion.com.ar/tecnologia/uber-afirma-que-su-servicio-es-legal-y-no-detiene-su-despliegue-en-buenos-aires-nid1887119.

2. I speak of framing in Callon's (1998) sense.

3. For an analysis of the emergence of this distinction, see Barry and Slater (2005: 13–14).

4. See Amoore (2020).

5. Chen et al (2015).

6. See Beer (2017).

7. See Barry and Slater (2005).

8. Evans (2014: 20).

9. Gunning (n.d.: 9), my emphasis.

10. Castle (1988).

11. Castle (1988: 28).

12. Gunning (n.d.: 7).

13. Cohen (1989: 93), see also Gunning (n.d.).

14. See Benjamin (1999).

15. Castle (1988: 39).

16. On iron and its relationship with the phantasmagoria of capitalism, see Cohen (2004: 212).

17. See Jennings (2003: 96).

18. Transcribed in Gunning (n.d.: 5).

19. See Cohen (1989, 2004).

20. Castle (1988: 30).

21. Alex Rosenblat, "Uber's Phantom Cabs," *Vice*, July 27, 2015, https://www.vice.com/en_us/article/mgbz5a/ubers-phantom-cabs. Rosenblat later published these findings in the peer-reviewed journal *Data and Society*.

22. See Mirowski (1989).

23. Cohen (2004: 209).

24. Castle (1988: 50).

25. Castle (1988: 51–56).

26. See Shore and Wright (2015) and Gillespie (2013).

27. See Rosenblat and Stark (2016), also Rosenblat (2018).

28. Thedvall (2015) examines the notion of "ethics of evaluation."

29. Carrier (2016: 22–37).

30. Strathern (2000) explores this dual sense of accountability.

31. Strathern (1997) analyzes the processes of making indexes targets.

32. On consistency and indicators, see Neyland (2013) and Wendland (2016).

33. Mirowski (2009).

34. Verran (2012: 118) develops the analogy with religious icons.

35. The example of the Egyptian peasant belongs to Mitchell (2002).

36. Amoore (2020: 13–14) examines the link between such propositions and truths.

37. Barry (2010) examines how calculation and metrological practices become political; Amoore (2020) examines the political foreclosure that algorithms effect.

Chapter 7

1. Latour (1999) develops the notion of trials of strength.

2. Kahn (2017: 6). On jurisdictional pragmatics, see also Latour (2010), Constable (2010), Maurer (2013), and Richland (2013).

3. Kahn (2017: 13).

4. Kahn (2017: 17) develops this notion of entextualization. On translation of conflicts into matters of law, see Latour (2010).

5. Kahn (2017) examines how different legal entries into a juridico-political order produce different legal subjectivities.

6. Richland (2013: 211) examines this legitimacy.

7. Pablo Tomino y Guillermo Tomoyose, "Polémica: La Ciudad acarreó un auto de Uber

y rastrea las oficinas para clausurarlas," *La Nación*, April 14, 2016, https://www.lanacion.com.ar/buenos-aires/la-ciudad-acarreo-un-auto-de-uber-y-rastrea-las-oficinas-para-clausurarlas-nid1889118; "La justicia ordenó frenar a Uber y hacen multas de hasta 77.000 pesos," *I Profesional*, April 14, 2016, https://www.iprofesional.com/legales/230803-taxi-multas-uber-La-Justicia-ordeno-frenar-a-Uber-y-hacen-multas-de-hasta-77000-pesos.

8. Ibid.

9. Jorgelina do Rosario, "Uber le responde al Gobierno con un mensaje a sus choferes: "Podés manejar tranquilo," *Infobae*, April 14, 2016, https://www.infobae.com/2016/04/14/1804396-uber-le-responde-al-gobierno-un-mensaje-sus-choferes-podes-manejar-tranquilo/.

10. "Justicia ordenó frenar a Uber."

11. The text in Spanish reads as follows: "Defendé tu #DerechoAElegir, ¡Viajá en Uber y todos tus viajes serán gratis!" *Uber Blog*, April 15, 2016, https://www.uber.com/es-AR/blog/defende-tu-derechoaelegir-viaja-en-uber-y-todos-tus-viajes-seran-gratis/.

12. Ibid.

13. Pablo Tomino y Guillermo Tomoyose, "Polémica: La Ciudad acarreó un auto de Uber y rastrea las oficinas para clausurarlas," *La Nación*, April 14, 2016, https://www.lanacion.com.ar/buenos-aires/la-ciudad-acarreo-un-auto-de-uber-y-rastrea-las-oficinas-para-clausurarlas-nid1889118.

14. See Braun and Whatmore (2010) and Latour (1993).

15. "Macri respaldó a taxistas en conflicto con Uber," *Ámbito Financiero*, April 14, 2016, https://www.ambito.com/informacion-general/macri-respaldo-taxistas-conflicto-uber-n3935216#:~:text=El%20presidente%20Mauricio%20Macri%20apoy%C3%B3,%22s%C3%ADmbolo%20de%20la%20Ciudad%22.

16. National news channel C5N's footage of the conflict is available at "C5N—Imágenes del allanamiento a las oficinas de Uber en Buenos Aires," uploaded to YouTube April 15, 2016, https://www.youtube.com/watch?v=H7nzVO7dDrc; Telefe Noticias's coverage is available at "Allanan oficinas de UBER—Telefe Noticias," uploaded to YouTube April 15, 2016, https://www.youtube.com/watch?v=bhx6Y16pZpo.

17. The interview was part of the radio show *Lanata sin filtro*, aired March 28, 2016. The relevant extract is available at "Sobre Uber y los taxistas: *Lanata sin filtro*," uploaded to YouTube March 28, 2016, https://www.youtube.com/watch?v=UkgWtW90ZaU.

18. Richland (2013: 218).

19. On jurisdictions and contingency, see Richland (2013), Cormack (2007), and Kahn (2017).

20. Richland (2013: 214).

21. Richland (2013).

22. Ternavasio (2009) and Halperín Donghi (1992: 24–25) examine this history.

23. Farmer (2003: 550).

24. Geertz (1975: 7).

25. Gramsci (1971) and Crehan (2011) examine the politics of common sense.

26. Barry (2010: 89).

27. Strictly speaking, Stengers (2010) speaks of ontology rather than order. See also Hetherington (2013).

28. Stengers (2010: 23).

29. See Mirowski (1989).

30. Foucault (2009: 19) and Cormack (2007).

31. On the emergence of propositions "from within," see Hetherington (2013).

32. Latour (1993, 1999).

33. See, for example, "Como pagar uber argentina ahora: Efectivo, tarjeta pre-paga," *Voy en Uber*, accessed January 16, 2021, http://www.voyenuber.com/revertir-bloqueo-tarjetas-argentinas/.

34. On the nature of this nature, see Carrier (1997).

35. On the simultaneous moral and natural violation of order, see Daston (2018).

36. Hetherington (2013: 83).

37. On the appropriate kind of relationships propositions put forward, see Hetherington (2013).

38. On these power relations, see Parikka (2012), Mitchell (2002), Lash (2007), and Anand (2017).

39. Natalia Zuazo, "Méndez: 'Cuando me reunía con Uber parecía que estaba nego-ciando con las FARC,'" *Brando*, May 29, 2018, https://www.lanacion.com.ar/lifestyle/mendez-cuando-me-reunia-con-uber-parecia-que-estaba-negociando-con-las-farc-nid2138985.

40. Ibid.

41. Latour (1993).

42. See del Nido (2019) on these expectations of modernity.

Chapter 8

1. On Eva's role in enabling these transferences, see Sarlo (2003).

2. On Macri's political emergence, see Forment (2007).

3. "Macri conformó su frente incorporando al Partido Justicialista," *Noticias Urbanas*, June 24, 2003, https://web.archive.org/web/20160129100807/http://www.noticiasurbanas.com.ar/noticias/4035de6d0f32ee0c0e897770168a0667/.

4. On Peronism as a mediation machine, see Novaro (2014a). On the last-hour messianic aura of Peronism, see (Healey 2012).

5. Sarlo (2011) thus describes Kirchner.

6. Laclau (2005) analyzed the logics of populism (covertly inspired on Peronism).

7. On Argentina's inception as a capitalist nation, see Wolf (1982: 319–23), Waisman (1987), and Rock (1985).

8. Alejandro Rebossio, "Denuncia contra Argentina ante la OMC por prácticas pro-teccionistas," *El País*, March 30, 2012, https://elpais.com/economia/2012/03/30/actuali-dad/1333140471_820812.html.

9. Kicillof: "No tengo el número de pobres, es una medida estigmatizante," *Perfil*, March 26, 2015, https://www.perfil.com/noticias/economia/kicillof-no-tengo-el-numero-de-pobres-es-una-medida-estigmatizante-20150326-0015.phtml.

10. Natalia Chientaroli, "Argentina presume de tener menos pobres que Alemania," *El Diario*, July 9, 2015, https://www.eldiario.es/internacional/Argentina-presume-tener-pobres-Alemania_0_396861018.html.

11. The relevant segment of Beatriz Sarlo's speech to Parliament is available as "Beatriz Sarlo en el Senado sobre la muerte del fiscal Nisman," uploaded to YouTube on February 12, 2015, https://www.youtube.com/watch?v=Ud4nG1uGhT0.

12. On women in Peronism, see Auyero (1999).

13. "Transcripción completa del discurso de Mauricio Macri," *La Nación*, December 10, 2015, https://www.lanacion.com.ar/1852996-transcripcion-completa-del-discurso-de-mauricio-macri.

14. Koselleck (2004).

15. I refer to punctuation in Guyer's (2007) sense.

16. On Argentine saving practices, see D'Avella (2014).

17. Berman (1983: 106).

18. Guyer (2007: 413).

19. Koselleck (2004: 34).

20. The interview was part of the radio show *Lanata sin filtro*, aired March 28, 2016. The relevant extract is available at "Sobre Uber y los taxistas: *Lanata sin filtro*," uploaded to YouTube March 28, 2016, https://www.youtube.com/watch?v=UkgWtW9oZaU.

21. See Ferguson (1990: 256). On the moralization of the political, see Mouffe (2005).

22. See Barry and Slater (2005).

23. On the depoliticized condition of myths, see Barthes (2010).

24. Maurer (2002).

25. Abélès and Badaró (2015: 85–92); also Rancière (1999).

26. Natalia Zuazo, "Méndez: 'Cuando me reunía con Uber parecía que estaba negociando con las FARC,'" *Brando*, May 29, 2018, https://www.lanacion.com.ar/lifestyle/mendez-cuando-me-reunia-con-uber-parecia-que-estaba-negociando-con-las-farc-nid2138985.

27. Corcoran (2010: 9–14).

28. Novaro (2014a).

29. Laclau (2005).

Conclusion

1. "La justicia porteña ordenó el bloqueo a nivel nacional del sitio y la app de Uber," *La Nación*, February 10, 2018, https://www.lanacion.com.ar/2108247-la-justicia-portena-ordeno-el-bloqueo-a-nivel-nacional-del-sitio-y-la-app-de-uber.

2. "La justicia porteña dio marcha atrás con el recurso que intentó bloquear a Uber," *La Nación*, June 21, 2018, https://www.lanacion.com.ar/2146323-la-justicia-portena-dio-marcha-atras-con-el-recurso-que-intento-bloquear-a-uber.

3. Gaspar Pisanu, "Bloqueo de aplicaciones en Argentina: Inseguridad jurídica en internet," *Access Now*, June 29, 2018, https://www.accessnow.org/bloqueo-de-aplicaciones-en-argentina-inseguridad-juridica-en-internet/, and "ASIET y GSMA expresan su preocupación por bloqueo a contenidos y servicios de internet en Argentina y solicitan que se deje sin efecto

el requerimiento de la Justicia de Buenos Aires," *ASIET*, May 29, 2018, http://asiet.lat/actualidad/noticias/asiet-gsma-expresan-preocupacion-bloqueo-contenidos-servicios-internet-argentina-solicitan-se-deje-sin-efecto-requerimiento-la-justicia-buenos-aires/ respectively.

4. This declaration is spelled out on Access Now's home page, accessed January 16, 2021, https://www.accessnow.org/.

5. Jorge Albertsen, "La Comisión Interamericana y la censura a Uber," *Infobae*, April 27, 2018, https://www.infobae.com/opinion/2018/04/27/la-comision-interamericana-y-la-censura-a-uber/.

6. Chhotray (2011: xvi) examines this "near-fanatical obsession."

References

Abélès, Marc, and Máximo Badaró. 2015. *Los encantos del poder: Desafíos de la antropología política*. Buenos Aires: Siglo XXI.

Adey, Peter. 2010. *Mobility*. New York: Routledge.

Amaral, Samuel. 2014. "La democracia y los orígenes del Peronismo." In *Peronismo y democracia: Historia y perspectivas*, edited by Marcos Novaro, 47–78. Buenos Aires: Edhasa.

Amoore, Louise. 2020. *Cloud Ethics: Algorithms and the Attributes of Ourselves and Others*. Durham, NC: Duke University Press.

Anand, Nikhil. 2017. *Hydraulic City: Water and the Infrastructures of Citizenship in Mumbai*. Durham, NC: Duke University Press.

Appadurai, Arjun. 1986. *The Social Life of Things: Commodities in Cultural Perspective*. Cambridge: Cambridge University Press.

Archetti, Eduardo. 1999. *Masculinities: Football, Polo and the Tango in Argentina*. Oxford: Berg.

Archetti, Eduardo. 2003. "O 'gaucho,' o tango, primitivismo e poder na formacao da identidade nacional argentina." *Mana* 9 (1): 9–29.

Aretxaga, Begoña. 1999. "A Fictional Reality: Paramilitary Death Squads and the Construction of State Terror in Spain." In *Death Squad: The Anthropology of State Terror*, edited by Jeffrey Sluka, 46–69. Philadelphia: University of Pennsylvania Press.

Argyle, John. 2008. "'Receiving Insiders' and 'Stranger Clients': African Additions to Austronesian Categories of Stranger-Kings." *Indonesia and the Malay World* 36 (105): 219–33.

Auyero, Javier. 1999. "Performing Evita: A Tale of Two Peronist Women." *Journal of Contemporary Ethnography* 27 (4): 461–93.

Bähre, Erik. 2014. "A Trickle Up Economy: Mutuality, Freedom and Violence in Cape Town's Taxi Associations." *Africa* 84 (4): 576–94.

Barry, Andrew. 2005. "The Anti-political Economy." In *The Technological Economy*, edited by Andrew Barry and Don Slater, 84–100. London: Routledge.

Barry, Andrew. 2010. "Materialist Politics: Metallurgy." In *Political Matter: Technoscience, Democracy and Public Life*, edited by Bruce Braun and Sarah J. Whatmore, 89–117. Minneapolis: University of Minnesota Press.

Barry, Andrew, and Don Slater. 2005. Introduction to *The Technological Economy*, edited by Andrew Barry and Don Slater, 1–27. London: Routledge.

Barthes, Roland. 2010. *Mythologies*. London: Random House.

Bass, Jeffrey. 2006. "In Exile from the Self: National Belonging and Psychoanalysis in Buenos Aires." *Ethos* 34 (4): 433–55.

Bauman, Zygmunt. 2014. "Desert Spectacular." In *The Flâneur*, edited by Keith Tester, 138–57. London: Routledge.

Beer, David. 2017. "The Social Power of Algorithms." *Information, Communication and Society* 20 (1): 1–13.

Berman, Marshall. 1983. *All That Is Solid Melts into Air: The Experience of Modernity*. London: Verso.

Block, Fred. 1990. *Postindustrial Possibilities: A Critique of Economic Discourse*. Oakland: University of California Press.

Bourdieu, Pierre. 1987. "The Force of Law: Toward a Sociology of the Juridical Field." *Hastings Law Journal* 38 (5): 805–53.

Bourdieu, Pierre. 1998. *Acts of Resistance: Against the Tyranny of the Market*. New York: New Press.

Braun, Bruce, and Sarah Whatmore. 2010. "The Stuff of Politics: An Introduction." In *Political Matter: Technoscience, Democracy and Public Life*, edited by Bruce Braun and Sarah Whatmore, ix–xl. Minneapolis: University of Minnesota Press.

Brennan, James. 1998a. Introduction to *Peronism and Argentina*, edited by James Brennan, ix–xiv. Wilmington, DE: Scholarly Resources.

Brennan, James. 1998b. *Peronism and Argentina*. Wilmington, DE: Scholarly Resources.

Brenneis, Don. 2006. "Reforming Promise." In *Documents: Artifacts of Modern Knowledge*, edited by Annelise Riles, 41–70. Ann Arbor: University of Michigan Press.

Buchrucker, Cristian. 1998. "Interpretations of Peronism: Old Frameworks and New Perspectives." In *Peronism and Argentina*, edited by James Brennan, 3–28. Wilmington, DE: Scholarly Resources.

Caldwell, Ian, and David Henley. 2008. "The Stranger Who Would Be King: Magic, Logic, Polemic." *Indonesia and the Malay World* 36 (105): 163–75.

Callon, Michel. 1998. *The Laws of the Markets*. Oxford: Basil Blackwell.

Callon, Michel, Pierre Lascoumes, and Yannick Barthe. 2009. *Acting in an Uncertain World: An Essay on Technical Democracy*. Cambridge: MIT Press.

Carrier, James. 1997. Introduction to *Meanings of the Market: The Free Market in Western Culture*, edited by James Carrier, 1–68. Oxford: Berg.

Carrier, James. 2012. "Simplicity in Economic Anthropology: Persuasion, Form and Substance." In *Economic Persuasions*, edited by Stephen Gudeman, 15–30. New York: Berghahn.

Carrier, James. 2016. *After the Crisis: Anthropological Thought, Neoliberalism and the Aftermath*. London: Routledge.

Cassagne, Juan Carlos. 2002. "Evolución de los principios aplicables a los servicios públicos y problemas actuales tras los procesos de privatización." *Revista de Administración Pública* 157:467–94.

Castells, Manuel, and Alejandro Portes. 1989. "World Underneath: The Origins, Dynamics, and Effects of the Informal Economy." In *The Informal Economy: Studies in Advanced and Less Developed Countries*, edited by Manuel Castells, Alejandro Portes, and Lauren Benton, 11–37. Baltimore: John Hopkins University Press.

Castle, Terry. 1988. "Phantasmagoria: Spectral Technology and the Metaphorics of Modern Reverie." *Critical Inquiry* 15 (1): 26–61.

Chen, Le, Alan Mislove, and Christo Wilson. 2015. "Peeking beneath the Hood of Uber." In *Proceedings of the 2015 Internet Measurement Conference*, edited by Kenjiro Cho and Kensuke Fukuda, 495–508. New York: Association for Computing Machinery, 2015.

Chhotray, Vasudha. 2011. *The Anti-politics Machine in India: State, Decentralization and Participatory Watershed Development*. London: Anthem Press.

Cohen, Margaret. 1989. "Walter Benjamin's Phantasmagoria." *New German Critique* 48:87–107.

Cohen, Margaret. 2004. "Benjamin's Phantasmagoria: The Arcades Project." In *The Cambridge Companion to Walter Benjamin*, edited by David Ferris, 199–220. Cambridge: Cambridge University Press.

Colloredo-Mansfeld, Rudi. 2002. "An Ethnography of Neoliberalism." *Current Anthropology* 43 (1): 113–37.

Constable, Marianne. 2010. "Speaking the Language of Law: A Jurisdictional Primer." *English Language Notes* 48 (2): 9–14.

Corcoran, Steven. 2010. "Editor's Introduction." In *Dissensus: On Politics and Aesthetics*, edited by Steven Corcoran, 1–24. London: Continuum.

Cormack, Bradin. 2007. *A Power to Do Justice: Jurisdiction, English Literature, and the Rise of Common Law, 1509–1625*. Chicago: University of Chicago Press.

Crampton, Jeremy. 2013. "Space, Territory, Geography." In *A Companion to Foucault*, edited by Christopher Falzon, Timothy O'Leary, and Jana Sawicki, 384–99. London: Blackwell.

Crehan, Kate. 2011. "Gramsci's Concept of Common Sense: A Useful Concept for Anthropologists?" *Journal of Modern Italian Studies* 16 (2): 273–87.

Cresswell, Timothy. 2006. *On the Move: Mobility in the Modern Western World*. New York: Routledge.

Crouch, Colin. 2004. *Post-democracy*. Cambridge: Polity Press.

Daston, Lorraine. 2018. *Against Nature*. Cambridge, MA: MIT Press.

D'Avella, Nicholas. 2014. "Ecologies of Investment: Crisis Histories and Brick Futures in Argentina." *Cultural Anthropology* 29 (1): 173–99.

de Heusch, Luc. 1991. "The King Comes from Elsewhere." In *Body and Space: Symbolic Models of Unity and Division in African Cosmology and Experience*, edited by Anita Jacobson-Widden, 109–17. Uppsala: Upsaliensis Academiae.

del Nido, Juan M. 2019. "Tecnología y ansiedad de modernidad: Notas etnográficas sobre el conflicto de Uber en Buenos Aires." *Hipertextos* 11 (7): 171–98.

Demetriou, Olga. 2007. "To Cross or Not to Cross? Subjectivization and the Absent State in Cyprus." *Journal of the Royal Anthropological Institute* 13 (4): 987–1006.

Domergue, Eric, and Julio Cabrera. 2010. *Historia del taxi porteño: 75 años de SPAT, 1935–2010*. Buenos Aires: La Imprenta.

Dore, Ronald. 1983. "Goodwill and the Spirit of Market Capitalism." *British Journal of Sociology* 34 (4): 459–82.

Douglas, Mary. 2002. *Purity and Danger: An Analysis of Concepts of Pollution and Taboo*. London: Routledge.

Du Gay, Paul. 1999. "Is Bauman's Bureau Weber's Bureau? A Comment." *British Journal of Sociology* 50 (4): 575–87.

Elyachar, Julia. 2013. "Mappings of Power: The State, NGOs, and International Organizations in the Informal Economy of Cairo." *Comparative Studies in Society and History* 45 (3): 571–605.

Eriksen, Thomas Hylland, James Laidlaw, Jonathan Mair, Keir Martin, and Soumhya Venkatesan. 2015. "The Concept of Neoliberalism Has Become an Obstacle to the Anthropological Understanding of the Twenty-First Century." *Journal of the Royal Anthropological Institute* 21 (4): 911–23.

Evans, Gillian. 2014. "Material Qualities: Introduction." In *Objects and Materials: A Routledge Companion*, edited by Penelope Harvey, Eleanor Conlin Casella, Gillian Evans, Hannah Knox, Christine McLean, Elizabeth B. Silva, Nicholas Thoburn, and Kath Woodward, 19–25. London: Routledge.

Evans-Pritchard, Edward Evan. 1965. *Witchcraft, Oracles and Magic among the Azande*. Oxford: Clarendon Press.

Farmer, Lindsay. 2003. "Whose Trial? Comments on 'A Theory of the Trial.'" *Law and Social Inquiry* 28 (2): 547–52.

Ferguson, James. 1990. *The Anti-politics Machine: Development, Depoliticization, and Bureaucratic Power in Lesotho*. Minneapolis: University of Minnesota Press.

Ferguson, James. 2009. "The Uses of Neoliberalism." *Antipode* 41 (1): 166–84.

Figueiro, Pablo. 2016a. "Los juegos de apuesta en la Argentina: La construcción de una mercancía entre la moral, la razón y la patología." *Antropolítica* 41:78–117.

Figueiro, Pablo. 2016b. "La quiniela: Una ludodicea de la vida cotidiana." *Apuntes de Investigación del CECYP* 28:96–129.

Forment, Carlos. 2007. "The Democratic Dribbler: Football Clubs, Neoliberal Globalization, and Buenos Aires' Municipal Election of 2003." *Public Culture* 19 (1): 85–116.

Foucault, Michel. 1985. *Discourse and Truth: The Problematization of Parrhesia*. Evanston, IL: Northwestern University Press.

Foucault, Michel. 1991. "Questions of Method." In *The Foucault Effect: Studies in*

Governmentality, edited by Graham Burchell, Colin Gordon, and Peter Miller, 73–87. Chicago: University of Chicago Press.

Foucault, Michel. 1994. *Dits et écrits: 1954–1988.* Vol. 4: *1980–1988.* Paris: Gallimard.

Foucault, Michel. 1995. *Discipline and Punish.* New York: Vintage.

Foucault, Michel. 2003. *Society Must Be Defended: Lectures at the Collège de France, 1975–1976.* New York: Picador.

Foucault, Michel. 2009. *Security, Territory, Population: Lectures at the Collège de France, 1977–78.* London: Palgrave Macmillan.

Frank, Thomas. 2002. *One Market under God: Extreme Capitalism, Market Populism, and the End of Economic Democracy.* London: Vintage.

Gago, Verónica. 2017. *Neoliberalism from Below: Popular Pragmatics and Baroque Economies.* Durham, NC: Duke University Press.

Gandolfo, Daniella. 2013. "Formless: A Day at Lima's Office of Formalization." *Cultural Anthropology* 28 (2): 278–98.

Garcia, Marie-France. 1986. "La construction sociale d'un marché parfait: Le Marché au Cadran de Fontaines-en-Sologne." *Actes de la Recherche en Sciences Sociales* 65:2–13.

García Fanlo, Luis. 2014. "La gubernamentalidad peronista." Paper presented at II Jornadas de Estudios de América Latina y el Caribe: "Desafíos y debates actuales," Facultad de Ciencias Sociales (UBA), Buenos Aires, September 26. https://www.aacademica.org/luis.garcia.fanlo/11.pdf.

Garguin, Enrique. 2007. "'Los Argentinos descendemos de los barcos': The Racial Articulation of Middle Class Identity in Argentina (1920–1960)." *Latin American and Caribbean Ethnic Studies* 2 (2): 161–84.

Geertz, Clifford. 1975. "Common Sense as a Cultural System." *Antioch Review* 33 (1): 5–26.

Gillespie, Tarleton. 2013. "The Relevance of Algorithms." In *Media Technologies: Essays on Communication, Materiality and Society*, edited by Tarleton Gillespie, Pablo J. Boczkowski, and Kirsten A. Foot, 167–93. Cambridge, MA: MIT Press.

Goldstein, Daniel. 2016. *Owners of the Sidewalk: Security and Survival in the Informal City.* Durham, NC: Duke University Press.

Gordillo, Agustín. 2013. *Teoría general del derecho administrativo: Tratado de derecho administrativo y obras selectas.* Buenos Aires: FDA.

Gorelik, Adrián. 2004. *Miradas sobre Buenos Aires.* Buenos Aires: Siglo XXI.

Gramsci, Antonio. 1971. *Selections from the Prison Notebooks.* Edited by Quintin Hoare and Geoffrey Nowell-Smith. London: Lawrence and Wishart.

Granovetter, Mark. 1985. "Economic Action and Social Structure: The Problem of Embeddedness." *American Journal of Sociology* 91 (3): 481–510.

Gunning, Tom. 2004. "Illusions Past and Future: The Phantasmagoria and Its Spectres." Paper presented at the First International Conference on the Histories of Art, Science and Technology. Archived at MediaArtHistories Archive. http://www.mediaarthistory.org/refresh/Programmatic%20key%20texts/pdfs/Gunning.pdf.

Gupta, Akhil, and James Ferguson. 1997. *Anthropological Locations: Boundaries and Grounds of a Field Science.* Berkeley: University of California Press.

Guyer, Jane. 2007. "Prophecy and the Near Future: Thoughts on Macroeconomic, Evangelical, and Punctuated Time." *American Ethnologist* 34 (3): 409–21.

Haidar, Julieta. 2013. "El estudio de los sindicatos en la ciencia política argentina." *Revista Temas y Debates* 17 (26): 147–66.

Halperín Donghi, Tulio. 1992. *Una nación para el desierto argentino*. Buenos Aires: Centro Editor de América Latina.

Hansen, Thomas Blom. 1999. *The Saffron Wave: Democracy and Hindu Nationalism in Modern India*. Princeton, NJ: Princeton University Press.

Hansen, Thomas Blom, and Oskar Verkaaik. 2009. "Introduction: Urban Charisma." *Critique of Anthropology* 29 (1): 5–26.

Hart, Keith. 1973. "Informal Income Opportunities and Urban Employment in Ghana." *Journal of Modern African Studies* 11 (1): 61–89.

Healey, Mark. 2012. *El peronismo entre las ruinas: El terremoto y la reconstrucción de San Juan*. Buenos Aires: Siglo XXI.

Helmke, Gretchen. 2004. *Courts under Constraints: Judges, Generals, and Presidents in Argentina*. Cambridge: Cambridge University Press.

Henley, David. 2004. "Conflict, Justice, and the Stranger-King Indigenous Roots of Colonial Rule in Indonesia and Elsewhere." *Modern Asian Studies* 38 (1): 85–144.

Henley, David, and Ian Caldwell. 2008. "Kings and Covenants: Stranger-Kings and Social Contract in Sulawesi." *Indonesia and the Malay World* 36 (105): 269–91.

Herzfeld, Michael. 1988. *Poetics of Manhood*. Princeton, NJ: Princeton University Press.

Hetherington, Kregg. 2013. "Beans before the Law: Knowledge Practices, Responsibility, and the Paraguayan Soy Boom." *Cultural Anthropology* 28 (1): 65–85.

Hirschman, Albert. 1977. *The Passions and the Interests: Political Arguments for Capitalism before Its Triumph*. Princeton, NJ: Princeton University Press.

Hobsbawm, Eric. 1994. *The Age of Empire, 1875–1914*. London: Abacus.

Humphrey, Caroline. 2007. "Alternative Freedoms." *Proceedings of the American Philosophical Society* 151 (1): 1–10.

James, Daniel. 2010. *Resistencia e integración: El peronismo y la clase trabajadora Argentina, 1946–1976*. Buenos Aires: Siglo XXI.

Jansen, Stef. 2009. "After the Red Passport: Towards an Anthropology of the Everyday Geopolitics of Entrapment in the EU's 'Immediate Outside.'" *Journal of the Royal Anthropological Institute* 15 (4): 815–32.

Jansen, Stef. 2014. "Hope for/against the State: Gridding in a Besieged Sarajevo Suburb." *Ethnos* 79 (2): 238–60.

Jansen, Stef. 2016. "Ethnography and the Choices Posed by the 'Affective Turn.'" In *Sensitive Objects: Affect and Material Culture*, edited by Jonas Frykman and Maja Povrzanovic Frykman, 55–79. Lund: Nordic Academic Press.

Jennings, Michael. 2003. "On the Banks of a New Lethe: Commodification and Experience in Benjamin's Baudelaire Book." *Boundary 2* 30 (1): 89–104.

Joseph, G. 2000. "Taking Race Seriously: Whiteness in Argentina's National and Transnational Imaginary." *Identities* 7 (3): 333–71.

Kahn, Jeffrey. 2017. "Geographies of Discretion and the Jurisdictional Imagination." *PoLAR: Political and Legal Anthropology Review* 40 (1): 5–27.

Kazin, Michael. 2017. *The Populist Persuasion: An American History.* Ithaca, NY: Cornell University Press.

Kian, Kwee Hui. 2008. "How Strangers Became Kings: Javanese-Dutch Relations in Java 1600–1800." *Indonesia and the Malay World* 36 (105): 293–307.

Koselleck, Reinhart. 2004. *Futures Past: On the Semantics of Historical Time.* New York: Columbia University Press.

Laclau, Ernesto. 2005. *On Populist Reason.* London: Verso.

Lash, Scott. 2007. "Power after Hegemony: Cultural Studies in Mutation?" *Theory, Culture and Society* 24 (3): 55–78.

Laszczkowski, Mateusz, and Madeleine Reeves. 2017. *Affective States: Entanglements, Suspensions, Suspicions.* Oxford: Berghahn.

Latour, Bruno. 1993. *We Have Never Been Modern.* Cambridge, MA: Harvard University Press.

Latour, Bruno. 1999. *Pandora's Hope: Essays on the Reality of Science Studies.* Cambridge, MA: Harvard University Press.

Latour, Bruno. 2010. *The Making of Law: An Ethnography of the* Conseil d'Etat. Malden, MA: Polity Press.

Lazar, Sian. 2012. "A Desire to Formalize Work? Comparing Trade Union Strategies in Bolivia and Argentina." *Anthropology of Work Review* 33 (1): 15–24.

Lazar, Sian. 2017. *The Social Life of Politics: Ethics, Kinship and Union Activism in Argentina.* Stanford, CA: Stanford University Press.

Lears, Jackson. 2003. *Something for Nothing: Luck in America.* London: Penguin.

Li, Tania Murray. 2001. "Relational Histories and the Production of Difference on Sulawesi's Upland Frontier." *Journal of Asian Studies* 60:41–66.

Lipsky, Michael. 1980. *Street-Level Bureaucracy: Dilemmas of the Individual in Public Services.* New York: Russell Sage.

López-Pedreros, A. Ricardo. 2019. *Makers of Democracy: A Transnational History of the Middle Classes in Colombia.* Durham, NC: Duke University Press.

Malkki, Liisa. 1994. "Citizens of Humanity: Internationalism and the Imagined Community of Nations." *Diaspora: A Journal of Transnational Studies* 3 (1): 41–68.

Marcus, George. 1997. "The Uses of Complicity in the Changing Mise-en-Scène of Anthropological Fieldwork." *Representations* 59:85–108.

Martínez Estrada, Ezequiel. 2017. *La cabeza de Goliat: Microscopía de Buenos Aires.* Buenos Aires: Interzona.

Maurer, Bill. 2002. "Repressed Futures: Financial Derivatives' Theological Unconscious." *Economy and Society* 31 (1): 16–36.

Maurer, Bill. 2013. "Jurisdiction in Dialect: Sovereignty Games in the British Virgin Islands." In *European Integration and Postcolonial Sovereignty Games: The EU Overseas Countries and Territories,* edited by Rebecca Adler-Nissan and Ulrik Pram Gad, 130–44. New York: Routledge.

Maybury-Lewis, David. 1991. "Becoming Indian in Lowland South America." In *Nation-States and Indians in Latin America*, edited by Greg Urban and Joel Sherzer, 207–35. Austin: University of Texas Press.

Mirowski, Philip. 1989. *More Heat Than Light: Economics as Social Physics; Physics as Nature's Economics.* Cambridge: Cambridge University Press.

Mirowski, Philip. 2009. "Postface: Defining Neoliberalism." In *The Road from Mont Pèlerin: The Making of the Neoliberal Thought Collective,* edited by Philip Mirowski and Dieter Plehwe, 417–55. Cambridge, MA: Harvard University Press.

Mitchell, Timothy. 2002. *Rule of Experts: Egypt, Techno-Politics, Modernity.* Berkeley: University of California Press.

Mouffe, Chantal. 1993. *The Return of the Political.* London: Verso.

Mouffe, Chantal. 2005. *On the Political.* London: Routledge.

Muir, Sarah. 2016. "On Historical Exhaustion: Argentine Critique in an Era of 'Total Corruption.'" *Comparative Studies in Society and History* 58 (1): 129–58.

Murmis, Miguel, and Juan Carlos Portantiero. 2011. *Estudios sobre los orígenes del peronismo.* Buenos Aires: Siglo XXI.

Mustapic, Ana María. 2002. "Del Partido Peronista al Partido Justicialista: Las transformaciones de un partido carismático." In *El asedio a la política: Los partidos latinoamericanos en la era neoliberal,* edited by Marcelo Cavarozzi and Juan Manuel Abal Medina, 137–61. Rosario: Homo Sapiens.

Navaro Yashin, Yael. 2002. *Faces of the State: Secularism and Public Life in Turkey.* Princeton, NJ: Princeton University Press.

Navaro-Yashin, Yael. 2012. *The Make-Believe Space: Affective Geography in a Postwar Polity.* Durham, NC: Duke University Press.

Neyland, Daniel. 2013. "An Ethnography of Numbers." In *A Companion to Organizational Anthropology,* edited by Douglas Caulkins and Ann T. Jordan, 219–35. Chichester, UK: John Wiley and Sons.

Nouzeilles, Gabriela, and Graciela Montaldo, eds. 2002. *The Argentina Reader.* Durham, NC: Duke University Press.

Novaro, Marcos. 2014a. "Introducción: Historia y perspectiva de una relación difícil." In *Peronismo y democracia: Historia y perspectivas de una relación compleja,* edited by Marcos Novaro, 15–47. Buenos Aires: Edhasa.

Novaro, Marcos. 2014b. *Peronismo y democracia: Historia y perspectivas de una relación compleja.* Buenos Aires: Edhasa.

Nuijten, Monique. 2004. "Between Fear and Fantasy: Governmentality and the Working of Power in Mexico." *Critique of Anthropology* 24 (2): 209–30.

O'Donnell, Guillermo. 2002. "Modernisation and Military Coups." In *The Argentina Reader,* edited by Gabriela Nouzeilles and Graciela Montaldo, 399–420. Durham, NC: Duke University Press.

Oksala, Johanna. 2013. "From Biopower to Governmentality." In *A Companion to Foucault,* edited by Christopher Falzon, Timothy O'Leary, and Jana Sawicki, 320–36. London: Blackwell.

Ormerod, Paul. 1994. *The Death of Economics*. London: Faber and Faber.

Oyler, Celia. 1996. "Sharing Authority: Student Initiations during Teacher-Led Read-Alouds of Information Books." *Teaching and Teacher Education* 12 (2): 149–60.

Padovan-Özdemir, Marta. 2016. "Racialised Entanglements of Teacher Professionalisation and Problematised Immigrant Schoolchildren: Crafting a Danish Welfare Nation State, 1970–2013." *Paedagogica Historica* 52 (5): 485–506.

Padovan-Özdemir, Marta, and Christian Ydesen. 2016. "Professional Encounters with the Post-WWII Immigrant: A Privileged Prism for Studying the Shaping of European Welfare Nation-States." *Paedagogica Historica* 52 (5): 423–37.

Parapugna, Alberto. 1980. *Historia de los coches de alquiler en Buenos Aires*. Buenos Aires: Corregidor.

Parikka, Jussi. 2012. "New Materialism as Media Theory: Medianatures and Dirty Matter." *Communication and Critical/Cultural Studies* 9 (1): 95–100.

Plotkin, Mariano Ben. 1998. "The Changing Perceptions of Peronism: A Review Essay." In *Peronism and Argentina*, edited by James Brennan, 29–54. Wilmington, DE: Scholarly Resources.

Plotkin, Mariano Ben, and Eduardo Zimmerman. 2012a. *Las prácticas del estado: Política, sociedad y elites estatales en la Argentina del siglo XX*. Buenos Aires: Edhasa.

Plotkin, Mariano Ben, and Eduardo Zimmerman. 2012b. *Los saberes del estado*. Buenos Aires: Edhasa.

Rajković, Ivan. 2019. "Balkanizing Sahlins: National Humiliation and Stranger Capitalism in a Semiperiphery." Paper presented at the Social Anthropology Seminar of the University of Manchester, April 1.

Rancière, Jacques. 1999. *Disagreement: Politics and Philosophy*. Minneapolis: University of Minnesota Press.

Rancière, Jacques. 2011. *The Politics of Aesthetics: The Distribution of the Sensible*. New York: Continuum.

Reeves, Madeleine. 2011. "Fixing the Border: On the Affective Life of the State in Southern Kyrgyzstan." *Environment and Planning D: Society and Space* 29 (5): 905–23.

Richland, Justin. 2013. "Jurisdiction: Grounding Law in Language." *Annual Review of Anthropology* 42:209–26.

Riles, Annelise. 2006. "Introduction: In Response," In *Documents: Artifacts of Modern Knowledge*, edited by Annelise Riles, 1–40. Ann Arbor: University of Michigan Press.

Rock, David. 1985. *Argentina, 1516–1982: From Spanish Colonization to the Falklands War*. Berkeley: University of California Press.

Roitman, Janet. 2005. *Fiscal Disobedience: An Anthropology of Economic Regulation in Central Africa*. Princeton, NJ: Princeton University Press.

Rosenblat, Alex. 2018. *Uberland: How Algorithms Are Rewriting the Rules of Work*. Oakland: University of California Press.

Rosenblat, Alex, and Luke Stark. 2016. "Algorithmic Labor and Information Asymmetries: A Case Study of Uber's Drivers." *International Journal of Communication* 10:3758–84.

Sahlins, Marshall. 1963. "Poor Man, Rich Man, Big-Man, Chief: Political Types in Melanesia and Polynesia." *Comparative Studies in Society and History* 5 (3): 285–303.

Sahlins, Marshall. 2008. "The Stranger-King, or, Elementary Forms of the Politics of Life." *Indonesia and the Malay World* 36 (105): 177–99.

Sahlins, Marshall. 2014. "Stranger Kings in General: The Cosmo-Logics of Power." In *Framing Cosmologies: The Anthropology of Worlds*, edited by Martin Holbraad and Allen Abramson, 137–63. Manchester: Manchester University Press.

Sarlo, Beatriz. 1988. *Una modernidad periférica: Buenos Aires, 1920 y 1930*. Buenos Aires: Ediciones Nueva Visión.

Sarlo, Beatriz. 2001. *Tiempo presente*. Buenos Aires: Siglo XXI.

Sarlo, Beatriz. 2003. *La pasión y la excepción*. Buenos Aires: Siglo XXI.

Sarlo, Beatriz. 2011. *La audacia y el cálculo: Kirchner, 2003–2010*. Buenos Aires: Sudamericana.

Savigliano, Marta. 1995. *Tango and the Political Economy of Passion: From Exoticism to Decolonization*. Boulder, CO: Westview.

Scalabrini Ortiz, Raúl. 2001. *Política británica en el Rio de la Plata*. Buenos Aires: Plus Ultra.

Schneider, Arnd. 1996. "The Two Faces of Modernity: Concepts of the Melting Pot in Argentina." *Critique of Anthropology* 16 (2): 173–98.

Scobie, James. 1964. *Argentina: A City and a Nation*. Oxford: Oxford University Press.

Scobie, James. 2002. "The Paris of South America." In *The Argentina Reader*, edited by Gabriela Nouzeilles and Graciela Montaldo, 170–81. Durham, NC: Duke University Press.

Scott, James. 1998. *Seeing Like a State: How Certain Schemes to Improve the Human Condition Have Failed*. Binghamton, NY: Vail-Ballou Press.

Seiler, Cotten. 2008. *Republic of Drivers*. Chicago: University of Chicago Press.

Shannon, Jennifer. 2007. "Informed Consent: Documenting the Intersection of Bureaucratic Regulation and Ethnographic Practice." *Political and Legal Anthropology Review* 30 (2): 229–48.

Sheller, Mimi, and John Urry. 2000. "The City and the Car." *International Journal of Urban and Regional Research* 24 (4): 737–57.

Shore, Chris, and Susan Wright. 2015. "Governing by Numbers: Audit Culture, Rankings and the New World Order." *Social Anthropology* 23:22–28.

Shiller, Robert. 2019. *Narrative Economics: How Stories Go Viral and Drive Major Economic Events*. Princeton, NJ: Princeton University Press.

Sidicaro, Ricardo. 2003. *Los tres peronismos: Estado y poder económico, 1946–55/1973–76/1989–99*. Buenos Aires: Siglo XXI.

Simmel, Georg. 1908. "The Stranger." InfoAmérica. https://www.infoamerica.org/documentos_pdf/simmel01.pdf.

Slobodian, Quinn. 2018. *Globalists: The End of Empire and the Birth of Neoliberalism*. Cambridge, MA: Harvard University Press.

Soriano, Osvaldo. 2002. "Living with Inflation." In *The Argentina Reader*, edited by Gabriela Nouzeilles and Graciela Montaldo, 481–86. Durham, NC: Duke University Press.

Spragens, Thomas. 1973. *The Politics of Motion: The World of Thomas Hobbes.* Lexington: Kentucky University Press.

Stafford, Charles. 2019. *Economic Life in the Real World: Logic, Emotion and Ethics.* Cambridge: Cambridge University Press.

Stawski, Martín. 2012. "Del equipo de asalto a la consolidación: Estado, elites y economía durante el primer peronismo, 1946–1955." In *Las prácticas del estado: Política, sociedad y elites estatales en la Argentina del siglo XX*, edited by Mariano Ben Plotkin and Eduardo Zimmerman, 93–130. Buenos Aires: Edhasa.

Stengers, Isabelle. 2010 *Cosmopolitics.* Minneapolis: University of Minnesota Press.

Strathern, Marilyn. 1987. "The Limits of Auto-Ethnography." In *Anthropology at Home*, edited by Anthony Jackson, 16–37. London: Tavistock.

Strathern, Marilyn. 1997. "'Improving Ratings': Audit in the British University System." *European Review* 5 (3): 305–21.

Strathern, Marilyn. 2000. "Introduction: New Accountabilities." In *Audit Cultures: Anthropological Studies in Accountability, Ethics and the Academy*, edited by Marilyn Strathern, 1–18. London: Routledge.

Swidler, Ann. 1979. *Organization without Authority: Dilemmas of Social Control in Free Schools.* Cambridge, MA: Harvard University Press.

Taylor, Charles. 2003. *Modern Social Imaginaries.* Durham, NC: Duke University Press.

Taylor, Julie. 1998. *Paper Tangos.* Durham, NC: Duke University Press.

Taylor, Julie. 2002. "Argentina and the 'Islas Malvinas': Symbolism and the Threat to Nationhood." In *The Best of Anthropology Today*, edited by Jonathan Benthall, 341–47. London: Routledge.

Ternavasio, Marcela. 2009. *Historia de la Argentina, 1806–1852.* Buenos Aires: Siglo XXI.

Thedvall, Renita. 2015. "Managing Preschool the Lean Way: Evaluating Work Processes by Numbers and Colours." *Social Anthropology* 23 (1): 42–52.

Thiranagama, Sharika, and Toby Kelly. 2010. "Introduction: Specters of Treason." In *Traitors: Suspicion, Intimacy, and the Ethics of State-Building*, edited by Sharika Thiranagama, and Toby Kelly, 1–23. Philadelphia: University of Pennsylvania Press.

Thrift, Nigel. 2004. "Driving in the City." *Theory, Culture and Society* 21 (4–5): 41–59.

Torre, Juan Carlos. 1989. "Interpretando (una vez más) los orígenes del peronismo." *Desarrollo Económico* 28 (112): 525–48.

Torre, Juan Carlos. 2012. *Ensayos sobre movimiento obrero y peronismo.* Buenos Aires: Siglo XXI.

Urry, John. 2000. *Sociology beyond Societies: Mobilities for the Twenty-First Century.* London: Routledge.

Usami, Koichi. 2004. "Transformation and Continuity of the Argentine Welfare State: Evaluating Social Security Reform in the 1990s." *Developing Economies* 42 (2): 217–40.

Venugopal, Rajesh. 2015. "Neoliberalism as Concept." *Economy and Society* 44 (2): 165–87.

Verran, Helen. 2012. "Number." In *Inventive Methods: The Happening of the Social*, edited by Celia Lury and Nina Wakeford, 110–24. New York: Routledge.

Waisman, Carlos. 1987. *The Reversal of Development in Argentina: Postwar Counter-revolutionary Policies and Their Structural Consequences.* Princeton, NJ: Princeton University Press.

Wasserman, Janek. 2019. *The Marginal Revolutionaries: How Austrian Economists Fought the War of Ideas.* New Haven, CT: Yale University Press.

Wendland, Claire. 2016. "Estimating Death: A Close Reading of Maternal Mortality Metrics in Malawi." In *Metrics: What Counts in Global Health*, edited by Vincanne Adams, 57–81. Durham, NC: Duke University Press.

Whyte, Jessica. 2019. *The Morals of the Market: Human Rights and the Rise of Neoliberalism.* London: Verso.

Wilson, Japhy, and Erik Swyngedouw. 2014. "Seeds of Dystopia: Post-politics and the Return of the Political." In *The Post-political and Its Discontents: Spaces of Depoliticisation, Spectres of Radical Politics,* edited by Japhy Wilson and Erik Swyngedouw, 1–22. Edinburgh: Edinburgh University Press.

Wolf, Eric. 1982. *Europe and the People without History.* Berkeley: University of California Press.

Wolf, Eric. 1990. "Distinguished Lecture: Facing Power—Old Insights, New Questions." *American Anthropologist* 92 (3): 586–96.

Wolff, Janet. 1993. "On the Road Again: Metaphors of Travel in Cultural Criticism." *Cultural Studies* 7:224–39.

Wright, Winthrop. 1974. *British-Owned Railways in Argentina: Their Effect on the Growth of Economic Nationalism, 1854–1948.* Austin: University of Texas Press.

Yablon, Charles. 1990. "Forms." *Cardozo Law Review* 11 (5): 1349–53.

Žižek, Slavoj. 2009. *The Ticklish Subject: The Absent Centre of Political Ontology.* London: Verso.

Index